14357

Contents

KEY SKILLS LEVELS MATRIX

Book section	Key Skills Level 1	2	3
1.1	✓		
1.2	✓		
1.3			✓
1.4			✓
2.1	✓		
2.2	✓		
2.3	✓		
2.4	✓		
2.5			✓
3.1	✓		
3.2	✓		
3.3	✓		
3.4	✓		
4.1		✓	
4.2		✓	
4.3		✓	
4.4	✓		
5.1	✓		
5.2	✓		
6.1	✓		
6.2		✓	
6.3		✓	
6.4		✓	
6.5		✓	
7.1	✓		
7.2		✓	
7.3		✓	
7.4		✓	
7.5		✓	
8.1	✓		
8.2	✓		
8.3		✓	
9	✓		

Book section	Key Skills Level 1	2	3
10.1	✓		
10.2		✓	
10.3		✓	
10.4			✓
10.5		✓	
10.6		✓	
10.7		✓	
10.8			✓
11.1		✓	
11.2			✓
11.3	✓		
11.4	✓		
12.1	✓		
12.2	✓		
12.3	✓		
12.4	✓		
12.5	✓		
12.6	✓		
12.7	✓		
13.1	✓		
13.2	✓		
13.3	✓		
13.4	✓		
13.5		✓	
13.6	✓		
14.1	✓		
14.2		✓	
14.3		✓	
14.4			✓
14.5		✓	
14.6		✓	
14.7			✓

Book section	Key Skills Level 1	2	3
15.1	✓		
15.2		✓	
15.3	✓		
15.4	✓		
15.5		✓	
15.6			✓
15.7			✓
16.1	✓		
16.2	✓		
16.3	✓		
16.4	✓		
16.5		✓	
17.1	✓		
17.2		✓	
17.3		✓	
17.4		✓	
18.1			✓
18.2			✓
19.1			✓
19.2			✓
19.3			✓
19.4			✓

Application of NUMBER

Second Edition

Brian Gaulter & Leslye Buchanan

OXFORD
UNIVERSITY PRESS

OXFORD
UNIVERSITY PRESS

Oxford University Press is a department of the University of Oxford.
It furthers the University's objective of excellence in research, scholarship,
and education by publishing worldwide in

Oxford New York

Athens Auckland Bangkok Bogotá Buenos Aires Calcutta
Cape Town Chennai Dar es Salaam Delhi Florence Hong Kong Istanbul
Karachi Kuala Lumpur Madrid Melbourne Mexico City Mumbai
Nairobi Paris São Paulo Singapore Taipei Tokyo Toronto Warsaw

with associated companies in Berlin Ibadan

Oxford is a registered trade mark of Oxford University Press
in the UK and in certain other countries

© B. Gaulter and L. Buchanan 1994

Database right Oxford University Press (maker)

First published 1994

Reprinted 1994, 1998, 1999

Second Edition 2000

British Library Cataloguing in Publication Data

Data available

ISBN 019-914796-5

Typeset and designed by Tech-Set Ltd.

Printed and bound in Great Britain by Butler & Tanner.

Introduction

The book is written for students studying a Key Skills unit. It is necessary for a student to show competence in *every* one of these skills.

One of the key skills is *Application of Number*, which is concerned with using Mathematics in the context of the real world.

There are different levels of Key Skills, each of which is broadly equivalent to a specific level of academic achievement:

- Key Skill Level 1 is comparable with study at GCSE standard.

- Key Skill Level 2 is comparable with study at the higher levels of GCSE.

- Key Skill Level 3 is comparable with study at AS or grade Es.

A complete list of the evidence required for each of the Levels is given on page vi.

This book is designed for students working at Levels 1, 2 and 3. Students who are competent in the key skills at their level are encouraged to extend their skills by working towards the next level. Students working at Application of Number Level 2 (or Level 1) should use the grid opposite, which gives the Key Skill level reflected in each topic.

There will be many circumstances where colleges feel that it is desirable for a student to have periods of teaching or workshop help, specifically to use learning material devoted to the key skills in Application of Number.

This book will be particularly useful as a resource for that purpose. A student should be able to identify weaknesses in a particular competence and then study that section in this book, either in a formal classroom situation or as part of a self-supported study programme.

The Application of Number competences need to be shown in a student's portfolio. These competences can usually be shown by means of assignments which students do as part of their study. It is important that the assignments are designed so that students can show all the competences required at their own key skill level. All students need to realise that they must produce, in their portfolio, work which clearly demonstrate their key skill competences.

At all levels, students also need to sit an externally set examination which assesses their ability on the whole of , Application of Number, Part A "What you need to know", at their key skill level.

At the end of this book is a section of assignments designed specifically to enable a student to demonstrate his or her key skill competences. This section is based on each of the 2000–01 GNVQ vocational areas, which also relate to many Advanced and Advanced Subsidiary subjects. However, it is intended primarily to be used as a guide. Each assignment should be regarded as the starting point in the student's study and developed into a more open-ended task. It is also essential that any assignment should relate closely to the topics which the student has followed in his or her study.

Students using textbooks sometimes worry if the solution at the end of the book differs slightly from their own answer. Very often this is caused by a misunderstanding about accuracy. In this book answers involving money should be given to the nearest penny and exact answers should always be given where possible. Where appropriate, other levels of accuracy can be required. As a guide, students should use at least four figures in their working and give answers to three significant figures. The answer must be rounded to the third figure.

As a guide, students should use at least four figures in their working and give answers to three significant figures. The answer must be rounded to the third figure.

We hope that this book will be of great benefit to lecturers and students alike. If you have any suggestions for enhancing its usefulness in future editions, please contact us via the Oxford office of OUP.

Brian Gaulter and Leslye Buchanan
Hampshire, 2000

Evidence required

The evidence required for each of the GNVQ levels is listed below.
A student needs to show all the evidence required at the appropriate level.

Application of Number Level 1

You must be able to:

- interpret straightforward information;
- carry out calculations, using whole numbers, simple decimals, fractions and percentages to given levels of accuracy;
- interpret the results of your calculations and present findings, using a chart and diagram.

Application of Number Level 2

You must be able to carry through a substantial activity that requires you to:

- select information and methods to get the results you need;
- carry out calculations involving two or more steps and numbers of any size, including use of formulae, and check your methods and levels of accuracy;
- select ways to present your findings, including use of a graph, describe methods and explain results.

Application of Number Level 3

You must be able to plan and carry through a substantial and complex activity that requires you to:

- plan your approach to obtaining and using information, choose appropriate methods for obtaining the results you need and justify your choice;
- carry out multi-stage calculations, including use of a large data set (over 50 items) and rearrangement of formulae;
- justify your choice of presentation methods and explain the results of your calculations.

Acknowledgements

The publisher and authors are grateful to the following organisations for permission to reproduce previously published material:

HMSO, for extracts from *Social Trends* and the *Annual Abstract of Statistics* (pages 101, 102, 147)
Jacobs Suchard Ltd, for the use of Toblerone (page 200)
The Office of Population Censuses and Surveys, for a table (page 108)
Southern Examining group for question on page 178

Every reasonable effort has been made to contact copyright owners, but we apologise for any unknown errors or omissions. The list will be corrected, if necessary, in the next reprint.

1 *Basic Numeracy*

Even in prehistoric times the basis of arithmetic was being developed. The earliest number system was one, two, many. When races began to settle and become farmers, craftsmen and traders, there was a need for more sophisticated number systems for counting, recording and calculation. As different civilisations evolved, they developed different number systems. Our system is based on the number 10. Other civilisations used different systems based on the number 60 (Babylonia), 20 (Mayan) or 5. The Romans used letters to represent numbers (e.g. I, V, X, C for 1, 5, 10, 100).

When trade and communication spread beyond the local area to the rest of the country and abroad, it became essential to have a common system of numbers which was efficient..

The **decimal** system, based on the number 10, was eventually accepted as the most convenient. Its advantages are that any number can be written using only ten symbols, 0, 1, 2, 3, 4, 5, 6, 7, 8, 9 (called **digits**) and **place value**.

1.1 *Integers and decimal fractions*

Place value

An abacus is a frame with beads sliding on wires, which was used as a counting aid before the adoption of the ten digits. It is still used for this purpose in parts of Asia.

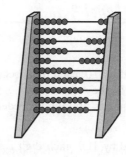

Beads on the first wire have the same value of 1 unit, but a bead on the second wire has a value which is the total of the beads on the first wire, i.e. 10. Each bead on the third wire then has the value $10 \times 10 = 100$, and so on.

The **decimal system** works in the same way, but with digits written in columns instead of beads on wires. Working from right to left, each column is worth 10 times the previous column:

$$15 = 5 \times 1 + 1 \times 10 = \text{fifteen}$$
$$352 = 2 \times 1 + 5 \times 10 + 3 \times 100 = \text{three hundred and fifty two}$$
$$1234 = 4 \times 1 + 3 \times 10 + 2 \times 100 + 1 \times 1000$$
$$= \text{one thousand, two hundred and thirty four}$$

If there is no digit in a particular column, the place is filled by **0**, which is called a **place-holder**.

$$105 = 5 \times 1 + 1 \times 100 = \text{one hundred and five}$$
$$150 = 5 \times 10 + 1 \times 100 = \text{one hundred and fifty}$$

Note. Whole numbers are also called **integers**.

Similarly, working from left to right, each column is worth one tenth of the previous column.

Each number in the column to the right of the units is worth $1 \div 10$, i.e. one tenth, which is a **decimal fraction**.

To separate whole numbers from decimal fractions a **decimal point** is used:

$$0.1 \quad = \tfrac{1}{10} \quad = \text{one tenth}$$
$$0.01 \quad = \tfrac{1}{100} \quad = \text{one hundredth}$$
$$0.001 = \tfrac{1}{1000} = \text{one thousandth}$$

Multiplication and division by 10, 100, 1000, etc., is very easy in the decimal system.

EXAMPLE 1

Multiply 34 by: **a** 10 **b** 1000

a When a number is multiplied by 10, each digit becomes worth 10 times more, i.e. moves **1 column** to the **left**.
The empty space in the units column is filled by a zero:
$34 \times 10 = 340$

b When a number is multiplied by 1000, each digit becomes worth $10 \times 10 \times 10$ more, i.e. moves **3 columns** to the **left**.
The three empty spaces in the units, tens and hundreds columns are filled by zeros:
$34 \times 1000 = 34000$

With numbers of more than four digits, it is usual to leave a small gap after each group of three digits, e.g. 34 000.

EXAMPLE 2

Divide 2030 by: **a** 10 **b** 100

a When a number is divided by 10, each digit becomes worth 10 times less, i.e. moves **1 column** to the **right**.
The zero in the units column is no longer needed:
$2030 \div 10 = 203$

b When a number is divided by 100, each digit is worth 10×10 times less, i.e. moves **2 columns** to the **right**.

The 3 in the tens column will move into the **tenths column**:
$2030 \div 100 = 20.30$ or 20.3

EXERCISE 1.1

1 What value do the following digits have in the given number?

   a 5 in 250   **d** 4 in 624

   b 7 in 1725   **e** 6 in 12.6

   c 3 in 3012   **f** 2 in 34.529

2 Write the following numbers in order of size, smallest first:

   a 54 17 45 10 21 86

   b 104 23 14 230 32 203

   c 60 6 600 61 610 601

   d 99 101 11 110 1001 999

   e 399 400 300 297 420

3 What is the largest number which can be made from the digits 1, 7, 5 and 0?

4 What is the smallest number which can be made from the digits 3, 9, 6 and 2?

5 Find the answers to the following multiplications:

   a 43×10 **d** 13.2×10 **g** 5.16×100

   b 167×100 **e** 5.8×100 **h** 7.03×1000

   c 20×100 **f** 93.58×10 **i** 0.13×1000

6 Find the answers to the following divisions:

   a $320 \div 10$ **d** $4030 \div 100$ **g** $2.7 \div 1000$

   b $300 \div 100$ **e** $65 \div 100$ **h** $0.51 \div 10$

   c $4000 \div 1000$ **f** $65 \div 1000$ **i** $0.02 \div 100$

7 What number is formed when:

   a 1 is added to 99   **b** 1 is added to 4099

   b 2 is added to 398   **d** 2 is added to 6198?

Decimals and the four rules

The four rules of arithmetic are **addition**, **subtraction**, **multiplication** and **division**. It is generally easiest to perform calculations involving decimals on a calculator (see Unit 2). However, in simple cases, you should also be able to find an answer without the aid of a calculator.

EXAMPLE 1

a Add 34.5, 9.7 and 56.12.

b Subtract 91.72 from 164.6.

First, write the numbers in a column so that the decimal points are in line, then each digit is in its correct place.

  a   34.5   **b** 164.60
        9.7   91.72
       56.12   72.88
     100.32

EXAMPLE 2

a Multiply 271.3 by 9.

b Divide 384.8 by 7.

  a   271.3   **b**   54.9
         9   7)384.3
     2441.7

EXERCISE 1.2

Calculate, without the aid of a calculator:

1   $36.2 + 5.7$

2   $104.9 + 75.4$

3   $6.7 + 51.09 + 76.18$

4   $72.9 - 56.2$

5   $89.13 - 72.42$

6   $121.6 - 69.85$

7   24.2×7

8   78.04×9

9   147.5×12

10   $54.6 \div 7$

11   $650.79 \div 9$

12   $526.46 \div 11$

Combining the four operations

Does $3 + 4 \times 2 = 7 \times 2 = 4$

or

does $3 + 4 \times 2 = 3 + 8 = 11$?

When more than one **operation** is used in a calculation there has to be an agreed order for combining the numbers.

The order used in the calculation is:

(i) brackets
(ii) multiplications and divisions
(iii) additions and subtractions

$\therefore \quad 3 + 4 \times 2 = 3 + 8 = 11$

EXAMPLE

Find: **a** $7 + 3 \times 6 - 1$ **b** $(7 + 3) \times 6 - 1$ **c** $7 + 3 \times (6 - 1)$

a $7 + 3 \times 6 - 1 = 7 + 18 - 1 = 24$

b $(7 + 3) \times 6 - 1 = 10 \times 6 - 1 = 60 - 1 = 59$

c $7 + 3 \times (6 - 1) = 7 + 3 \times 5 = 7 + 15 = 22$

EXERCISE 1.3

The answers to questions 1–10 should be found without the aid of a calculator. (You may use a calculator to check your answers.)

1	$5 + 7 \times 3$	6	$(21 + 17 - 10) \div 4$
2	$(5 + 7) \times 3$	7	$16 \div 4 - 20 \div 5$
3	$10 \div (5 - 3)$	8	$528 \div (150 - 142)$
4	$10 \div 5 - 1$	9	$150 - 90 \div 45 - 15$
5	$11 - 15 \div 3 \times 2$	10	$(150 - 90) \div (45 - 15)$

11 An artist buys 9 paint brushes costing 56p each.
How much change will be received from a £10 note?

12 Canvas costs £3.50 per square metre.
How many square metres can be bought for £14?

13 An office buys two computers for £889.08 each (including VAT) and a laser printer costing £1643.83. The budget for this expenditure is £3500. How much money remains after the purchases?

14 A theatre can seat 564 people in the stalls, 228 in the circle, and 196 in the balcony.

a How many people can the theatre seat in total?

Seats in the stalls cost £4.50, circle seats cost £6.50, and balcony seats cost £3.75.

b How much will the theatre take in ticket sales if it has a full house?

15   A freelance typist works at 60 wpm. She charges 0.25p per word.

    a How long will she take to type a document which is 7620 words long?

    b How much will she receive for this document?

16   Packs of 40 nappies cost £6.95.
How many packs can be bought for £50?
How much change will be received?

17   Mrs Halliday uses her own estate car when she delivers meals on wheels
and keeps a record of her mileage.

Week of 24/1/00	Mon	Wed	Fri	Sun
Mileage	12.3	11.5	13.9	9.8

For the week shown above:

    a what was her total mileage for the week?

    b how much does she claim for the week if she claims 27.2p per mile?

18   The diagram shows an extract from a holiday brochure:

Hotel Dates	Golden Sands		Park Royal		Ocean Lodge	
	14 days	21 days	14 days	21 days	14 days	21 days
Mar 2–Mar 29	323	368	337	382	284	321
Mar 30–Apr 26	373	425	387	439	334	377
Apr 27–May 24	338	385	352	400	299	339
May 25–Jun 21	367	418	382	434	329	372
Jun 22–Jul 19	399	455	414	470	361	408
Single room supp.	£2.30 per day		£2.70 per day		£2.90 per day	

Find the cost of a holiday for three adults staying at the Park Royal for
14 days from May 25. The third adult will require a single room.

19   It costs £44.50 per day to hire a car plus £0.06 per mile travelled.
How much does it cost to hire a car for 3 days to travel 450 miles?

20   A foundry makes accessories for fireplaces. A pair of brass fire dogs
weighs 1.7 kg, a set of fire irons weighs 2.04 kg, and a fire screen weighs
3.65 kg.

    a What is the total weight of the accessories for one fireplace?

A van carries a load of up to 1000 kg.

    b How many sets of the above accessories can the van carry?

21   A machine buts lengths of hollow metal rod for lamps. Each section is
20.6 cm long.

    a How many sections can be cut from a 200 cm length of rod?
    b What length of rod will be wasted?

1.2 *Directed numbers*

The negative sign has two distinct uses in mathematics:

(i) as a **subtraction** operation, e.g. $6 - 4 = 2$,
(ii) as a **direction** symbol, e.g. $-7\,°C$.

If we wish to show a temperature which is $7\,°C$ *below* zero, we can write $^-7\,°C$ *or* $-7\,°C$.

If a car travels 20 miles in one direction and then 15 miles in the reverse direction, we can write the distances travelled as $^+20$ **miles** and $^-15$ **miles**.

The numbers $^-7$, $^+20$ and $^-15$ are called **directed numbers**.

On your calculator you will see that there are two keys with negative symbols:

$\boxed{-}$ for subtraction

$\boxed{+/-}$ for direction.

Directed numbers can be represented on a horizontal or a vertical number line.

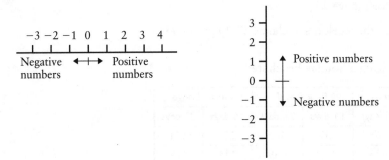

Addition and subtraction

Think of additions and subtractions of numbers as movements *up* and *down* the vertical number line.

Start at zero, move up 7 and then down 3.
Your position is now 4 *above* zero.

$$\text{i.e.} \quad 7 + (-3) = +4$$

Subtracting two numbers is the same as finding the difference between them:

$$5 - (-3)$$

is the difference between being 3 *below* zero and being 5 *above* zero on the number line.

From 3 below to 5 above you must move up 8. Therefore

$$5 - (-3) = +8 \ or \ 5 - (-3) = 5 + 3 = 8$$

(Note that $-(-3) = +3$.)

$$-4 - (-2)$$

is the difference between being 2 below zero and being 4 below zero.

From 2 *below* to 4 *below* you must move DOWN 2, i.e.

$$-4 - (-2) = -2$$

or use the rule $- \times - = +$ to give

$$-4 - (-2) = -4 + 2 = -2$$

EXERCISE 1.4

Find the answers to the following, without the aid of a calculator.

1 **a** $-5+7$ **c** $-2+-8$ **e** $-21+27$ **g** $-19+19$

   b $3+(-7)$ **d** $16+(-12)$ **f** $35+5$ **h** $-35+(-14)$

2 **a** $7-8$ **c** $-9-4$ **e** $-10+(-7)$ **g** $25-(-25)$

   b $12-(-5)$ **d** $11-(-9)$ **f** $-15-(-15)$ **h** $100-64$.

Multiplication and division

Going *up* 2 three times would mean you were now 6 *above* zero. So

$$(+2) \times 3 = +6$$
$$\text{or} \quad 2 \times 3 = 6 \qquad \text{also} \quad 3 \times 2 = 6$$

Going *down* 2 three times would mean you were now 6 *below* zero. So

$$(-2) \times 3 = -6$$
$$\text{or} \quad -2 \times 3 = -6 \qquad \text{also} \quad 3 \times -2 = -6$$

But what is $(-2) \times (-3)$?

Remember that $-(-6) = +6$
and $(-2) \times 3 = -6 = -(2 \times 3)$
$\therefore$ $(-2) \times (-3) = -(2 \times -3) = -(-6) = +6$

i.e. the reverse of moving 6 *down* is moving 6 *up*.

The rules for multiplication and division are similar:

Two numbers with like signs give a positive answer.
Two numbers with unlike signs give a negative answer.

EXAMPLE 1

Find the product of $-4 \times -7 \times -3$

$$(-4 \times -7) \times -3 = +28 \times -3$$
$$= -84$$

EXAMPLE 2

Evaluate $(-12 \div 4) \times -6$

$$(-12 \div 4) \times -6 = -3 \times -6$$
$$= +18$$

EXERCISE 1.5

Do *not* use a calculator in the following questions:

1 **a** -3×6 **d** $-7 \div -4$ **g** $8 \div \frac{1}{2} \div -2$ **j** $\dfrac{20 \times -6}{-4 \times -3}$

   b $15 \div -5$ **e** $10 \times -3 \div 2$ **h** $(-3 + -6) \times -4$

   c -7×-4 **f** $-3 \times -3 \times -3$ **i** $-7 \div (3 - (-4))$

1.3 *Powers and roots*

Powers

Patterns of dots like this

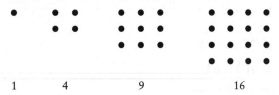

form squares, and the numbers 1, 4, 9, 16, ... are called the **square numbers**.

The square numbers are also formed by finding the product of an integer with itself:

$$1 \times 1 = 1$$
$$2 \times 2 = 4$$
$$3 \times 3 = 9$$
$$4 \times 4 = 16, \text{ etc.}$$

The sums of odd numbers also produce the square numbers:

$$1 \qquad\qquad = 1$$
$$1 + 3 \qquad\quad = 4$$
$$1 + 3 + 5 \qquad = 9$$
$$1 + 3 + 5 + 7 \quad = 16$$
$$1 + 3 + 5 + 7 + 9 = 25, \text{ etc.}$$

If any number is multiplied by itself, the product is called the square of the number. For example:

the square of 1.2 is 1.44
the square of $\sqrt{2}$ is 2.

The square of 3 or 3 squared $= 3 \times 3 = 3^2$, and the 2 is called the **index**.

Similarly:

the cube of $4 = 4$ cubed $= 4 \times 4 \times 4 = 4^3$

and

the fourth power of $2 = 2 \times 2 \times 2 \times 2 = 2^4$

Roots

The square of $4 = 4 \times 4 = 16$.

The number 4, in this example, is called the **square root** of 16, i.e. the number which when squared will give 16.

16 has another square root because $-4 \times -4 = 16$.

Hence the square roots of 16 are $+4$ and -4.

The symbol $\sqrt{}$ indicates the positive square root and hence $\sqrt{16} = +4$.

Similarly, the cube root of a number is the number which when multiplied by itself three times equals the given number. For example:

the cube root of 64 or $\sqrt[3]{64} = 4$
(since $4^3 = 4 \times 4 \times 4 = 64$)

EXERCISE 1.6

1 Write down the first 10 square numbers.

2 Write down the first 6 cube numbers.

3 Find the positive square roots of the following numbers:

   a 25   **b** 121   **c** 625   **d** 225   **e** 196

4 **a** Find the cube root of (i) 27 (ii) $^{-}64$ (iii) 729

   b Find the fifth root of 32.

   c Find the fourth root of (i) 82   (ii) 625

5 Write 25 as the sum of a sequence of odd numbers.

6 What is the third power of 2?

7 What is 3 cubed?

8 Write down the cube root of:

   a 8   **b** 27   **c** 216   **d** $\frac{1}{8}$ **e** $^{-}64$

9 What is the fourth root of 81?

10 Evaluate $5^2 \times \sqrt{16}$.

1.4 *Factors and multiples*

A **factor** is an integer which divides into a given number exactly, i.e. there is no remainder.

For example: 3 and 4 are factors of 12.

A **multiple** of a number is the number multiplied by any integer.

For example, multiples of 6 are 12, 18, 24, and so on.

12 is a multiple of 3 and of 4, since 3 and 4 are factors of 12.

EXAMPLE 1

Find all the factors of 42 and list them in pairs, the product of which is 42.

The factors of 42 are 1, 2, 3, 6, 7, 14, 21, 42.

Listed in pairs they are 1×42, 2×21, 3×14, 6×7.

EXAMPLE 2

Which of the following numbers are multiples of 9?

a 63   **b** 732   **c** 1944

a $63 \div 9 = 7$ means that 63 is a multiple of 9.

b $732 \div 9 = 81.3$ means that 732 is not a multiple of 9.

c $1944 \div 9 = 216$ means that 1944 is a multiple of 9.

Exercise 1.7

1   Find all the factors of each of the following and list the factors in pairs, the product of which is the number itself:

   a 15 **b** 27 **c** 36 **d** 64 **e** 100

2   **a** Write down the factors of (i) 48 (ii) 72.

   b List the factors which are common to 48 and 72.

3   Of which of the following numbers is 4 a factor?

   34 64 144 642 116 2620

4   State which of 5, 10, 20, 25 are factors of the following:

   a 300 **b** 1050 **c** 470 **d** 875 **e** 2360

5   Which of the following numbers are divisible by **a** 3, **b** 6, **c** 15?

   125 240 87 96 146 255 1073

2 *Using a Calculator*

2.1 *Approximations*

Most calculators display answers of up to 10 digits.

In most cases, this is too many digits. Therefore, when using a calculator, it is necessary to give an *approximate* answer which contains fewer digits (but which has a sensible degree of accuracy).

There are two methods in common usage:
rounding to a number of **decimal places** (e.g. 2 decimal places or 2 d.p.) and rounding to a number of **significant figures** (e.g. 3 significant figures or 3 s.f.).

The rule for rounding to, for example, 2 decimal places is:

If the digit in the third decimal place is **5 or more, round up,** i.e. increase the digit in the second decimal place by 1.

If the digit in the third decimal place is **less than 5, round down,** i.e. the digit in the second place remains the same.

EXAMPLE 1

Give the following numbers from a calculator display, to 2 d.p.
7.92341, 25.675231, 0.06666. ., 0.9999999. .

Calculator display	Degree of accuracy required (2 d.p.)	Answer correct to 2 d.p.
7.92341	7.92|341	7.92
25.675231	25.67|5231	25.68
0.066666 .	0.06|6666.	0.07
0.9999999 . .	0.99|99999..	1.00

The rules for significant figures are similar, but you need to take care with zeros.

Zeros at the beginning of a decimal number or at the end of an integer are not counted as significant figures, but must be included in the final result. All other zeros are significant.

For example, 70 631.9 given correct to 3 significant figures is 70 600.

The three significant figures are 7, 0 and 6. The last two zeros are not significant (i.e. do not count as fourth and fifth figures), but are essential so that 7 retains its value of 70 thousand and 6 its value of 6 hundred.

EXAMPLE 2

Give the following numbers, from a calculator display to 3 s.f.
7.92341, 25.675231, 0.066666. ., 24380.., 0.999999. .

Calculator display	Degree of accuracy required (3 s.f.)	Answer correct to 3 s.f.
7.92341	7.92|341	7.92
25.675231	25.6|75231	25.7
0.066666 .	0.0666|66 . .	0.0667
24380.	243|80.	24400
0.9999999. .	0.999|999..	1.00

In the last example, the digit 1 becomes the first significant figure, and the two zeros are the second and third figures.

EXERCISE 2.1

Give each of the following numbers to the accuracy requested in brackets:

1   9.736 (3 s.f.)

2   0.36218 (2 d.p.)

3   147.49 (1 d.p.)

4   28.613 (2 s.f.)

5   0.5252 (2 s.f.)

6   4.1983 (2 d.p.)

7   1245.4 (3 s.f.)

8   0.00425 (3 d.p.)

9   273.6 (2 s.f.)

10   459.97314 (1 d.p.)

2.2 *Estimation*

The answer displayed on a calculator will be correct for the values you have entered, but a calculator cannot tell you if you have pressed the wrong key or entered your numbers in the wrong order.

Each number you enter into the calculator should be checked for accuracy and the final answer should be checked by comparing it with an *estimated* answer.

EXAMPLE

Estimate the value of 31.41×79.6.

31.41 is approximately 30
79.6 is approximately 80

An estimated value is therefore $30 \times 80 = 2400$.

If the calculator displays, for example, 25002.36, a mistake has been made with the decimal point, and the answer should read 2500.236.

EXERCISE 2.2

1   By rounding all numbers to 1 significant figure, find an estimated value of each calculation:

a 52.2×67.4 d $607 \div 1.86$ g $\dfrac{520.4 \times 8.065}{99.53}$

b 6143×0.0381 e $48.2 \div 0.203$

c 607×1.86 f $3784 \div 412$ h $\dfrac{807}{391.2 \times 0.38}$

2   Find an estimate for each of the following calculations, by choosing an appropiate approximation for each number:

a $82.3 \div 9.1$ b $0.364 \div 6.29$ c $\dfrac{31.73 \times 6.282}{7.918}$

3   By finding an estimate of the answer, state which of the following calculations are obviously incorrect. (Do not use a calculator.)

a $8.14 \times 49.6 = 403.74$ f $\dfrac{42.3 \times 3.97}{1635} = 10.27$

b $23.79 \div 5.57 = 4.27$

c $324 \div 196 \times 0.5 = 226$ g $\sqrt{1640} = 40.5$

d $3.14 \times 9.46^2 = 882.35$ h $\sqrt{650} = 80.6$

e $23.79 \div 0.213 = 11.169$ i $(0.038)^2 = 0.00144$

j $(0.205)^3 = 0.0862$

2.3 *Degrees of accuracy*

Whenever you solve a numerical problem, you must consider the accuracy required in your answer, especially if you cannot obtain an exact answer. In Section 2.1, you saw how to correct an answer to a number of significant figures or decimal places. Section 2.3 shows you how to select an appropriate degree of accuracy.

Sometimes the answer to a numerical problem is an integer, and this gives you an exact answer. Fractions are also exact, but their decimal equivalents are often inexact. For example, suppose you were able to buy sixteen pencils for £3 but wanted to buy only one. Each pencil would cost £$\frac{3}{16}$.

As a decimal this would be 18.75 pence, but obviously you cannot pay 18.75 pence for an individual pencil. The shopkeeper would work in the smallest unit of currency, which is one penny. To make sure that she did not lose money she would round up the price to 19p.

EXAMPLE 1

A netball club is hiring a number of minibuses to go to an away match. Each minibus can carry 15 passengers and 49 members of the club wish to travel. How many minibuses are needed?

The number of minibuses is $\frac{49}{15} = 3.26667$
3.26667 is rounded up to the nearest integer.

The netball club needs 4 minibuses.

Sometimes you will need to **round down** a mathematical answer as the following example shows.

---**EXAMPLE**---

Pam changes 9413 French francs into pounds at the rate of 10.9 francs to £1. The bank, not wishing to be generous, decides to round down to the nearest penny the money it will give Pam.

How much does Pam receive?

$$9413 \text{ French francs} = \frac{9413}{10.9} = £863.577\,98$$

∴ Pam receives £863.58

EXERCISE 2.3

1 Twelve pens cost £6.20. What would be charged for one pen?

2 A tin of paint covers 12 m^2.
How many tins are required to cover an area of 32 m^2 with two coats of paint?

3 Sara gives each of her 35 friends a chocolate biscuit. Each packet of chocolate biscuits contains 8 biscuits. How many packets of chocolate biscuits must Sara open?

4 An office orders plastic sleeves which cost £2.67 for a box of 100.
How much should be charged:

   a for ten   **b** for one?

5 A TV room 5.6 m^2 is to be carpeted. The carpet chosen is 3 m wide and is sold in metre lengths. How many metres should be bought?

6 Visitors to a day centre pay £1.70 per week of five days towards the cost of tea and biscuits. How much should someone visiting for one day be charged, if the centre is not to make a loss?

7 Eleven students receive a bill for £120 after an evening out.
How much should each pay?

8 A booking agency normally sells a block of four tickets for £55.43. It agrees to sell them individually.
How much should it charge for one ticket if it does not wish to lose money through individual sales?

9 A factory used 26 818 units of electricity at 5.44p per unit.
What is the cost of the electricity used?

10 In a car factory, pieces of glass fibre 0.9 m are cut from a roll which is 24 m long.
How many pieces can be cut from one roll?

2.4 *The keys of a calculator*

To use your calculator most effectively, you must become familiar with the keys and their functions.

The booklet that accompanies your calculator will tell you the order in which the keys are used for calculations.

For example, to find $\sqrt[4]{5}$ the keys required on most calculators are

| 5 | INV | x^y | 4 | = |

Other useful keys are

a the memory keys $\boxed{\text{Min}}$ $\boxed{\text{MR}}$ $\boxed{\text{M+}}$ $\boxed{\text{M−}}$ (can you use them correctly?)

b brackets,   e.g. $\dfrac{36 \times 14}{21 \times 4}$ is $36 \times 14 \div (21 \times 4)$

   or $36 \times 14 \div 21 \div 4$

   not $36 \times 14 \div 21 \times 4$

c The $\boxed{\text{AC}}$ key clears the calculator (except the memories) before beginning a new calculation.

d The $\boxed{\text{C}}$ or $\boxed{\text{CE}}$ key is used to correct an entry error (i.e. if the wrong key has been pressed).

The key clears the last entry made (either a figure or an operation), provided it is pressed immediately after the error has been made.

The correct entry can then be made and the sequence continued.

For example, $6 + 3$ $\boxed{\text{C}}$ $2 =$ will produce the answer to $6 + 2$.

EXERCISE 2.4

1 $386.9 \div 32.87$ (to 1 d.p.)

2 $2576 \div 0.03741$ (to 3 s.f.)

3 $\sqrt{\dfrac{79.5}{10.9}}$ (to 3 s.f.)

4 0.000356×385.7 (to 3 d.p.)

5 $(7.1 + 4.01) \times 8$ (to 3 s.f.)

6 $\dfrac{1}{0.0345}$ (to 3 s.f.)

7 $(4.63)^2$ (to 3 s.f.)

8 $2.1 + 3.41 \times 7.01$ (to 3 s.f.)

9 $\dfrac{3.8 \times 2.9}{17.1 \times 0.82}$ (to 3 d.p.)

10 $\frac{1}{2}(246.3 + 1092.8 + 376.4 + 49.8)$

11 $\dfrac{3.1 \times 15.2}{7.01 \times 8.11}$ (to 3 d.p.)

12 $\sqrt{\pi \times 38.4}$ (to 2 s.f.)

13 $\sqrt[3]{4 + 3.7 + 28.1}$ (to 1 d.p.)

2.5 *Standard form*

Standard form is used when dealing with very large or very small numbers.

In standard form the number is always written as a number between 1 and 10 multiplied by a power of 10, i.e. as

$$A \times 10^n \text{ where } 1 \leqslant A < 10 \text{ and } n \text{ is an integer.}$$

This form is also known as **scientific notation**.

EXAMPLE 1

The velocity of light is 300 000 000 metres per second.
Write this number in standard form.

   (i) Write down A, the number between 1 and 10: 3.0

  (ii) Count the number of places to the *right* which the decimal point must be moved to give the velocity of light: 8 places.

 (iii) Write the number in standard form: 3.0×10^8

or
$$300\,000\,000 = 3.0 \times 100\,000\,000$$
$$= 3.0 \times 10^8$$

EXAMPLE 2

0.000 000 000 000 000 000 000 000 001 67 kg is the mass of a hydrogen atom.

Write this number in standard form.

   (i) $A = 1.67$

  (ii) In this case the decimal point must be moved 27 places to the *left*, $n = -27$

 (iii) In standard form, the mass $= 1.67 \times 10^{-27}$ kg.

EXAMPLE 3

Convert 3.15×10^4 to a 'normal' number.

$n = 4$ so the decimal point must be moved 4 places to the right:
$$3.15 \times 10^4 = 31\,500$$

or $3.15 \times 10^4 = 3.15 \times 10\,000$
$$= 31\,500$$

EXAMPLE 4

Multiply (2.7×10^4) by (5×10^{-2})

$(2.7 \times 10^4) \times (5 \times 10^-2) = (2.7 \times 10\,000) \times (5 \div 100)$
$$= 13.5 \times 100$$
$$= 1.35 \times 1000$$
$$= 1.35 \times 10^3$$

Using a calculator:

$(2.7 \times 10^4) \times (5 \times 10^-2) = 2.7$ $\boxed{\text{EXP}}$ 4 $\boxed{\times}$ 5 $\boxed{\text{EXP}}$ 2 $\boxed{+/-}$

(On some calculators the exponential button is $\boxed{\text{EE}}$.)

Calculator display is   1350
$$= 1.35 \times 10^3 \text{ (in standard form)}$$

If it is possible to use your calculator in scientific mode, the same sequence of operations will produce the answer in standard form displaying

1.35   03   or possibly 1.35^{03}

which is then written as 1.35×10^3.

(Some calculators round calculations to 2 s.f. displaying the answer as 1.4^{03}, which is then written as 1.4×10^3.)

EXAMPLE 5

Divide (2.7×10^4) by (5×10^{-2}).

$$
\begin{aligned}
(2.7 \times 10^4) \div (5 \times 10^{-2}) &= 27\,000 \div 0.05 \\
&= 540\,000 \\
&= 5.4 \times 10^5 \text{ (in standard form)}
\end{aligned}
$$

Using your calculator gives
$$(2.7 \times 10^4) \div (5 \times 10^{-2}) = 2.7 \boxed{\text{EXP}} \; 4 \div 5 \; \boxed{\text{EXP}} \; 2 \; \boxed{+/-}$$

$$
\begin{aligned}
&= 540000 \\
&= 5.4 \times 10^5 \text{ (in standard form)}
\end{aligned}
$$

Working in the scientific mode will give the correct answer 5.4^{05}

which is conventionally written as 5.4×10^5.

Numbers in standard form can be added and subtracted, provided the power of 10 is the same in each number.

If the powers of 10 are *not* the same, convert each number to a normal number before adding or subtracting or convert to a common power of 10.

EXAMPLE 6

Evaluate $(4.3 \times 10^4) - (8.7 \times 10^3)$

$$
\begin{aligned}
(4.3 \times 10^4) - (8.7 \times 10^3) &= 43\,000 - 8700 \\
&= 34\,300 \\
&= 3.43 \times 10^4
\end{aligned}
$$

EXERCISE 2.5

1   Write the following numbers in standard form:

   a 790 000   **g** 15.7×1000

   b 0.0046   **h** 4700×10000

   c 31 300   **i** $0.000\,34 \times 100$

   d 0.000 0941   **j** $0.0027 \div 1000$

   e 100 000   **k** $5000 \div 10000$

   f 0.000 282   **l** $0.000\,029 \div 200$

2   Write the following numbers in normal form:

   a 7.53×10^3 **f** 4.042×10^4

   b 2.4×10^2 **g** 3.192×10^6

   c 1.9×10^{-3} **h** 9.74×10^{-4}

   d 8.37×10^{-1} **i** 6.8×10^{-6}

   e 4.51×10^{-2}

3   Evaluate the following, giving your answers in standard form:

    a $(3 \times 10^2) \times (2 \times 10^2)$ **f** $(3.6 \times 10^4) \div (9.0 \times 10^5)$

    b $(1.4 \times 10^{-3}) \times (3.7 \times 10^3)$ **g** $(2.7 \times 10^{-2}) \times (1.6 \times 10^{-3})$

    c $(8 \times 10^3) \div (2 \times 10^2)$ **h** $(3.3 \times 10^4) - (4.6 \times 10^3)$

    d $(5.3 \times 10^3) + (8.2 \times 10^3)$ **i** $(4.5 \times 10^{-3}) - (5.0 \times 10^{-3})$

    e $(4.6 \times 10^3) \times (5.9 \times 10^{-1})$ **j** $(1.32 \times 10^{-1}) \div (2.2 \times 10^{-3})$

4   The distance from the Earth to the Sun is about 9.29×10^7 miles and from the Earth to the Moon is about 2.38×10^5 miles.
How many times greater is the distance to the Sun than the distance to the Moon?

5   Light travels at a speed of 3.0×10^8 metres per second.

If the distance from the Earth to the Sun is approximately 1.5×10^8 km, how long does it take the Sun's light to reach the Earth?

EXERCISE 2.6

1   The weight of 100 m of fine thread is 2.3 g.

    a Find the weight of 1 m and state this weight in kg in standard form.

    b Find the length of thread which has weight 2×10^{-4} kg.

2   A mill produces 350 m of a particular material.
State this length (in cm) in standard form.

One designer buys 8.34×10^3 cm.
How many metres of the material does the mill have left?

3   The revenue of the budget in West Samoa in 1990 was W\$ 1.21×10^8.
The population was 1.6×10^5.
What was the revenue raised per person?

4   The capacity of a computer is 40 megabytes where 1 megabyte is 10^3 kilobytes. 1 kilobyte is 1.024×10^3 bytes.
Express the capacity of the computer in bytes in standard form.

5   In Peter's blood there are 4.7×10^{12} blood cells per litre. Peter's body contains 4.9 litres of blood.
How many red blood cells are there in Peter's body?

6   The population of the USA in 1992 was 2.55×10^8, of whom $\frac{1}{19}$ were over 75 years old.
How many were over 75?

7   The number of people attending a sports centre is 132 000 during a year:

    a Give this number in standard form.
    b Find the average number of people attending on each day.

8   The length of a round-the-world yacht race is 3.3×10^4 miles. A boat
    averages 311 miles per day.
    How many days does the yacht take to complete the race?

9   In 1992, Martinique imported goods worth $\$1.7 \times 10^9$. The population
    of the island was 3.7×10^5.
    What was the value of the goods imported per person (to the nearest
    dollar)?

10 In 1991 the coal reserves in the USA were estimated to be 2.15×10^{11}
    tons. The production was 9.44×10^8 tons.
    At this rate of production, how many years would the reserves last?

3 *Fractions*

3.1 *Types of fraction*

A fraction is a number which can be written as a ratio, with an integer divided by an integer, e.g. $\dfrac{7}{9}$ or $-\dfrac{2}{3}$.

If a shape is divided into a number of equal parts and some of those parts are then shaded, the shaded area can be written as a fraction of the whole.

 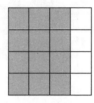

$$\begin{array}{cccc} \text{Fraction} \\ \text{shaded} \end{array} = \quad \frac{3}{8} \qquad\qquad \frac{12}{16} \qquad\qquad \frac{2}{6}$$

The **denominator** (lower integer) denotes the number of parts into which the shape was divided.

The **numerator** (upper integer) denotes the number of parts which have been shaded.

Fractions which have a smaller numerator than denominator are called **proper** fractions, e.g. $\dfrac{1}{2}, \dfrac{5}{12}, -\dfrac{28}{60}$.

If the numerator is larger than the denominator, the fraction is an **improper** fraction, e.g. $\dfrac{12}{5}, -\dfrac{7}{2}, \dfrac{72}{18}$.

A **mixed number** is a number composed of an integer and a proper fraction, e.g. $3\dfrac{1}{2}, -24\dfrac{3}{4}, 4\dfrac{5}{6}$.

3.2 *Equivalent fractions*

We could consider the larger square above to be divided into four columns instead of sixteen squares.

The shaded area is then $\dfrac{3}{4}$ of the whole. This means that $\dfrac{12}{16} = \dfrac{3}{4}$.

$\dfrac{12}{16}$ and $\dfrac{3}{4}$ are called **equivalent fractions** because they have the same value.

EXAMPLE 1

Complete $\dfrac{6}{7} = \dfrac{?}{28}$ to give equivalent fractions.

The 7 in the denominator must be increased four times to give 28.

The numerator must be treated similarly and be increased four times:

$$\frac{6}{7} = \frac{6 \times 4}{7 \times 4} = \frac{24}{28}$$

EXAMPLE 2

Reduce $\dfrac{32}{72}$ to its lowest terms.

$$\frac{32}{72} = \frac{32 \div 8}{72 \div 8} = \frac{4}{9}$$

(4 and 9 have no common factor therefore the fraction is in its lowest terms.)

EXAMPLE 3

Convert $13\frac{2}{5}$ to an improper fraction.

$$13\frac{2}{5} = 13 + \frac{2}{5}$$
$$= (13 \times \frac{5}{5}) + \frac{2}{5}$$
$$= \frac{65}{5} + \frac{2}{5}$$
$$= \frac{65 + 2}{5}$$
$$= \frac{67}{5}$$

EXAMPLE 4

Convert $\dfrac{141}{22}$ to a mixed number.

$$22)\overline{141}$$
$$\qquad\qquad 6 \text{ remainder } 9$$
$$\frac{141}{22} = 6\frac{9}{22}$$

EXERCISE 3.1

1 Complete each of the following to give equivalent fractions:

   a $\dfrac{4}{5} = \dfrac{?}{10}$ **d** $\dfrac{1}{4} = \dfrac{?}{36}$

   b $\dfrac{2}{3} = \dfrac{?}{12}$ **e** $\dfrac{21}{30} = \dfrac{?}{10}$

   c $\dfrac{3}{4} = \dfrac{?}{24}$ **f** $\dfrac{16}{18} = \dfrac{8}{?}$

2 Reduce the following fractions to their lowest terms:

   a $\dfrac{10}{15}$ **b** $\dfrac{18}{24}$ **c** $\dfrac{22}{99}$ **d** $\dfrac{21}{33}$

   e $\dfrac{75}{100}$ **f** $\dfrac{40}{60}$ **g** $\dfrac{30}{65}$ **h** $\dfrac{64}{96}$

3 A particular shade of green paint is made by mixing 60 g of blue powder paint with 30 g of yellow powder paint.
What fraction of the mixture is blue paint?

4 A secretary's working day is 8 hours long. On one particular day, $4\frac{1}{2}$ hours were spent typing and $1\frac{1}{2}$ hours on the telephone.
What fraction of the working day was spent:
   a typing   **b** telephoning?

5 A dental chart shows that a patient with a full set of 32 teeth has 6 fillings.
What fraction of the teeth are filled?

6 In a group of 240 tourists travelling on a charter flight, 180 requested seats in the non-smoking section.
What fraction of the passengers were in the smoking section?

7 A printing firm produces 350 books in a day. 200 of these are to be exported.
What fraction of the day's production is exported?

8 Convert the following mixed numbers to improper fractions:

   a $2\dfrac{2}{9}$ **b** $5\dfrac{1}{6}$ **c** $4\dfrac{11}{12}$ **d** $11\dfrac{1}{10}$

   e $8\dfrac{3}{4}$ **f** $12\dfrac{2}{3}$ **g** $7\dfrac{3}{20}$ **h** $20\dfrac{3}{7}$

9 Convert the following improper fractions to mixed numbers, in their lowest terms:

   a $\dfrac{9}{7}$ **b** $\dfrac{36}{5}$ **c** $\dfrac{30}{9}$ **d** $\dfrac{61}{8}$

   e $\dfrac{153}{11}$ **f** $\dfrac{127}{12}$ **g** $\dfrac{132}{15}$ **h** $\dfrac{94}{4}$

3.3 *Operations involving fractions*

Addition and subtraction

Only fractions *of the same type* can be added or subtracted, i.e. they must have the same denominator.

The method for addition or subtraction is:

(i) Find the smallest number which is a multiple of all the denominators.

(ii) Change each fraction to an equivalent fraction with the new denominator.

(iii) Add and/or subtract the fractions.

(iv) If the answer is an improper fraction, convert to a mixed number.

(v) Give the answer in its lowest terms.

EXAMPLE 1

Evaluate $\dfrac{5}{8} - \dfrac{3}{4} + \dfrac{1}{5}$

40 is the smallest number that is a multiple of all the denominators.

The sum in equivalent fractions is $\dfrac{5 \times 5}{8 \times 5} - \dfrac{3 \times 10}{4 \times 10} + \dfrac{1 \times 8}{5 \times 8} = \dfrac{25}{40} - \dfrac{30}{40} + \dfrac{8}{40}$

$$= \dfrac{3}{40} \text{ which is a fraction in its lowest terms.}$$

EXAMPLE 2

Evaluate $1\dfrac{2}{3} + \dfrac{3}{4} - 2\dfrac{1}{12}$

$$1\dfrac{2}{3} + \dfrac{3}{4} - 2\dfrac{1}{12} = 1 + \dfrac{2}{3} + \dfrac{3}{4} - \left(2 + \dfrac{1}{12}\right)$$

$$= 1 + \dfrac{2}{3} + \dfrac{3}{4} - 2 - \dfrac{1}{12}$$

The smallest multiple of all the denominators is 12.

The sum in equivalent fractions is $\dfrac{12}{12} + \dfrac{8}{12} + \dfrac{9}{12} - \dfrac{24}{12} - \dfrac{1}{12}$

$$= \dfrac{12 + 8 + 9 - 24 - 1}{12}$$

$$= \dfrac{4}{12} = \dfrac{1}{3} \text{ in its lowest terms}$$

EXERCISE 3.2

Evaluate the following:

1 $\dfrac{2}{5} + \dfrac{3}{4}$ 2 $\dfrac{7}{8} - \dfrac{5}{6}$ 3 $\dfrac{5}{12} + \dfrac{1}{4}$ 4 $1\dfrac{1}{2} - \dfrac{3}{4}$

5 $4\dfrac{1}{6} - 3\dfrac{2}{3}$ 6 $3\dfrac{4}{5} + 1\dfrac{1}{4}$ 7 $3\dfrac{1}{2} - 4\dfrac{1}{4} + 2\dfrac{3}{4}$ 8 $3\dfrac{5}{8} - 1\dfrac{1}{4} - 1\dfrac{1}{2}$

9 A clear glaze for pottery is made by mixing feldspar, flint, whiting and china clay.
One half of the mix is feldspar and one fifth is china clay. Flint and whiting are mixed in equal amounts.
What fraction of the mix is flint?

10 a Photographic prints $4\dfrac{1}{2}$ in wide by $3\dfrac{1}{2}$ in are to be mounted in an album which has pages $9\dfrac{3}{4}$ in wide by $13\dfrac{1}{4}$ in.
How many prints can be mounted on one page?
b The photographs are to be equally spaced on the page. What width are the margins:
a across the page   b down the page?

11 Three quarters of an office's stationary budget is spent on paper, one sixth on envelopes, and the remainder on miscellaneous items.
What fraction is spent on miscellaneous items?

12 To encourage customers to pay their bills, a firm gives a discount of $\dfrac{1}{20}$ of the bill if it is paid on time and a further discount of $\dfrac{1}{12}$ of the bill for early payment.
What fraction of the bill is deducted for early payment?

13 A dietician, advising clients on suitable diets, found that $\dfrac{3}{4}$ of her clients were overweight, $\dfrac{1}{6}$ suffered from arthritis and the remainder from coeliac disease.
a What fraction were coeliac sufferers?
b If her clients numbered 36 at the time, how many needed a gluten-free diet?

14 A cold remedy is sold as a powder in sachets. $\dfrac{4}{5}$ of each powder is aspirin and $\dfrac{2}{25}$ is ascorbic acid. The remainder is caffeine.
a What fraction is caffeine?
b How much of each ingredient does 500 mg of powder contain?

15 The proprietor of a B & B establishment mixes his own breakfast cereal. This consists of $2\dfrac{1}{2}$ cups of oats, $\dfrac{1}{4}$ of a cup of wheat germ, and $\dfrac{2}{3}$ of a cup of raisins and nuts.
What is the total number of cups in this mixture?

16 During a three-day holiday break, $1\dfrac{1}{2}$ in of rain fell on the first day, $1\dfrac{3}{4}$ in on the second day and $3\dfrac{3}{4}$ in on the third day.
How much rain fell altogether?

17 An axle of diameter $2\dfrac{3}{4}$ inches is fitted into the centre of the hub of a wheel which has a diameter of $3\dfrac{1}{8}$ inches.
How much clearance is there between the axle and the inside of the hub on each side?

18 In a self-assembly unit, a wood top, $\dfrac{5}{8}$ in thick, is screwed to a metal frame $1\dfrac{1}{4}$ in thick.
What is the maximum length of screw that can be used?

Multiplication and division

The rules for multiplication and division of fractions are very different from those for addition and subtraction.

The fractions do not have to have the same denominator, but they must not be mixed numbers.

Answers should be given in their lowest terms and as mixed numbers, if necessary.

To divide by a fraction, invert it and then multiply by the inverted fraction.

EXAMPLE 1

Multiply $\dfrac{18}{25}$ by $\dfrac{5}{6}$

$$\frac{18}{25} \times \frac{5}{6} = \frac{18 \times 5}{25 \times 6} = \frac{90}{150} = \frac{3}{5} \qquad or \qquad \frac{18}{25} \times \frac{5}{6} = \frac{\overset{3}{\cancel{18}} \times \overset{1}{\cancel{5}}}{\underset{5}{\cancel{25}} \times \underset{1}{\cancel{6}}} = \frac{3 \times 1}{5 \times 1} = \frac{3}{5}$$

EXAMPLE 2

Evaluate $1\dfrac{3}{4} \times 2\dfrac{2}{7}$

The mixed numbers are converted to improper fractions:

$$\frac{7}{4} \times \frac{16}{7} = \frac{7 \times 16}{4 \times 7} = \frac{112}{28} = 4 \qquad or \qquad \frac{7}{4} \times \frac{16}{7} = \frac{\overset{1}{\cancel{7}} \times \overset{4}{\cancel{16}}}{\underset{1}{\cancel{4}} \times \underset{1}{\cancel{7}}} = \frac{1 \times 4}{1 \times 1} = 4$$

EXAMPLE 3

Evaluate $\dfrac{5}{9} \div \dfrac{2}{3}$

$$\frac{5}{9} \div \frac{2}{3} = \frac{5}{9} \times \frac{3}{2} = \frac{15}{18} = \frac{5}{6}$$

or

$$\frac{5}{9} \div \frac{2}{3} = \frac{5}{9} \times \frac{3}{2} = \frac{5 \times \overset{1}{\cancel{3}}}{\underset{3}{\cancel{9}} \times 2} = \frac{5 \times 1}{3 \times 2} = \frac{5}{6}$$

EXAMPLE 4

Divide $3\dfrac{1}{6}$ by $\dfrac{2}{3}$

$$3\frac{1}{6} \div \frac{2}{3} = \frac{19}{6} \div \frac{2}{3} = \frac{19}{6} \times \frac{3}{2} = \frac{57}{12} = 4\frac{9}{12} = 4\frac{3}{4}$$

or

$$3\frac{1}{6} \div \frac{2}{3} = \frac{19}{6} \div \frac{2}{3} = \frac{19}{\underset{2}{\cancel{6}}} \times \frac{\overset{1}{\cancel{3}}}{2} = \frac{19 \times 1}{2 \times 2} = \frac{19}{4} = 4\frac{3}{4}$$

EXERCISE 3.3

Evaluate the following:

1 $\dfrac{7}{8} \times \dfrac{4}{5}$ **2** $1\dfrac{2}{3} \times \dfrac{4}{5}$ **3** $6 \div \dfrac{1}{2}$ **4** $\dfrac{5}{6} \div \dfrac{3}{4}$ **5** $2\dfrac{1}{5} \times 3\dfrac{1}{4}$ **6** $5\dfrac{1}{7} \div 3$

7 The length of the head of an adult is about $\frac{1}{8}$ of the adult's height.
For a baby, the head is about $\frac{1}{3}$ of the total height.

  a An artist draws the figure of a lady which is $4\frac{4}{5}$ inches in length.
  What, approximately, should be the length of the head?

  b In the same picture, a baby is drawn with a head length of $\frac{1}{2}$ inch.
  What, approximately, should be the length of the baby from neck to foot?

8 A silversmith designs a kilt pin which is a sword $6\frac{1}{4}$ cm long. The hilt is $\frac{1}{5}$ of the total length and the cross-piece is $\frac{3}{5}$ of the blade.
What is the length of:

  a the hilt

  b the cross-piece?

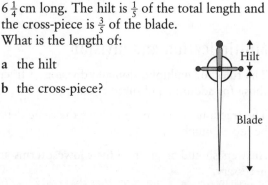

9   In a small business, overtime is paid at one and a third (see Section 7.2). The basic hourly rate is £5.70 per hour.

What is the overtime rate of pay per hour?

10 A5 paper is half the size of A4, which is half the size of A3.

a What fraction of A3 size paper is A5?

b How many sheets of A3 should be cut to make two dozen sheets of A5?

11 In a healthy person approximately $\frac{1}{15}$ of their weight is body fat.
How much body fat should a healthy person of $11\frac{1}{4}$ stones have?

12 Approximately $\frac{1}{7}$ of virgin oil consists of saturates.
Approximately, how many grams of saturates are contained in:

a a 91 g bottle of oil

b a $5\frac{1}{4}$ g helping of oil?

13 A large bowl contains three times the B & B proprietor's cereal mixture (see question 15, Exercise 3.2). Each guest receives $\frac{3}{4}$ of a cup of cereal for breakfast.
How many guests can be served with the contents of the bowl?

14 A travel company charges children $\frac{2}{3}$ of the cost of an adult's holiday price.

a How much is charged for a child if the adult price is £432?

b How many children are the equivalent, in cost, of ten adults?

15 A $1\frac{7}{8}$ in long screw has a thread which is $\frac{3}{5}$ of the length of the screw.
How long is the thread?

16 A toy manufacturer makes sets of boxes which nest inside one another. One set is rectangular in shape and the length of each box is $1\frac{2}{3}$ times the width.

a If the width of the largest box in the set is $4\frac{1}{2}$ inches, what is the length?

b If the length of the smallest box is $4\frac{1}{6}$ inches, what is the width?

3.4 *The conversion between fractions and decimal fractions*

The fraction $\frac{7}{8}$ may be stated as $7 \div 8$.

Using a calculator, $7 \div 8 = 0.875$, and this is the **decimal fraction** which is equivalent to $\frac{7}{8}$.

EXAMPLE 1

Convert $3\frac{5}{6}$ to a decimal.

The integer part of the mixed number remains the same. Only the fractional part needs to be converted.

On the calculator $5 \div 6 = 0.833\,3333$ which is a recurring decimal.

$$3\frac{5}{6} = 3.8\dot{3} \text{ or } 3.83 \text{ (to 3 s.f.)}$$

All fractions convert to either a terminating or a recurring decimal. The dot above the 3 indicates that the 3 is a recurring decimal.

EXAMPLE 2

Convert 0.35 to a fraction in its lowest terms.

$0.35 = \dfrac{35}{100} = \dfrac{7}{20}$ (dividing numerator and denominator by 5)

EXERCISE 3.4

1   Write down the shaded area as (i) a fraction, (ii) a decimal fraction of the whole area.

   a   b   c

2   Convert the following fractions to decimals:

   a $\dfrac{1}{10}$ b $\dfrac{1}{2}$ c $\dfrac{3}{4}$ d $1\dfrac{9}{20}$

   e $4\dfrac{21}{25}$ f $2\dfrac{5}{6}$ g $7\dfrac{4}{9}$ h $3\dfrac{1}{7}$

3   Convert the following decimals to fractions:
   a   0.5   f   2.8
   b   0.25   g   3.6
   c   1.$\dot{6}$ h   2.15
   d   1.$\dot{3}$ i   0.125
   e   1.3   j   0.375

4   Investigate the relationships between the fractional and decimal forms of:

   a   Halves, quarters and eighths

   b   thirds, sixths and ninths.

5   Describe a quick method of converting to decimals:

   a   tenths   b   fifths   c   hundredths

   d   twentieths   e   twenty-fifths.

In questions 6–11, where appropriate, write the answer:

   (i)   as a mixed number in its lowest terms

   (ii) as a decimal correct to 2 d.p.

6   A designer draws a sketch for a new design of car. The length of the car on the sketch is $4\frac{1}{2}$ inches. The actual length of the car is 153 inches. How many times larger is the actual car than the sketch?

7   a   A chemist sells toothpaste in two sizes: 75 g and 125 g.
       How many times larger is the 125 g tube than the 75 g tube of toothpaste?

   b   If the cost of the 75 g tube of paste is 48p what should the equivalent price of the 125 g tube be?

8   Traditionally, 1 quire of paper = 24 sheets
                       1 ream of paper = 20 quires
   Nowadays, however, a ream is generally 500 sheets.

   a   How many extra sheets are there in a ream?

   b   How many quires are there in a ream?

9   On a hospital ward, 40 minutes is spent every day checking patients' temperatures and blood pressures.
   How many hours are spent on this activity in a 7-day week?

10   A tour bus driver has to travel 112 miles on the first leg of the journey. The driver expects to travel at an average speed of 35 mph.
   What is his estimate of the time for this part of the journey?

11   A piece of machinery has two interlocking cogs.
   Cog A has 35 teeth.   Cog B has 20 teeth.
   How many turns does Cog B make for each turn of Cog A?

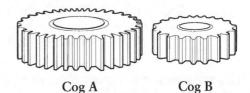

   Cog A   Cog B

4 *Ratio and Proportion*

4.1 *Ratio*

Carmen's parents give her a weekly allowance of £3.60.
Her younger brother, Leroy, is given an allowance of £1.20.
Carmen receives three times as much allowance as Leroy.
Here is another way of saying the same thing:

The ratio of Carmen's allowance to Leroy's allowance is **3:1**.

Ratios can be written with a colon between the amounts, like this:

First quantity : Second quantity

or as a fraction, like this: $\dfrac{\text{First quantity}}{\text{Second quantity}}$

EXAMPLE 1

When Leroy is older, his parents decide that the ratio between his
allowance and his sister's should now be 2:3.
If Carmen receives £3.90 per week, how much should they give Leroy?

Leroy's allowance : Carmen's allowance $= 2 : 3 = \dfrac{2}{3}$

Leroy should receive $\dfrac{2}{3}$ of Carmen's allowance

Leroy's allowance $= \dfrac{2}{3} \times £3.90 = £2.60$

EXAMPLE 2

A large jar of coffee costs £2.38 and a small jar costs 84p.
Express these prices as a ratio in its lowest terms.

Converting both prices to pence gives the ratio

Large jar : small jar $= 238 : 84$

The ratio can be reduced if 238 and 84 can both be divided by the same
number (called a common factor).

The largest factor which is common to 238 and 84 may not be
immediately obvious, in which case the reduction to lowest terms can be
carried out in stages.

2 is a common factor of 238 and 84. Dividing by 2 reduces the ratio to
119 :42

Possible factors of 42 are 2, 3, 6 and 7.
Only 7 is also a factor of 119.

Dividing by 7 gives the ratio in its lowest terms

$= 17 : 6$

Exercise 4.1

In questions 1–3, write all ratios in their lowest terms.

1 Two brothers have £20 and £24 in their respective savings accounts.
   Express these amounts as a ratio.

2 Miss Morgan has £320 in her current account, £400 in her deposit account, and £800 in her savings account.
   Express these amounts as a ratio.

3 A pound of grapes costs £1.60 and a pound of pears 72p. Write these prices as a ratio.

4 Write each pair of quantities as a ratio in its lowest terms:

   a 60 m, 40 m   f 15 cm, 10 cm

   b £2, 20p   g 750 g, 2 kg

   c 0.6 cm, 0.05 cm   h 39 litres, 26 litres

   d 0.4 m, 1.6 m   i 32 mph, 48 mph

   e 1 ft, 9 in

5 Complete the following ratios:

   a 3 : 4 = 6 : ?   d 240 : 400 = ? : 1

   b 18 : 9 = ? : 1   e 20 : 1 = 64 : ?

   c ? : 1 = 12 : 10   f : ? = 5 : 13

6 Spring bulbs are planted in a border in the ratio of 3 yellow tulips to 2 pink tulips to 5 grape hyacinths.
   If 615 yellow tulip bulbs are planted, how many pink tulip bulbs and how many grape hyacinth bulbs are planted?

7 Two terracotta pots have volumes in the ratio of 2 : 9. The smaller can hold 3 kg of peat.
   What weight of peat can the larger pot hold?

8 The width of a marigold flowerhead in a photograph is 9 mm. In an enlargement the width is 6 cm.
   Write these widths as a ratio.

9 Carl, Stephanie and Joanne deal with 425 clients in a year. The number of clients are in the ratio of 2 : 5 : 10.
   a How many clients has Stephanie?
   b How many more clients has Joanne than Carl?

10 The cost of a drug to a hospital is 75p and a rest home pays £4 for the same drug.
    Write these prices as a ratio.

11 The daily feeds of two new born babies are in the ratio of 3 : 4. The smaller baby needs 21 fl oz per day.
    How much milk does the larger baby need?

12 In a leisure centre, the width and height of a locker are 9 inches and 6 feet. Write these measurements as a ratio.

13 Sara, Richard and Francesca hire cars on their holidays. The number of miles travelled by them are in the ratio 4 : 3 : 6. The total mileage travelled is 3120 miles.

    a How many miles does Richard travel?

    b How many more miles does Francesca travel than Sara?

14 The length of a hacksaw blade is 32 cm and its width is 8 mm. Write these measurements as a ratio.

15 A garage dealing in Ford cars sells Fiestas, Escorts and Mondeos in the ratio of 4 : 5 : 2. In one month 363 of these cars are sold.
    How many were Mondeos?

4.2 *Division in a given ratio*

FAIR SHARES FOR ALL!!

This does not necessarily mean equal shares for all.

For example, if three partners invest different amounts of money in a business, they might expect the profits to be shared in proportion to their investment.

EXAMPLE 1

Divide £672 between Emily, Faye and Geoff in the ratio 7 : 5 : 9 respectively. How much does each person receive?

Method
 (i) Find the total number of shares.
 (ii) Find the amount of one share.
 (iii) Find the amount each receives.

Calculation
 (i) Total number of shares = $7 + 5 + 9$ = 21

 (ii) Amount of one share = $\dfrac{£672}{21}$ = £32

 (iii)
      Emily receives   £32 × 7   = £224
      Faye receives   £32 × 5   = £160
      Geoff receives   £32 × 9   = £288

(*Check.* 224 + 160 + 288 = 672.)

EXAMPLE 2

Three partners, A, B and C, invest money in a small business. The amounts they invest are £10 000, £12 000 and £6000, respectively.

At the end of the first year of trading the profits from the business are £14 350.

They each receive profits in proportion to their investment. How much does each partner receive?

The investments are in the ratio 10000 : 12000 : 6000
                                 = 5 : 6 : 3
The total number of shares   = 5 + 6 + 3   = 14
One share of the profits   = £14350 ÷ 14 = £1025
A receives 5 shares   = £1025 × 5   = £5125
B receives 6 shares   = £1025 × 6   = £6150
C receives 3 shares   = £1025 × 3   = £3075

(*Check.* 5125 + 6150 + 3075 = 14350.)

EXERCISE 4.2

1   Divide £650 in the ratio 2 : 3.

2   Divide £12 000 in the ratio 1 : 3 : 4.

3   Divide £104 in the ratio 6 : 4 : 3.

4   Mrs Chandra shared £4000 among her three children in the ratio 7 : 5 : 4.
How much did each receive?

5   The Shang Dynasty in China was making bronze artifacts more than three thousand years ago.

The bronze they used was an alloy of copper and zinc in the ratio (by weight) of 17 : 3. What weights of copper and zinc were used to make a bronze bowl weighing 1.6 kilograms?

6   The number of necklaces, bracelets and earrings made by a jeweller are in the ratio of 4 : 5 : 8. In one week, she made 68 pieces of jewellery.
How many of the pieces made were bracelets?

7   X and Y invested money in a home computing business. X put in £6000, but Y could only afford £4000. The profits were divided in the same ratio as their investment.

  a At the end of the first year the profits were £10 530.
    How much did each receive?

  b At the end of the second year X's share of the profits was £9456.
    How much was the total profit?

  c After two years Y increased his investments to £5000. At the end of the year his share of the profits was £8270.
    How much did X receive?

8   Four office workers run a pools syndicate and each week pay £4.95, £6.60, £3.30 and £4.95 respectively for their entry. When they win £104 616 they divide the winnings in the ratio of their weekly contribution.
    How much does each receive?

9   A drug company representative gives 72 trial samples of a drug to two doctors in the ratio of 3 : 5.
    How many samples does each doctor receive?

10 On one day, a hospital casualty department saw 140 accident victims. The ratio of casualties caused by motor accidents, accidents in the home, sporting accidents and others was 4 : 5 : 3 : 2.
    How many casualties were the result of motor accidents?

11 a Every summer, Grandma gives her grandchildren money to spend on holiday in the ratio of their ages. When David is 10 years old, Emily is 6 years old.

    (i) What is the ratio of their ages, in its simplest form?

    (ii) If Grandma gives the children £12 to share, how much does each child receive?

  b Next year the children again share £12 between them in the ratio of their ages. How much (to the nearest 1p) does each receive?

12 The cost of hiring a coach from Bournemouth to London for a day trip was £78. The breakdown of the cost into labour, fuel, overheads and profit was in the ratio of 4 : 4 : 3 : 2.
    How much of the cost was for the driver?

13 On one day, a toy manufacturer makes 2072 fashion dolls dressed either in disco wear or in riding gear. The ratio of dolls in disco wear to riding gear is 7 : 1.
    How many dolls are wearing disco wear?

14 A company makes 1056 television sets. The number of portable, small screen and large screen models is in the ratio of 4 : 15 : 3.

  a How many portable television sets are made?

  b How many of the televisions are small screen models?

4.3 *Direct proportion*

If two quantities increase, or decrease, at the same rate, they are said to be in **direct proportion.**

For example, if you double your speed of walking you will travel twice as far in the same period of time.

EXAMPLE

Mrs Wall usually buys 12 pints of milk each week and pays the milkman £4.92. In a week when she has visitors, she buys 3 extra pints. How much is her milk bill for that week?

   12 pints of milk cost £4.92

   1 pint of milk costs $\dfrac{£4.92}{12}$ (=41p)

   (12 + 3) pints of milk cost $\dfrac{£4.92}{12} \times 15$

   = £6.15

EXERCISE 4.3

1 Find the cost of 6 lb of apples if 4 lb cost £2.12.

2 The baker's shop sells cheese biscuits for £1.52 per quarter pound.
How much would 7 oz cost? ($\frac{1}{4}$lb=4oz).

3 Pic'n'Mix sweets cost 56p per quarter pound.
How much would you be charged for 9 oz.?

4 A printer charges £1.15 for 25 posters.
How much should be charged for 40 posters?

5 A designer sells coasters in packs of 18 for £19.80. In order to increase sales, the designer decides to offer them also in packs of 4.
How much should he charge for a pack of coasters?

6 A tax adviser charges clients per letter sent.
John pays £352 when 16 letters are sent.
How much should Camilla pay if her tax affairs require 11 letters?

7 An accountant charges £369 for 12 hours of her professional services.
How much should she charge for 14 hours?

8 A rest-home needs 24 care assistants when there are 6 residents.
How many assistants does it need when there are 11 residents?

9 Amy burns up 75 calories when she swims for 15 minutes.
How many calories does she use up when she swims for 40 minutes?

10 On an organised hike, it is estimated that hikers take $3\frac{1}{2}$ hours to walk $10\frac{1}{2}$ miles.
How long will it take them to walk 12 miles at the same speed?

11 A timeshare agent is paid for each person he persuades to look at a new development.
Alastair sends 32 people and is paid £1312.
How much does Jason receive when he sends 45 people?

12 A carpenter uses 48 screws to fit 4 doors.
How many screws does he need to fit 7 doors?

13 Two spanners are in the ratio of 4 : 11. The smaller is $\frac{1}{4}$".
What size is the larger spanner?

4.4 *Scale diagrams and models*

Scale Diagrams

Scale diagrams are two-dimensional representations of three-dimensional shapes. If the scale diagram is to be a faithful representation of the original, all the corresponding measurements of the original and the scale diagram must be in the same proportion.

The **scale** is the proportion by which each measurement has been reduced.

In order to fit a diagram onto paper, the measurements have to be 'scaled down'.

Once this has been done, you have a 'scale diagram'.

A scale is expressed either as a comparison between 2 lengths:

e.g. 1 cm : 2 m

or as a ratio:

e.g. 1 : 200.

For example, a scale of 2 centimetres to 1 metre means that every length of 1 metre on the original is represented by a length of 2 centimetres on the scale diagram, i.e. the measurements are all in the ratio of 1 : 50 and all the measurements of the scale diagram are $\frac{1}{50}$ of those of the original.

EXAMPLE 1

The scale of a diagram is 1 : 5. AB in the scaled diagram is 4 cm.
Find the original length AB.

$$\text{Original length} = 5 \times 4 \, \text{cm}$$
$$= 20 \, \text{cm}$$

EXAMPLE 2

A scale diagram of a playing field is drawn on a scale of 1 : 500.

a What distance on the ground is represented by 6.3 cm on the scale diagram?

b What distance on the scale diagram represents 82 m on the ground?

a 1 cm represents 500 cm

6.3 cm represents $500 \times 6.3 \, \text{cm} = 3150 \, \text{cm} = \dfrac{3150}{100} \, \text{m}$

$$= 31.5 \, \text{m}$$

Actual distance = Scale × Length on scale diagram

b $500 \, \text{cm} = \dfrac{500}{100} \, \text{m} = 5 \, \text{m}$

5 m is represented by 1 cm
1 m is represented by 0.2 cm
82 m is represented by $82 \times 0.2 \, \text{cm} = 16.4 \, \text{cm}$

or   **Length on diagram** $= \dfrac{\textbf{actual length}}{\textbf{Scale of diagram}}$

$$= \dfrac{82 \times 100}{500} \, \text{cm}$$

$$= 16.4 \, \text{cm}$$

EXAMPLE 3

The length of a kitchen is 4.8 m. The length on a scale diagram is 6 cm.
Find the scale used.

$$\text{Scale} = \dfrac{\textbf{Original length}}{\textbf{Scaled length}}$$

Converting all units to centimetres gives

$$\text{Scale} = \dfrac{4.8 \times 100}{6}$$

$$= 80$$

The scale of the diagram is 1 : 80.

EXERCISE 4.4

1 Convert the following actual lengths to scale diagram lengths using the scales given:

Actual length	Scale
a 5 metres	1 : 500
b 120 metres	1 : 2500
c 11 metres	1 : 10
d 14.4 centimetres	1 : 5

2 Convert the following diagram lengths to the original lengths using the scales given:

Diagram length	Scale
a 2 centimetres	1 : 10
b 3.1 centimetres	1 : 40
c 2.8 centimetres	1 : 60
d 3 inches	1 : 300
e 4.5 inches	1 : 20

3 The end of a roll of dress material is shown below on a scale of 1 : 40.

Find: a the width of the material

b the length of one pattern of the material (before it repeats).

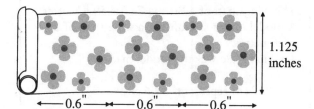

1.125 inches

◄— 0.6" —►◄— 0.6" —►◄— 0.6" —►

4 A designer sketches a dress.
The height of the model on whom the dress will be shown is 5' 9". Find:
a the scale used in drawing the sketch
b the length of the dress.

5 The plan of an office is shown on a scale of 1 : 60.

a What are the dimensions of a desk in metres?

b What is the minimum distance between the two desks?

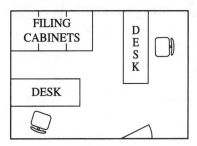

FILING CABINETS

DESK

DESK

6 A company is hoping to build a 'brown-field site factory'. On an Ordnance Survey map scale 1 : 2500, the rectangular plot of land is 4 cm by 18 cm.
What are the actual dimensions of the field?

7 The plan of a room in a rest-home is shown below on a scale of 1 : 80.
Find the area of the room in m^2.

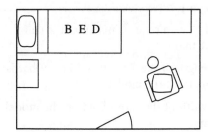

B E D

8 The plan of a ward in a cottage hospital is shown below.
The beds are 3' by 6'. Find:

a the scale of the plan

b the size of the ward.

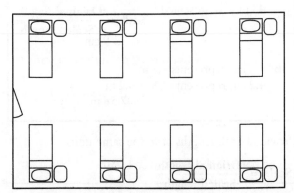

9   The diagram shows the accurate drawing of a car to a scale of 1 : 50. Find the length and height of the car in metres.

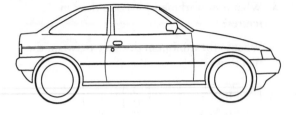

10 The plan shows the machine-tool section of a manufacturing company. Each work station is at least 2.4 m from the next work-station. Find:

a   the scale of the plan

b   the area of a work-station.

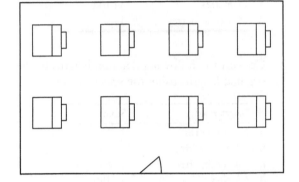

Models

A model is a replica, usually much smaller in size, of an original object. As with scale diagrams, if the model is to be a faithful representation of the original, all the corresponding measurements of the original and the model must be in the same proportion.

EXAMPLE 1

A model of an aircraft is made to a scale of 1 cm : 1.8 m.

a   The length of the aircraft is 43 m. What is the length of the model?

b   The width of the cargo hold on the model is 4.2 cm.
    What is the width of the cargo hold on the aircraft?

a   1.8 m is represented by 1 cm

1 m is represented by $\dfrac{1}{1.8}$ cm

43 m is represented by $\dfrac{1}{1.8} \times 43$ cm

$$= 23.9 \text{ cm}$$

b   1 cm represents 1.8 m
    4.2 cm represents 1.8 × 4.2 m
    $$= 7.56 \text{ m}$$

EXAMPLE 2

The wing-span of a Boeing 747 is 59.6 metres. A model of the aircraft has a wing-span of 29.8 centimetres.
To what scale was the model made?

29.8 cm represents 59.6 m

1 cm represents $\dfrac{59.6}{29.8}$ m $= 2$m $= 200$cm

The scale is '1 cm represents 200 cm' or 1 : 200

Provided both lengths have the same units,

$$\text{Scale} = \frac{\textbf{Original length}}{\textbf{Scaled length}}$$

EXERCISE 4.5

1 A doll's house is made to a scale of 1
   centimetre representing 30 centimetres.

   a What are the measurements, in the doll's
      house, of the following:

      (i) a 2.1 m high door

      (ii) a carpet measuring 4.2m × 3.6m

      (iii) a plate of diameter 24 cm?

   b What would be the full-scale sizes of the
      following doll's house furnishings:

      (i) a chair of height 3.1 cm

      (ii) a candlestick 4.5 mm high

      (iii) a picture 23mm × 20mm?

2 a When Alice ate a cake marked 'Eat me' she
      found herself enlarged on a scale of 1 to 1.9.
      If she was previously 4 ft 10 in tall, how tall
      was she after eating the cake?

   b When Alice drank the contents of the bottle
      labelled 'Drink me', she shrank to a height of
      10 inches.
      If the miniature Alice had feet which were
      3.6 cm long, how long were the feet on the
      enlarged Alice?

3 An 'N' gauge model railway is made to a scale of
   $\frac{1}{150}$. The roof of a model station is 136 mm long.

   a How long would the actual station roof be?

   b Taking 30cm = 1foot, calculate the actual
      length of the roof in feet.

4 A model of a stage set is made to a scale of
   1 : 20.

   a A table is 1.2 m by 0.6 m.
      What are its dimensions on the model?

   b A bed on the model is 6.2 cm wide.
      What is its actual width?

5 An architect produces a model of a housing
   development to a scale of 1 : 125.

   a A house will be 11 m wide.
      What is its width on the model?

   b A road on the model is 4 cm wide.
      What will be its actual width?

6 In a children's home, the children produce a
   model of an outside play area using Lego
   bricks. A roundabout in the model is 6 cm wide
   and represents an actual roundabout 9 m wide.

   a What is the scale of the model?

   b A slide is 4 m long.
      What should be its length in the model?

7 A travel agent made a window display of the
   Pyramids to promote a special offer. The height
   of the tallest display pyramid is 3 feet. The
   actual pyramid is 90 m high.

   a What is the scale of the display?

   b Each side of the pyramid's base is 188 m.
      What should be the base length of the
      pyramid in the window?

8 A model replica of a plane is shown below. The
   length of the plane is 47 m.

   a What is the scale of the model?

   b What is the width of the model?

   c What is the width of the plane?

5 *Measurement*

5.1 *Metric and imperial units*

In 1971 the British monetary system was decimalised. We stopped using pounds, shillings and pence (£ s d) and started using pounds and 'new' pence (£ p). Since then, many more units have changed from imperial to metric units:

We now buy petrol in litres, not gallons.
We buy material in metres instead of yards.
The standard length of a ruler is 30 centimetres, not 12 inches.
The weather forecast gives temperatures in degrees Celsius rather than in degrees Fahrenheit.

We do, however, still use some imperial measures:

Distances are given in miles and speed restrictions in miles per hour.
Although most grocery items are labelled with weights in both grams and ounces, fruit, vegetables and sweets are priced in pounds and ounces as well as in kilograms.
Milk and beer are still sold in pints.
Carpets are often sold in feet and yards.

The advantage of the metric system over the imperial is the ease with which one unit can be converted to another.

The USA still uses imperial units.

Metric units

The metric system is a decimal system and units are converted by multiplying or dividing by powers of 10 (i.e. 10, 100, 1000).

Each prefix to a standard measure (e.g. metre, gram, litre) indicates the relative size:

kilo (k)   means $1000 \times$ deci (d) means $\frac{1}{10} \times$

hecto (H) means $100 \times$

deka (D) means $10 \times$ centi (c) means $\frac{1}{100} \times$

milli (m) means $\frac{1}{1000} \times$

The most common metric units in everyday use are:

Length Metre (m)	Weight Gram (g)	Capacity Litre (l)
1 kilometre = 1000 metres	1 kg = 1000 g	1 litre = 100 cl
1 centimetre = 10 millimetres	1 g = 1000 mg	1 litre = 1000 ml
1 metre = 100 centimetres	1 tonne = 1000 kg	1 cl = 10 ml
1 metre = 1000 millimetres		

EXAMPLE

a Convert 2.75 kg to g.

b Convert 6.3 ml to cl.

c Convert 56 cm to km.

a 1 kg = 1000 g, so

$$2.75\,kg = 1000 \times 2.75\,g = 2750\,g$$

b 1 ml = $\dfrac{1}{10}$ cl, so

$$6.3\,ml = \frac{1}{10} \times 6.3\,cl = 0.63\,cl$$

c 1 cm = $\dfrac{1}{100}$ m = $\dfrac{1}{1000} \times \dfrac{1}{100}$ km, so

$$56\,cm = \frac{1}{1000} \times \frac{1}{100} \times 56\,km$$

$$= 0.000\,56\,km$$

Estimation of measurements

You should be able to estimate many familiar measurements – for example, the length of a room. You may then use an accurate measurement to check your estimation.

EXAMPLE

Estimate the height of a room.

Most houses have a ceiling height of between 2.3 m and 2.4 m. Suitable estimates would be:
2 m, using one significant figure:
2.3 m or 2.4 m, using two significant figures
or $2\frac{1}{2}$ m.

An estimate of 3 m would be too large, and 2.34 m would be too great a degree of accuracy.

EXERCISE 5.1

1 Estimate, in turn, each of the following (or substitute your own choice):

  a the height of a friend

  b the length of the classroom

  c the length of a sheet of A4 paper

  d the width of a sheet of A5 paper

  e the length of your stride

  f your handspan

g the circumference of your wrist

h the dimensions of the college car park.

When you have estimated the lengths, measure them, to an appropriate
degree of accuracy and record the results on a table:

Object	Estimated length	Actual length	Measuring device
a Height of student			
b Length of room			
etc.			

2 Choose the most appropriate metric unit to
measure:

a the height of a building

b the capacity of a bottle of ink

c the weight of a baby

d the length of a journey

e the thickness of a brass screw.

3 Place the following lengths in order, beginning
with the smallest:
750 m, $\frac{1}{2}$ km, 5000 mm, 4860 cm.

4 Which is larger: $\frac{3}{8}$ kg or 370 g?

5 Change:

a 1232 m to km   e 1.62 cl to ml

b 0.032 m to mm   f 12.7 km to m

c 626 g to kg   g 59.1 ml to litres

d 0.731 litres to cl h 3.4 tonnes to kg

6 The weight of sliced meat is marked on the
packet as 0.23 kg.
What is the weight in grams?

7 A hotel restaurant uses 100 kg of potatoes per
day.
A load of 2 tonnes is delivered.
How many days supply is this?

8 A silver ingot weighs 1550 g.
How many kg is this?

9 A length of cable has a diameter of 26.5 mm.
What is its diameter in cm?

10 A bottle of disinfectant holds 739 ml.
To make up a solution for cleaning the floors.
5 ml of disinfectant are added to 4.5 litres of
water.
How many litres of solution can be made from
the bottle?

Imperial units

The most common imperial units in everyday use are:

Length	Weight	Capacity
1 mile = 1760 yards	1 ton = 20 hundredweight	1 gallon = 8 pints
1 yard = 3 feet (ft or ')	(cwt)	1 pint = 20 fluid
1 foot = 12 inches (in or ")	1 cwt = 112 pounds (lb)	ounces
	1 lb = 16 ounces (oz)	(fl oz)
	1 stone = 14 pounds	

EXAMPLE

a Convert 76″ to feet and inches.

b Convert 6 lb 5 oz to ounces.

c Convert 18 pints to gallons.

a $12\,\text{in} = 1\,\text{ft}$, so $76'' = \dfrac{76}{12}\,\text{ft} = 6\dfrac{4}{12}\,\text{ft} = 6'\ 4''$

b $1\,\text{lb} = 16\,\text{oz}$, so $6\,\text{lb}\ 5\,\text{oz} = (6 \times 16) + 5\,\text{oz} = 101\,\text{oz}$

c $8\,\text{pt} = 1\,\text{gal}$, so $18\,\text{pt} = \dfrac{18}{8}\,\text{gal} = 2.25\,\text{gal}$

EXERCISE 5.2

1 Repeat question 1 of Exercise 5.1 using imperial units for the measurements.

2 Change:

    a 39 in to feet   **e** 3 lb 7 oz to oz

    b 40 oz to lb and oz   **f** 20 pints to gallons

    c $16\frac{1}{2}$ ft to yards   **g** $3\frac{1}{2}$ gallons to pints

    d 2 ft 3 in to inches   **h** 0.7 pint to fluid ounces

3 A recipe requires 15 fluid ounces of water, but the measuring jug is calibrated in pints. How many pints of water should be measured?

4 The dimension of a room are 12′ 9″ by 10′ 6″. What is the perimeter of the room in:

    a feet   **b** yards?

5 A grocery store divides a block of cheese weighing 4 lb 9 $\frac{1}{2}$ oz into twelve equal portions. How much does each portion weigh?

6 A 'flat' for a stage set is 15 ft high by $7\frac{1}{2}$ ft wide.
What are its dimensions in yards?

7 Churns of milk in a dairy hold 5 gallons.
How many one pint bottles can be filled from each churn?

8 A baby's bottle holds 8 fluid ounces of milk. How many bottles can be filled from 2 pints of milk?

9 A cricket pitch has a length of 1 chain = 22 yd. Ian knows that his stride is about 1 yard in length, so he paces out the distance between the wickets by taking 22 strides.
In fact, his stride is 34 inches in length.
What is the actual length of his pitch in yards, feet and inches?

10 An 18″ TV has a screen which is 18 inches wide and 14 inches high.
What are the dimensions of the screen in feet? Give your answer correct to 2 d.p.

5.2 *Conversion between metric and imperial units*

It is often necessary, for comparison, to convert from imperial to metric units
or vice versa.

If a rough comparison is all that is required, an approximate conversion factor
can be used. For large quantities, or where a correct comparison is required, a
conversion factor of the appropriate degree of accuracy should be used.

Approximate conversion	More accurate conversion
5 miles ≈ 8 km	1 mile = 1.608 km
1 yard ≈ 1 m	1 yard = 0.914 m
1 foot ≈ 30 cm	1 foot = 30.48 cm
1 inch ≈ $2\frac{1}{2}$ cm	1 inch = 2.54 cm
1 kg ≈ 2 lb or 2.2 lb	1 kg = 2.205 lb
1 litre ≈ $1\frac{3}{4}$ pints	1 litre = 1.76 pt
	1 gallon = 4.55 litres

EXAMPLE 1

The contents of a packet of sugar weigh 250 g.
What weight, in ounces, should be printed on the packet?

Merchandise must carry an accurate description, and therefore the
weight given must be correct to a reasonable degree of accuracy.
The weight stated on a packet, tin, etc., is usually the minimum weight
of the contents.

$$\text{The conversion is } 1\,\text{kg} = 2.205\,\text{lb}$$
$$\therefore\ 1000\,\text{g} = 2.205 \times 16\,\text{oz} = 35.28\,\text{oz}$$
$$1\,\text{g} = 0.035\,28\,\text{oz}$$
$$250\,\text{g} = 0.035\,28 \times 250\,\text{oz}$$
$$= 8.82\,\text{oz}$$

The minimum weight of the sugar is 8.8 oz.

EXAMPLE 2

A family, on a self-catering holiday in Europe, wish to buy the equivalent
in weight of 3 lb of potatoes and $\frac{1}{2}$ lb of butter.
How much of each item should they buy?

Exact weights are not required.

$$\text{The conversion used is } 2\,\text{lb} \approx 1\,\text{kg}$$
$$\text{or } 1\,\text{lb} \approx 0.5\,\text{kg}$$
$$\text{so } 3\,\text{lb} \approx 1.5\,\text{kg}$$
$$\text{and } \tfrac{1}{2}\,\text{lb} \approx 0.25\,\text{kg} = 250\,\text{g}$$

They should buy $1\frac{1}{2}$ kg of potatoes and 250 g of butter.

EXERCISE 5.3

1 Which is greater: 5 miles or 9 kilometres?

2 Vegetables are sold in tins of various sizes. What weight, in ounces to the nearest 0.1 oz, should be printed on a tin if the contents weigh:

   a 425 g   b 440 g   c 415 g?

3 A shop prepacks its groceries and labels the packets with both metric and imperial weights. For each of the following items, calculate the missing weight:

   a 1 lb of mince

   b 150 g of cooked ham

   c 5 lb of potatoes

   d 0.74 lb of cheese

   e 14.2 g of dried herbs.

4 a What is the equivalent of 1 litre of petrol in gallons?

   b A driver buys 20 litres of petrol. Approximately how many gallons of petrol does he buy (correct to 1 d.p.)?

5 The specifications for a particular make of ambulance give the petrol consumption as 16 miles per gallon.
   How many miles per litre is this?

6 One type of loft insulation has a thickness of 6 in, a width of 370 mm and a length of 5.22 m. Find:

   a the thickness in millimetres

   b the width in inches

   c the length in feet.

7 When you tow a caravan or trailer, the maximum permitted speed is 50 miles per hour. What is this speed in kilometres per hour?

8 The luggage allowance when travelling by air is 20 kg per person. A passenger weighs his case on scales at home and finds the weight is 3 stones.

   a What is the weight of his case in pounds?

   b By how many pounds is he under the allowance?

9 Gary is designing a storage unit for a collection of CDs.
   What is the minimum width of shelving, to the nearest inch, he can use to accommodate CDs which are 14.1 cm wide?

10 Pottery clay is generally sold in lumps of 56 lb. What is this weight in kilograms?

11 An advertisement for cabin crew requires applicants to:

   a have a height 5 ft 3 in–6 ft

   b be capable of swimming 25 yd.

   Convert these imperial measures to suitable metric measures.

12 Precious metals and gems are weighed in troy ounces. 1 troy ounce = 31.104 g.

   a What is the weight in grams of a gold necklace weighing 2.5 troy ounces?

   b What is the weight in troy ounces of a silver bracelet weighing 18 g?

13 Lengths of nails used to be measured in inches. What are the metric equivalents (to the nearest millimetre) for the following lengths?

   $2\frac{1}{4}$ inches

   $3\frac{1}{2}$ inches

   $\frac{7}{8}$ inch

   $1\frac{1}{4}$ inches

14 A medicine spoon holds 5 ml.
   How many doses of medicine can be measured out from a quarter-pint bottle?

Measurements are found by using an appropriate measuring device, such as a thermometer or expanding tape, or by reading from a scale, as on a speedometer, weighing machine or voltmeter. In the following exercise, you are required to read measurements from the diagrams.

EXERCISE 5.4

1 What length has been measured on the rule?

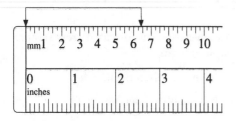

2 What is the reading on the following sets of dials?

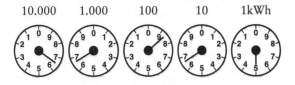

3 What is the weight of the parcel?

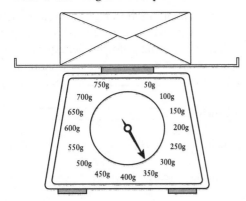

4 What temperatures is shown on the clinical thermometer?

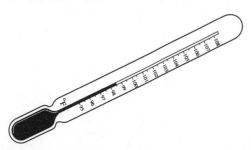

5 What time is recorded on the stopwatch?

6 A vehicle's speedometer is shown below. At what speed is it travelling:

a in miles per hour

b in kilometres per hour?

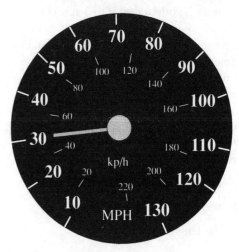

7 A lorry's tyres should have an air pressure of 75 psi (pounds per square inch).
By how much should the pressure be increased if the present pressure is shown on the gauge below?

5.3 *Compound measures*

A **compound measure** connects two different measurements.

Examples of compound measures are
Density which connects weight and volume and
Speed which connects distance and time.

Compound measures are normally given as a rate.

Rate

In Unit 4 (page 30), an intermediate step in the calculation was to find the **cost of one unit**: e.g. one pound, the time taken to make one article, the amount of work done in one day.

If the information given is already in this form, it is called a **rate**. For example:

A speed of 50 miles per hour is a rate of travel
American dollars $1.61 per £1   is a rate of exchange
£423 per week   is a rate of pay
Time and a half is   an overtime rate
5 kg per m^3 is a density

Given the basic rate, it is a simple calculation to find any other amount required.

EXAMPLE 1

A firm pays an overtime rate of time and a half for work done on a Saturday.
The firm's basic rate of pay is £3.42 per hour.
How much is paid for $6\frac{1}{2}$ hours of work on a Saturday?

Basic rate of pay   = £3.42 per hour
Overtime rate of pay = 1.5 × £3.42 per hour
    = £5.13 per hour
Saturday pay   = £5.13 × 6.5
    = £33.35

EXAMPLE 2

An electric fire uses 18 units of electricity over a period of $7\frac{1}{2}$ hours.
What is the hourly rate of consumption of electricity?

$$\text{Hourly rate of consumption} = \frac{\text{Number of units used}}{\text{Time}}$$
$$= \frac{18 \text{ units}}{7.5 \text{ hours}}$$
$$= 2.4 \text{ units per hour}$$

EXAMPLE 3

The density of glass is 2.74 g/cm^3
Find the weight of 740 cm^3 of glass.

Weight is 2.74 × 740 g
    = 2027.6 g
    = 2.03 kg

EXERCISE 5.5

1 Carrots cost 18p per pound.
How much would $4\frac{1}{2}$ lb of carrots cost?

2 A man earns a basic wage of £10.70 per hour.
What is his basic weekly pay for a 35-hour week?

3 A car uses petrol at the rate of 36 miles per gallon.

  a How many miles can the car travel on $2\frac{1}{2}$ gallons of petrol?

  b How many gallons of petrol (to the nearest gallon) would be needed for a journey of 240 miles?

  c One gallon is approximately 4.55 litres. What is the car's rate of consumption in miles per litre?

4 At the current rate of exchange there are 10.73 French francs to the pound sterling. How much would 1800 francs be worth in pounds?

5 The speed limit on a motorway is 70 mph. What is the shortest possible journey time from Dover to Glasgow, a distance of 470 miles?

6 Lawn sand should be applied at a rate of 136 g per square metre.
How much lawn sand is required for a lawn 9.5 m × 7.5 m? (Give your answer to the nearest 0.1 kg.)

7 a The toll charged for a car travelling on a motorway was £33.60 for a journey of 420 kilometres.
What was the rate per kilometre?

  b Cars with trailers are charged double. How much would it cost for a car and caravan to travel 264 kilometres?

8 A sheet of perspex of thickness 3 cm measures 1 m by 70 cm, and weighs 24.6 kg.
Find the density of perspex in grams per cubic centimetre.

Speed or velocity

Speed is the rate of travel.

Common measures of speed are miles per hour (mph); kilometres per hour (km/h); metres per second (m/s).

To calculate speed you need to know the distance travelled and the time taken:

$$\text{Speed} = \frac{\text{Distance travelled}}{\text{Time taken}}$$

Unless the speed is constant over the whole distance, this will be an **average speed** for the journey.

Rearranging this formula will give:

$$\text{Distance travelled} = \text{Speed} \times \text{Time taken}$$

and

$$\text{Time taken} = \frac{\text{Distance travelled}}{\text{Speed}}$$

EXAMPLE 1

A car travelling at a speed of 65 miles per hour takes $2\frac{1}{2}$ hours for a journey.

What distance has the car covered in this time?

  In 1 hour the car travels 65 miles
  In $2\frac{1}{2}$ hours the car travels $65 \times 2\frac{1}{2}$ miles
  $\qquad\qquad\qquad\qquad = 162.5$ miles

or Distance = Speed × Time = $65 \times 2\frac{1}{2}$ miles
  $\qquad\qquad\qquad\qquad = 162.5$ miles

EXAMPLE 2

A family travelling with a car and caravan in France cover a journey of 238 kilometres travelling at an average speed of 70 kilometres per hour.

How long does the journey take?

To travel 70 km takes 1 hour

To travel 1 km takes $\dfrac{1}{70}$ hour

To travel 238 km takes $\dfrac{1}{70} \times 238$ hours

$\qquad\qquad\qquad = 3.4$ hours

$\qquad\qquad\qquad = 3$ hour 24 minutes

or $\quad$ Time $= \dfrac{\text{Distance}}{\text{Speed}} = \dfrac{238 \text{ km}}{70 \text{ km/h}}$

$\qquad\qquad\qquad = 3$ hours 24 minutes

EXERCISE 5.6

1 Find the average speed, in the most appropriate units, for each of the following:

   a a journey of 162 miles which took 3 hours

   b a 1500 m race which was won in a time of 2 minutes 54.4 seconds.

   c a journey of 286 km which took $3\frac{1}{4}$ hours.

2 Find the distance covered:

   a by a car travelling at 85 km/h for 2.4 hours

   b by an aircraft travelling at 600 mph for 4 hours 36 minutes

3 Find the time taken

   a to travel 186 km at an average speed of 62 km/h

   b to travel 306 miles at an average speed of 40 mph

4 Andy goes running every evening for 45 minutes.
If he runs at a speed of 10 mph, how far does he run?

5 **a** A race for small yachts has three 'legs' of distances 8 km, 6 km and 10 km. The average speed for the winning yacht was 6.2 kilometres per hour.
How long did it take the winning yacht to complete the course?

   b The second yacht finished 8 minutes after the winner.
What was its average speed?

6 *Percentages*

> 'Inflation now stands at 2.3%.' 'Ford have given their workforce a 3.5% rise.'
> 'Unemployment in Winchester is less than 2%.'

Percentages are a part of our everyday lives. They are often quoted in the media, particularly in connection with money matters.

Percentages often help us make comparisons between numbers, but we must know exactly what a 'percentage' is.

6.1 *Percentages*

A percentage is a fraction with a particular number divided by 100:

$$20\% \text{ means } \frac{20}{100}$$

A decrease of 20% would be a decrease of $\frac{20}{100}$, which is the same thing as a decrease of $\frac{1}{5}$, a fifth.

$$\frac{1}{4} = \frac{1}{4} \times \frac{25}{25} = \frac{25}{100} \text{ which is } 25\%$$

To convert a fraction to a percentage multiply by 100.
To convert a percentage to a fraction, divide by 100.

EXAMPLE 1

Convert **a** $\frac{3}{5}$, **b** $\frac{9}{11}$ to percentages.

a $\frac{3}{5}$ as a percentage $= \frac{3}{5} \times 100 = 60\%$

b $\frac{9}{11}$ as a percentage $= \frac{9}{11} \times 100 = 81.82\%$ (to 2 d.p.)

┌─ **EXAMPLE 2** ────────────────────────────────────┐

Convert 65% to a fraction in its lowest terms.

$$65\% = \frac{65}{100} = \frac{13}{20}$$

└──┘

EXERCISE 6.1

1 Convert the following fractions to percentages:

a $\dfrac{1}{5}$ b $\dfrac{1}{8}$ c $\dfrac{7}{10}$ d $\dfrac{13}{20}$

e $\dfrac{2}{3}$ f $\dfrac{9}{25}$ g $1\dfrac{3}{4}$ h $2\dfrac{1}{2}$

2 Convert the following percentages to fractions:

a 60%   b 25%   c 10%   d 85%

e 15%   f 130%   g $37\dfrac{1}{2}\%$ h $33\dfrac{1}{3}\%$

3 Copy and complete the following table to give each quantity in its fractional, decimal and percentage form.

	Fraction	Decimal	Percentage
a	$\frac{3}{4}$		
b		0.5	
c	$\frac{1}{8}$		
d			$33\frac{1}{3}$
e		0.375	
f	$\frac{7}{10}$		
g			35
h		0.6	
i	$\frac{3}{5}$		
j			62.5

6.2 *Finding a percentage of an amount*

┌─ **EXAMPLE 2** ────────────────────────────────────┐

Julian reads in the newspaper that the average pocket money for 12-year-olds has increased nationally by 14% in the last year.
Julian's 12-year-old daughter Gilly has been given £1.60 per week for the last two years. How much more per week should he provide for a 14% increase?

$$14\% = \frac{14}{100}$$

$$14\% \text{ of } £1.60 = \frac{14}{100} \times £1.60$$

$$= 0.14 \times £1.60 = 22.4\text{p}$$

Increase in pocket money = 22.4p = 22p (to the nearest 1p)
Note. See Section 2.1 for a further explanation of approximations.

└──┘

EXERCISE 6.2

1   Calculate the following percentages to the nearest 1p.

    a 10% of £13.75   **e** 123% of £4.20

    b 50% of £637.24   **f** 121% of £69.80

    c 7% of £316   **g** 10.80% of £900

    d 15% of £92.72   **h** 34.3% of £128.50

6.3 *Increasing an amount by a given percentage*

┌─ **EXAMPLE** ─────────────────────────────────

TRAIN FARES TO RISE BY 6%

What does this mean in cash terms to the 20 000 long-distance commuters who travel to London every day?

If an InterCity season ticket costs £2632 now, how much will it cost after the rise?

Method 1
To find the new cost of a ticket we can find 6% of £2632 and then add this to the original:

$$6\% \text{ of } £2632 = \frac{6}{100} \times £2632$$

Increase in fare = £157.92

New cost of fare = £2632 + £157.92

$$= £2789.92$$

Method 2
Consider the original amount of £2632 as 100%. Increasing it by 6% is the same as finding 106% of the original cost.

$$106\% = \frac{106}{100} = 1.06$$

Therefore the quickest way of increasing the original fare by 6% is to multiply it by 1.06.

$$106\% \text{ of } £2632 = 1.06 \times £2632$$

New cost of fare = £2789.92

EXERCISE 6.3

Give all answers to the nearest 1p.

1   Increase the following rail fares by 10%.

    a £9.20   **d** £9.81

    b £3.70   **e** £9.13

    c £5.00

2   Increase the given amount by the required percentage.

    a £72.12 by 50%   **d** £220 by $6\frac{1}{4}$%

    b 95p by 10%   **e** £124.80 by 25%

    c £360 by 120%   **f** £19.99 by $8\frac{1}{2}$%

6.4 *Decreasing an amount by a given percentage*

---**EXAMPLE**---

The marked price of this sweater is £24.90.
What is its sale price?

Method 1

$$\text{The reduction} = 20\% \text{ of } £24.90$$

$$= \frac{20}{100} \times £24.90$$

$$= £4.98$$

$$\text{The sale price} = £24.90 - £4.98$$

$$= £19.92$$

Method 2

£24.90 is the equivalent of 100% and so decreasing the price by 20% is equivalent to finding 80% of the original price.

$$\frac{80}{100} \times £24.90 = 0.80 \times £24.90$$

$$\text{Sale price} = £19.92$$

EXERCISE 6.4

Give all answers to the nearest 1p.

1 Reduce the following marked prices by 20% to find the sale prices:

   a £30.00   **d** 45p

   b £10.50   **e** £12.99

   c £17.60

2 Decrease the given amount by the required percentage:

   a £54.10 by 8%   **d** £27.15 by $12\frac{1}{2}\%$

   b 84p by 30%   **e** £99.05 by 40%

   c £128 by 60%   **f** £1.62 by 33%

6.5 *Expressing one quantity as a percentage of another*

In a survey of insurance companies it was found that the most common type of car accident was one car running into the back of another.

Out of 35 000 claims, 6280 were for this type of accident.

Information of this type is usually quoted as a percentage.

EXAMPLE 1

Find 6280 as a percentage of 35 000.

First express 6280 as a fraction of 35 000:

$$\frac{6280}{35\,000}$$

Then multiply this fraction by 100 to express it as a percentage:

6280 as a percentage of 35 000

$$= \frac{6280}{35\,000} \times 100\%$$

$$= 17.9\% \ (3 \ \text{sf})$$

This means that almost 18% of car accidents are caused by cars running into the backs of other vehicles.

Note. See Unit 2 for a further explanation of significant figures.

EXAMPLE 2

A shop buys wallpaper from a wholesaler at £6 per roll and sells it to customers at £8.20 per roll.

What is the percentage increase in price?

The **increase** in price is £8.20 − £6.00 = £2.20

This is $\dfrac{£2.20}{£6.00}$ as a fraction of the **original** price.

$$\text{Percentage increase} = \frac{£2.20}{£6.00} \times 100\%$$

$$= 36.7\%$$

EXAMPLE 3

By what percentage has the marked price of £4.70 been decreased to give a sale price of £3.80?

The **decrease** in price is expressed as a fraction of the **original** price and then multiplied by 100.

$$\text{Decrease in price} = 90\text{p}$$

$$\text{Percentage decrease} = \frac{90\text{p}}{£4.70} \times 100\%$$

$$= \frac{£0.90}{£4.70} \times 100\% \ \text{(both quantities must be in the same units)}$$

$$= 19.1\%$$

EXERCISE 6.5

Give all answers correct to 3 significant figures.

1 Express the first quantity as a percentage of the second:

   a 20, 25   d 54, 108

   b 3, 87   e 60p, £1.10

   c 140, 80   f £16.25, £12.50

2 Find the percentage by which the first amount is increased or decreased to give the second amount:

   a £65, £80   d £499, £399

   b £250, £300   e £1.23, 67p

   c 20p, 95p   f £24.50, £138.20

Exercise 6.6

1 A dress made by a Paris Fashion House has a recommended retail price of £870. A London shop advertises it at £710.
By what percentage has the shop reduced the price?
Give your answer to the nearest integer.

2 Linda and Mario are discussing the students at their Art College.

   a Linda says that 60% of the students are female and Mario says that there are 52 more females than males.
   How many students are there at the college?

   b Linda says that $\frac{2}{5}$ of the students attend on Wednesday only in the morning and Mario knows that 30% of the students attend all day on Wednesday.
   How many students do not go into college on Wednesday?

3 A watch has a MRRP (maker's recommended retail price) of £32.99, but a jeweller's shop advertises it for £28.99.
By what percentage has the shop reduced the price (to the nearest whole number)?

4 In a town of 25 000 inhabitants, 80% are over 18 years of age.

   a How many of the inhabitants are over 18?

   Of these, $37\frac{1}{2}$ usually shop in the town's supermarket.

   b How many shop in the supermarket?

   7240 people over 18 living in the town use hypermarkets regularly.

   c What percentage of people over 18 shop in hypermarkets?

5 A survey on teenage smoking found that 70% of girls of secondary school age tried smoking and that 36% of those who tried it became addicted.

   In a secondary school with 580 female students:

   a how many girls would you expect to find had tried smoking?

   b how many girls would you expect to find had become addicted to smoking?

6 The 36 residents in a rest-home each pay £231 per week. 28% of the total income of the home is spent on nursing care. The rest-home employs its nurses for a total of 588 hours per week. What is the hourly rate of pay for each nurse?

7 Restaurants often add a service charge of 12% to your bill. A meal for two costs £28.60. How much service charge will be added?

8 'Sunny Tours' offers a 5% discount on all holidays booked before 31 December the previous year.

   How much will a family of 2 adults and 2 children aged 11 and 15 pay for a holiday whose advertised price is £380 each with a 30% reduction for children under 14 years of age?

9 In the survey of 3500 accidents at work, 17.6% happened on a Friday.
How many of the accidents occurred on a Friday?

10 Mr Robinson invested £32 000, together with money raised from a loan from his bank, in a manufacturing enterprise. He spent 65% on buildings, with an additional 28% on equipment. How much did he have left to spend on materials?

7 *Wages and Salaries*

7.1 *Basic pay*

All employees receive a wage or salary as payment for their labour.

A **wage** is paid weekly and is calculated on a fixed hourly rate.
A **salary** is paid monthly and is calculated on a fixed annual amount.

Many wage earners are required to work a fixed number of hours in a week,
and they are paid for these hours at the basic hourly rate.

EXAMPLE 1

Simon works in a hairdressers. His basic pay is
£3.75 per hour for a 40-hour week.
Calculate his weekly wage.

Weekly wage = Rate of pay × Hours worked

$$= £3.75 \times 40$$

$$= £150$$

EXAMPLE 2

Layla's gross weekly wage (i.e. her wage before
deductions) is £166.95. She works a 35-hour
week.
What is her hourly rate of pay?

$$\text{Hourly rate of pay} = \frac{\text{Weekly wage}}{\text{Hours worked}}$$

$$= \frac{£166.95}{35}$$

$$= £4.77$$

EXERCISE 7.1

1 Calculate Donna's gross weekly wage if she
   works for 42 hours per week at a rate of pay of
   £4.10 per hour.

2 Daniel's yearly salary is £5756.
   How much is he paid per month?

3 A basic working week is 36 hours and the
   weekly wage is £231.48.
   What is the basic hourly rate?

4 An employee's gross monthly pay is £965.20.
   What is his annual salary?

5 Carrie is an outworker and is paid £3.73 per
   hour to produce a wall-hanging tapestry.
   When Carrie works 36 hours, how much is she
   paid?

6 Calculate how much Phillipa is paid per year if
   her monthly pay as a graphics designer is
   £1975 per month.

7 In one month, Mustafa earns £610 as a secretary.
   What is Mustafa's annual income?

8 A shop assistant, Kayley, usually works $48\frac{1}{2}$
   hours a week and is paid £221. One week
   Kayley attends a family wedding and can work
   only 41 hours.
   How much is Kayley paid for that week?

9 As a part-time nurse, Annabel earns £437 per
   month.
   What is Annabel's annual income?

10 Annabel's brother James works as a porter at
   the same hospital. He is paid £4.52 per hour.
   How much is James paid for a week in which
   he works 43 hours?

11 For her work as a travel courier, Morag is paid
   £210 per week. She normally works a 38-hour
   week.
   What is Morag's hourly rate of pay?

12 As a maintenance worker at Stonehenge, Nicholas is paid £3.89 per hour. How much is Nicholas's gross pay when he works $9\frac{1}{2}$ hours in a day?

13 Derek is paid £192 when he works a 45-hour week in a factory making parts for a shipyard. How much is Derek paid per hour?

14 The basic week in a factory is 35 hours. Find the weekly wage of the following employees whose basic hourly rate of pay is:

a a machine operator, basic rate £7.42 per hour

b a trainee, basic rate £4.45 per hour

c a supervisor, basic rate £12.60 per hour.

7.2 *Overtime rates*

An employee can increase a basic wage by working longer than the basic week, i.e. by doing overtime.
A higher hourly rate is usually paid for these additional hours.
The most common rates are **time and a half** and **double time**.

EXAMPLE

Mr Arkwright works a basic 36-hour week for which he is paid a basic rate of £5.84 per hour. In addition, he works 5 hours overtime at time and a half and 3 hours overtime at double time.

Calculate his gross weekly wage.

36 hours basic pay = £5.84 × 36 = £210.24

5 hours overtime at time and a half = (£5.84 × 1.5) × 5 = £43.80

3 hours overtime at double time = (£5.84 × 2) × 3 = £35.04

∴ Grosspay = £289.08

EXERCISE 7.2

1 Jim Cooper's basic wage is £6.20 per hour, and he works a basic 5-day, 40-hour week. If he works overtime during the week, he is paid at time and a half. Overtime during the weekend is paid at double time. Calculate Jim's gross wage for the week when he worked five hours overtime during the week and four hours overtime on Saturday.

2 **a** The basic weekly wage of employees in a small firm is £171 for a 38-hour week.
What is the basic hourly rate?

b All overtime is paid at time and a half.
Calculate the number of hours of overtime worked by Ms Wiley during a week when her gross pay was £198.

3 Jenny, a machinist for a dressmaker, receives £3.91 per hour for her basic pay. One week she works a basic week of 36 hours, together with 8 hours overtime at time and a half.
What is her gross pay for this week?

4 The number of hours worked by an employee is often calculated from a clock card similar to the one shown below. Harold Meyer works a basic eight-hour day, five days a week and his basic hourly rate is £4.15.

DAY	IN	OUT	IN	OUT	CLOCK HOURS	O/T HOURS
SAT	0730	1200	1230	1400	6	6
SUN	0800	1200				
MON	0730	1200	1300	1700		
TUES	0730	1200	1300	1730		
WED	0800	1200	1300	1730		
THURS	0730	1200	1245	1815		
FRI	0730	1200	1230	1600		

Overtime is paid at the following rates:
Time and a quarter for Monday to Friday
Time and a half for Saturday
Double time for Sunday
Calculate Harold's gross pay for this week.

5 Collette normally works 38 hours per week helping to restore 'old masters'. One week she works five hours overtime at double time and receives a gross pay of £269.76.
What is her hourly rate of pay for a weekday evening when Collette is paid time and a half?

6 Janine, a hotel receptionist, is paid £4.70 per hour for her basic 38-hour week. Overtime on Sundays is paid at double time, while other overtime is paid at time and a half.
How much is Janine's gross pay when she works 47 hours in a week, 5 hours of which are on a Sunday?

7 Samantha is an assistant in a personnel section, earning £223.92 when she works a basic 36-hour week. One week she has to produce a summary of last year's appointments and works six hours overtime paid at time and a half.
Calculate Samantha's gross pay for that week.

8 Emily, an assistant in a convalescent home, is paid £3.90 per hour for her basic 38-hour week. During a particularly busy week she does four hours overtime at time and a half and six hours overtime at double time.
Calculate Emily's gross weekly pay.

9 Joanna, a dental assistant, earns £201.60 when she works her basic 36-hour week. In a week after the holidays she also worked 8 hours overtime at time and a half.
Calculate Joanna's gross pay during that week.

10 A swimming pool attendant is paid £3.70 per hour for his basic 36-hour week. He is paid overtime at time and a half.
How much does he earn in a week in which he does 6 hours overtime?

11 Ruth is a waitress who earns £210.90 when she works a basic 38-hour week. In one week, she had to work five hours overtime (paid at double time) as the restaurant was hosting a wedding reception.
Calculate Ruth's gross pay that week.

12 The basic working week in a small factory is 35 hours (i.e. 7 hours per day) and the basic rate of pay is £4.98 per hour. The overtime rate is time and a half from Monday to Friday and double time on Saturdays. The table shown below shows the hours worked by five employees. For each employee, calculate the gross weekly pay.

	MON	TUES	WED	THUR	FRI	SAT
Andrews A J	7	7	8	9	8	0
Collins F	8	8	9	9	7	5
Hammond C	9	9	9	10	10	0
Jali Y	8	10	11	11	9	4
Longman B H	9	10	10	9	7	6

13 Carol works on a production line making televisions. When she works her basic week of 38 hours together with 4 hours overtime at double time, Carol receives a gross pay of £250.70.
What is Carol's basic pay?

7.3 *Commission*

People who are employed as salespersons or representatives and some shop assistants are paid a basic wage plus a percentage of the value of the goods they have sold.

Their basic wage is often small, or non-existent, and the **commission** on their sales forms the largest part or all of their gross pay.

EXAMPLE

A salesman earns a basic salary of £690 per month plus a commission of 5% on all sales over £5000.
Find his gross income for a month in which he sold goods to the value of £9400.

He earns commission on (£9400 − £5000) worth of sales

$$\text{Commission} = 5\% \text{ of } (£9400 - £5000)$$

$$= 0.05 \times £4400$$

$$= £220$$

$$\text{Gross salary} = \text{Basic salary} + \text{Commission}$$

$$= £690 + £220$$

$$= £910$$

EXERCISE 7.3

1 An estate agent charges a commission of $1\frac{1}{2}\%$ of the value of each house he sells. How much commission is earned by selling a house for £104 000?

2 Calculate the commission earned by a shop assistant who sold goods to the value of £824 if her rate of commission is 3%.

3 Find the gross monthly pay of Jasmine, who has a basic salary of £855 per month plus a commission of 2% of her monthly sales. She sells £51 410 of goods during the month.

4 A sculptor agrees to pay a studio 6% commission on all sales of her work.

How much commission does the sculptor pay the studio when it sells a sculpture for £8220.

5 Andrina is paid a basic wage of £50 per week by a group of knitters to sell their hand-knitted jumpers. She is also paid 17% commission on all her sales. In one week she sells 160 jumpers at £40 each.
How much is Andrina paid for that week?

6 An insurance representative is paid a commission of 8% on all insurance sold up to a value of £4000 per week. If the value of insurance sold exceeds £4000 per week, he is paid a commission of 18% on the excess. Calculate his gross pay for the 4 weeks in which his sales were £3900, £4500, £5100 and £2700.

7 Two firms place advertisements for an insurance representative:
Firm A offers an annual salary of £5000 plus a company car (worth £2500 per year) and 4% commission on sales over £200 000 per annum.
Firm B offers an annual salary of £7000 and 3.4% commission on sales over £150 000 per annum.

a Which is the better job if sales of £350 000 per year can be expected?

b If, in a good year, sales rose to £500 000 per year, which job would pay the higher amount and by how much?

8 A nurse at a doctor's surgery is paid a basic wage of £220 per week plus a commission of £2.05 for every vaccination she gives. In one week she givers 31 vaccinations. What is her gross pay for that week?

9 A dentist pays his technician Rachel commission for sealing the teeth of children to prevent tooth decay. Rachel is paid £4 per child up to the first 10 in that week and £3 for each child thereafter.
How much commission does Rachel receive in a week in which she seals the teeth of 28 children?

10 Collette, a hairdresser, is paid 12% commission on her work. In one day, her clients pay £500. How much is Collette paid on that day?

11 An agent is paid 5% commission on all tickets sold for shows, and 8% for all coach trips. The agent sells tickets for shows to the value of £900 and £680 worth of coach trips.
Find his commission.

12 A car salesman is paid 21% commission on his weekly sales over £6000. In one particular week he sold two cars for £7520 and £10 640. What was his commission for that week?

13 In addition to his basic salary of £210 per week, a double-glazing salesman is paid 11% commission on his sales. In one week he negotiates 4 sales of £1250, £180, £3850 and £6100 respectively.
Find his gross income for that week.

7.4 *Piecework*

Some employees, particularly in the manufacturing and building industries, are paid a fixed amount for each article or piece of work they complete. This is known as **piecework**.

They may also receive a small basic wage and, in addition, some are paid a bonus if production exceeds a stipulated amount.

┌─ **EXAMPLE** ───

Workers in a pottery firm who hand-paint the plates are paid a basic weekly wage of £120 and a piecework rate of 80p for every plate over 30 which they paint in a day.

Calculate the weekly wage of an employee whose daily output was as follows:

Day 1   35 plates   Day 2   38 plates   Day 3   40 plates
Day 4   45 plates   Day 5   39 plates

No. of plates over 30 painted $= 5 + 8 + 10 + 15 + 9$
$= 47$

Piecework bonus $= 80p \times 47$ Weekly gross pay $= £120 + £37.60$
$= £37.60$ $= £157.60$

└───

EXERCISE 7.4

1   A firm employs casual labour to deliver advertising leaflets door to door. The rate of pay is £4.80 for every 100 leaflets delivered. How much is earned by someone who delivers 1230 leaflets?

2   Karl is paid £3.60 per hour plus a bonus of 80 pence for every sack of rubbish collected. In one day Karl collects 30 sacks when he works 9 hours. How much is his gross pay for that day?

3   A seamstress receives a bonus of 57 pence for every 2 fashion waistcoats made in excess of 15 per day.
What bonus is received if she makes 30 waistcoats in a day?

4   Mr Ansell, a picture framer, works a basic 40-hour week at £3.78 per hour, plus a bonus of £1.25 for every picture framed. In five successive days he frames 10, 11, 16, 17 and 8 pictures.
What is Mr Ansell's gross wage?

5   A freelance computer operator is paid £7 for each page of Basic program which is converted into MAC Basic. In one day she complete 26 pages. How much is she paid for that day?

6   To prepare and complete a tax return, an accountant, Francine, charges a basic £70 plus £4, for every letter sent or received, and £5 for every phone call. In dealing with one client's return, Francine sends 25 letters, receives 18 letters in return and handles 24 phone calls. What is Francine's charge?

7   In addition to his basic salary, a doctor is paid £11.50 for each daytime home visit and £28 for each night call.
How much extra does he receive during a weekend when he makes 14 visits of which 5 are during the night?

8   Anya is paid by a charity to deliver lunches to housebound pensioners. Her rate of pay is £1.50 per lunch delivered plus £10 per day. Calculate her pay on a day when she delivers 14 lunches.

9   A timeshare tout is paid £20 for each person she persuades to visit a development. In one week she sends 22 people to the development. How much does the tout receive?

10 Pierre is a guide showing tourists around the Roman amphitheatre in Arles. He is paid 100 francs per group plus a bonus of 10 francs per person. On one day there are 23, 18, 11, 17 and 21 tourists in the six groups he takes on guided tours of the amphitheatre.
How much does Pierre earn that day?

11 A bricklayers receives a bonus of 64 pence for every 10 bricks laid in excess of 350 per day. What bonus does he receive if he lays 3070 bricks in a six-day week?

12 The Rapid Fix Tyre Company pays its fitters £4.60 per hour plus 80p for each tyre fitted. In one day Ahmed works 9 hours and fits 71 tyres.
What is Ahmed's gross pay for that day?

7.5 *Deductions from pay*

Employees do not usually receive all the money they have earned.

Certain amounts of money are **deducted** from the gross pay and the pay the employee receives is the **net pay** or **take-home pay**.

The main deductions are:

- **Income Tax**
- **National Insurance**
- **Pension** (also called **Superannuation**)

Income tax (lowest rate)

Income tax is used to finance government expenditure.

It is a tax based on the amount a person earns in a tax year that begins on 6 April and ends on 5 April the following year.

Most people have income tax deducted from their pay before they receive it, by their employer, who then pays the tax to the Government. This method of paying income tax is called **PAYE** (Pay As You Earn).

Certain amounts of each person's income are not taxed. These amounts are called **tax allowances**.

The Tax Office sends the employee and the employer a PAYE Code which tells them the value of the allowances. For example, a tax code of 0450L would be given to a single person who has allowances of £450 × 10 = £4500.

$$\text{Gross income} - \text{Tax allowances} = \text{Taxable income}$$

The **lowest** rate of income tax in 1999–2000 was 10p in the pound on taxable income up to £1520.

The Personal tax allowance (in 2000–2001) was £4385.

In addition you may have a tax allowance by reason of expenses connected with your work (e.g. union contributions) or caring for a dependent relative.

EXAMPLE

Mr Brown earns £5500 per year, which is his only source of income.

Find   **a** his tax allowance,   **b** his taxable income,
c the tax paid per annum.

a Personal tax allowance = £4385

b Taxable income = Gross income − Tax allowance
$$= £5500 - £4385$$
$$= £1115$$

c Tax paid $= \dfrac{1.0}{100} \times £1115$

$$= £111.50$$

EXERCISE 7.5

Assume that the earnings stated in the following questions are the only source of income.

1 Find
   (i) the total tax allowance,
  (ii) the taxable income,
 (iii) the yearly tax paid , for:

  a someone earning £4500 per annum

  b someone earning £4950 per annum

  c someone earning £67 per week.

2 Find the yearly income tax payable by Mrs Bailey, who earns £5705 per annum and has a total tax allowance of £4385.

3 Miss Davis earns £6462 per year. She is entitled to the personal allowance plus an allowances of £960 per year for expenses necessary in her work. Calculate her monthly tax bill.

4 Find the yearly income tax payable by:

  a Ulrika, a single art gallery attendant, who earns £5243 per annum and has a total tax allowance of £4385

  b Ashley, a married graphics artist, who earns £105 per week and has a total tax allowance of £4395.

5 A trainee in a design studio is paid £473 per month. His personal allowance is £4385. Calculate the tax paid per month.

6 Zoe's husband is unemployed. Zoe works in a county council office and earns £5750 per year. Calculate her annual tax bill.

7 Jason, an unmarred office junior, earns £530 per month. He has a personal allowance of £5165. Calculate Jason's monthly tax bill.

8 Find:

   (i) the total tax allowance

  (ii) the taxable income

 (iii) the yearly tax paid, for:

  a Sanjay, a married care assistant earning £5200 per annum

  b Francesca, a single nurse, earning £111 per week.

9 Ben, a charity worker, earns £702 per month. He has a personal allowance of £7260. Calculate his monthly tax bill.

10 A travel consultant is paid £460 per month and has a tax-free allowance of £4398. How much tax does he pay per month?

11 A waitress is paid £125 per week. Her personal allowance is £5165. How much tax does she pay per week?

12 Find the annual income tax payable by Malcolm, a single apprentice, working in a steel plant, who earns £6800 per year and has a total tax allowance of £5325.

13 Anna is a trainee machine operator who earns £590 per month. If her personal allowance is £5620, calculate Anna's monthly tax bill.

Income tax (lowest rate and basic rate)

Most people who pay income tax earn more than £5905, and hence have a taxable income in excess of £1520.

Taxable income between £1520 and £28 400 is taxed at 22p in the pound, i.e. 22%. Since most people pay the majority of their income tax at this rate, the 22p rate is known as the basic rate.

EXAMPLE

Mr Jackson is an engineer and earns £21 250 per year. His personal tax allowance is £4557. How much income tax does he pay per year?

Annual taxable income = Annual gross pay − Total allowance
$$= £21250 − £4557 = £16693$$

Income taxable at basic rate = Taxable income − £1520 (maximum at lowest rate)

$$= £15\,173$$

Income tax at lowest rate	= 10p × 1520	= £152
Income tax at basic rate	= 22p × 15 173	= £3338.06
Total annual income tax		= £3490.06

EXERCISE 7.6

1 Find the yearly tax paid by:

   a Andrea, a single girl, earning £12 050 a year

   b Philip, a single man, earning £182 per week

   c Sarah and John, a married couple, earning £21 470 between them. Both earn more than £8000.

2 Jane and Denis live together. Denis earns £13 185 per annum and Jane earns £10 585 per annum.

   a What was their total tax bill for the year 2000–2001, if they claimed only the standard allowances?

   b How much tax would they have paid if they had been married?

3 If, in the next budget, the Chancellor changes the basic rate of tax from 22% to 21%, but wages remain the same, how much less tax would be paid by the employees in question 1 above?

4 Sally is a design artist earning £27 850 per annum. Her tax allowance is £3445. How much is Sally's annual tax bill?

5 Julian, an advertising agent, is paid a basic annual wage of £21 500. She also receives £325 per month in commission. How much is Julian's monthly tax bill?

6 Mark, an accountant, earns £31 500 per year. His tax allowance is £5248. How much tax does he pay each year?

7 Find the monthly tax bill payable by Ingrid, who has a company car and is therefore taxed as if she had an additional income of £2700. Ingrid earns £1995 per month and her tax allowance is £4445.

8 Find the monthly income tax paid by Asif, a staff nurse, who has a tax allowance of £4385 and earns £16 500.

9 Asif's brother Salman is a porter in the same hospital. His basic wage is £420 per week, and he has a second income of £120 per month. Salman's tax allowance is £4385. How much tax does he pay each month?

10 Marcel, a restaurant owner, has an income of £2310 per month. His tax allowances is £5255. How much is Marcel's annual tax bill?

11 Ross, the manager of a health club in an hotel, earns £18 500 per year plus £7450 in bonuses. His tax allowance is £3855. How much is Ross's monthly tax bill?

12 Richard, a window fitter, is paid £285 per week. He also works on Saturdays and admits to an income of £310 per month from this extra work. His tax allowance is £4652. How much tax does Richard pay each month?

13 As the manager of the 'Exhausts in an Instant' agency, Alf earns a basic salary of £26 150 per year. He is also paid a commission which averages £96 per week. Alf's tax allowance is £4385. How much tax does Alf pay per year?

National Insurance

National Insurance (NI) is paid by both the **employee** and the **employer**. It helps to pay for:

National Health Service
Statutory sick pay
Pensions
Unemployment benefits

The amount paid in National Insurance depends on your gross pay and whether or not you are 'contracted out' of the State Pension Scheme.

Employees who are 'contracted out' pay less National Insurance. On retirement, these employees can claim only the basic State Pension, but they will receive an employment pension.
Employees who are not 'contracted out' receive the basic State Pension plus an earnings-related state pension.

The level of employees' National Insurance contributions was changed in the 2000 budget and from 6 April 2000 is as follows:

Weekly earnings (£)	Monthly earnings (£)	Rate of National Insurance contribution
0–75.99	0–329	Nil
76–535	329–2318	10% †of earnings in excess of £76 per week (or £329 per month)
Above 535	Above 2318	10% of £459 per week (or £1989 per month)

†8.4% for employees who are contracted out.

EXAMPLE 1

Mr Day's annual salary is £15 978. Calculate his monthly National Insurance contribution if he is contracted out.

Mr Day's monthly salary = £15978 ÷ 12 = £1331.50

He earns over £277 per month and will pay the rate of 8.4% (because he is contracted out) on his earnings over £329, i.e. on £1331.50 − £329 = £1002.50.

He pays
$$8.4\% \text{ of } £1002.50 = £1002.50 \times 0.084 = £84.21$$

Total monthly contribution $\qquad = £84.21$

EXAMPLE 2

Mrs Fielding earns a gross weekly wage of £87.90. Calculate her National Insurance contribution.

Mrs Fielding will pay 10% on her earnings over £76,
i.e. on £87.90 − £76 = £11.90.

She pays
$$10\% \text{ of } £11.90 = £11.90 \times 0.10 = £1.19$$

Total weekly contribution $\qquad = £1.19$

It is expected that in the budget in the year 2001 the starting point for paying income tax and for paying National Insurance will become the same. Hence in April 2001 the threshold for paying National Insurance is expected to rise to £87 per week. This will be equal to the anticipated personal tax allowance of £4524 per annum.

EXERCISE 7.7

1   Using the table on page 61, calculate the National Insurance contributions for:

    a Alice, who earns £112.70 per week

    b Charlie, who earns £586.40 per month

    c David, who is contracted out and earns £971 per month

    d Anne, who is contracted out and earns £428.64 per month

    e Maria, who earns £4.30 per hour for a 28-hour week.

2   Mrs Ferry earned £82 per week for her part-time job.
Calculate:

    a her yearly National Insurance contribution

    b her net income for the year.

3   Nadia earns £4.60 per hour for a 40-hour week. Her income tax payment for the week is £29.25. Calculate:

    a her gross weekly wage

    b her weekly National Insurance contribution

    c her net pay for the week.

Note. Section 7.5 takes into account the changes announced in the Spring Budget for the financial year 2000–2001. Readers using this book during or after the financial year 2000–2001 should make themselves aware of any further changes introduced by the Chancellor of the Exchequer.

8 *Travel*

8.1 *Foreign currency*

Currency exchange

If you plan a trip abroad for business or holiday, you must decide the money you will need and the form in which you will take it.

Most people take a limited amount of cash in the currency of each country to be visited. They take the remainder in the more secure form of traveller's cheques. Alternatively, they use credit cards to obtain cash.

In the UK British currency (pounds sterling) is usually exchanged for foreign currency at a bank or travel agency. Exchange rates between one currency and other currencies change frequently and are published daily in newspapers and displayed where money is exchanged.

By consulting the **selling price** you can calculate the amount of foreign currency you will be sold for your pounds and from the **buying price** you can calculate the amount of pounds you will receive in return for your foreign currency.

EXAMPLE

Mr Oztürk is to travel on a business trip to Greece. He changes £350 into Greek drachma on a day when the bank selling price is 502.2.

On returning home he changes his remaining 105 500 drachma into sterling. The bank buying price is 528.9 to £1.

Calculate:

a the amount of drachma he receives
b the amount of pounds he receives on his return.

a The bank pays 502.2 drachma for every £1 it buys

For £350 he will receive 502.2 × 350 drachma

$$= 175\,770 \text{ drachma}$$

b The bank charges 528.9 drachma for every £1 it sells

For 105 500 drachma he will receive $£\dfrac{105\,500}{528.9}$

$$= £199.47$$

EXERCISE 8.1

1 Using the bank selling price, change:

   a £12 to Croatian kunas

   b £140 to Latvian lats

   c £96.50 to American dollars.

2 Using the bank buying price, calculate the sterling equivalent of:

   a 200 Swiss francs

   b 11 100 Canadian dollars

   c 650 Japanese yen.

EXCHANGE RATES		
	Bank buys	Bank sells
Australia	2.56	2.42
Canada	2.44	2.30
Croatia	12.85	11.48
Czech Republic	58.21	55.31
Greece	528.9	502.2
Japan	170.2	160.8
Latvia	0.971	0.916
Lithuania	6.60	6.30
Norway	8.208	7.715
Poland	6.916	6.522
South Africa	9.67	9.12
Slovenia	330.7	300.2
Switzerland	2.62	2.48
Turkey	837 700	787 440
USA	1.65	1.58

3   Geraldine and Peter ate a meal in a restaurant while on holiday in Rhodes.
The meal for two cost 4256 drachma. Use the bank selling price to calculate the cost of the meal in pounds.

4   The Andersons spent a holiday touring in Switzerland. While travelling they used 200 litres of petrol which cost 1.04 francs per litre. The exchange rate was 2.59 Swiss francs to £1.

   a How much did the petrol cost them in pounds?

   b What was the price per litre of the petrol in pence?

5   Before going on holiday to Eastern Europe, the Williams family changed £600 into Polish zloty. While in Poland they spent 1840 zloty and then changed their remaining zloty into Latvian lats as they crossed the border.
The exchange rate was 0.1405 lats to 1 zloty. Calculate:

   a the number of zloty they received

   b the number of lats they bought.

6   If Mr Oztürk (in the example on page 63) had postponed his trip to Greece until the following week the bank selling price would have been 508.4 drachma to the pound.
On his return, the buying price would have been 534.8 drachma to the pound.

   a How many drachma would he have received?

   b How many drachma would he have had left on his return to Britain (assuming that he would have spent the same amount)?

   c How many pounds would he have received on his return?

   d How much money would he have saved by travelling the following week?

7   a Mr Elton changed £100 into Norwegian krone for a day trip to Norway. How many krone did he receive?

   b Unfortunately the excursion was cancelled and so he changed all his krone back to pounds. How many pounds did he receive?

   c How much money did he lose because of the cancellation?

Commission

In practice, the banks also charge commission for each currency exchange.

The commission is £1 on currency exchanges up to the value of £200 and 0.5% of the value above £200.

On traveller's cheques the commission is £2 for up to £200 in value and 1% of the value above £200.

EXERCISE 8.2

Questions 1 and 2 refer to Exercise 8.1.

1   a How much commission did Mr Elton pay when changing pounds to krone?

   b How much commission did he pay when changing the krone back to pounds?

   c How much did his cancelled trip cost him, including commission charges?

2   a How much commission did the Williams family pay for their zloty?

   b How much commission would they have paid if they had taken the £600 in traveller's cheques?

3 **a** For a three-week holiday, touring Croatia, Switzerland and Slovenia, a group of four friends decided to take the equivalent of £900 abroad.
At the bank they changed £110 into Croatian kuna, £100 into Swiss francs and £120 into Lithuanian litas. How much of each currency did they receive (after commission was deducted)?

b After buying the foreign currencies, they changed as much as possible of the remaining money into traveller's cheques.

The smallest value of traveller's cheque which can be bought is £10.
   (i) How much did they exchange for traveller's cheques?
   (ii) How much commission did they pay for the cheques?

c What was the total cost per person of the foreign currencies and cheques?

8.2 *Time*

There are two methods in general use for showing the time:

 (i) the 12-hour clock   (ii) the 24-hour clock.

With the 12-hour clock the day is divided into two periods, from midnight to noon (am) and noon to midnight (pm).

The 24-hour clock uses a single period of 24 hours, starting at midnight. The time is written as a four-digit number, without a decimal point, and there is no need to specify morning (am) or afternoon (pm).

This method is always used for timetables and is in common use on video recorders and digital clocks.

EXAMPLE

Write the times
a ten to nine in the evening,
b twenty past seven in the morning, using both the 12-hour and 24-hour clocks.

a The 12-hour clock time is 8.50 pm.
The 24-hour clock time is 2050 (i.e. 8.50 + 12 hours).

b The 12-hour clock time is 7.20 am.
The 24-hour clock time is 0720 (note the zero at the beginning to make a four-digit number).

EXERCISE 8.3

In the following exercise the time is written using words, the 12-hour clock or the 24-hour clock.
For each question, give the time using the other two methods.

1	Six fifteen in the morning	6	2220
2	11.10 pm	7	Ten to ten in the evening
3	0930	8	10.45 am
4	1.40 am	9	Twenty-five past midnight
5	1350	10	1656

EXAMPLE

The 0745 train from Newcastle is scheduled to arrive in Southampton at 1516.
How long is the journey?

Method 1

From 0745 to 0800	= 15 mins
From 0800 to 1500	= 7 hours
From 1500 to 1516	= 16 mins
Total journey time	= 7 hours + 15 mins + 16 mins
	= 7 hours 31 mins

Method 2

Hours Mins   Hours Mins

	Hours	Mins		Hours	Mins	
Train arrives	15	16	=	14	76	(76=16+60)
Train departs	7	45		– 7	45	
Time taken			=	7	31	

The journey time is 7 hours 31 minutes.

EXERCISE 8.4

1 Mr Little catches the 0654 train to London. If he arrives at the station at twenty to seven, how long does he wait?

2 Miss Brothers travels on the 0704 train. She arrives at the station nine minutes before the train is due.
At what time does she arrive at the station?

3 Mr Ghosh arrives at the airport at 8.35 am and his plane takes off 55 minutes later.
At what time does the plane take off?

4 At what time does the 0929 train at Coventry arrive if it is 13 minutes late?

5 **a** Mrs Richardson's afternoon train is scheduled to arrive in Birmingham at eight minutes past four, but it is 15 minutes late. At what time, on the 24-hour clock, does she arrive?

b Her connecting train leaves at 1651. How long does she have to wait?

6 Chris has an appointment in London at 2.15 pm. The train journey from his local station takes 1 hour and 10 minutes. He allows a further 20 minutes to travel on the underground to his place of appointment. In case there are any delays on the journey, he allows an extra 15 minutes travelling time. What length of time should Chris allow from his local station?

7 **a** The boat from Dover to Calais departs at 1715. The crossing takes $1\frac{1}{2}$ hours and French time is 1 hour ahead.
At what time does the boat dock in France, French time?

b The same boat leaves Calais for Dover at 2000.
At what time does it arrive in England, British time?

8.3 *Timetables*

All timetables use the 24-hour clock.

EXERCISE 8.5

Mondays to Saturdays

BASINGSTOKE (Bus Station) ⇆			0730	0840	0935	1035	1135	1235	1335	1435	1535
Basingstoke (Winton Square)			0735	0845	0940	1040	1140	1240	1340	1440	1540
Worting Road (South Ham)			0739	0849	0944	1044	1144	1244	1344	1444	1544
Worting (White Hart)			0743	0853	0948	1048	1148	1248	1348	1448	1548
Newfound (Fox Inn)			0747	0857	0952	1052	1152	1252	1352	1452	1552
Deane Gate			0753	0903	0958	1058	1158	1258	1358	1458	1558
Overton (Post Office) ⇆		0756	0758	0908	1003	1103	1203	1303	1403	1503	1603
Laverstoke (Mill)		0802	0802	0912	1007	1107	1207	1307	1407	1507	1607
Whitchurch (Square)		0809	0809	0919	1014	1114	1214	1314	1414	1514	1614
Whitchurch (Bere Hill Estate)	0650		0813	0923		1118		1318		1518	
Whitchurch (Square)	0654	0809	0817	0927	1014	1122	1214	1322	1414	1522	1614
Hurstbourne Priors (Portsmouth Arms)	0659	0814	0822	0932	1019	1127	1219	1327	1419	1527	1619
The Middleway		0821			1026		1226		1426		1626
Longparish (Plough Inn)	0708		0831	0941		1136		1336		1536	
Longparish (Station Hill)	0712		0835	0945		1140		1340		1540	
London Road (Admirals Way)	0723*	0825	0843	0953	1030	1148	1230	1348	1430	1548	1630
ANDOVER (Bridge Street) arr.	0727	0829	0847	0957	1034	1152	1234	1352	1434	1552	1634
ANDOVER (West Street) ⇆ arr.	0729C			0959C		1154C		1354C			

ANDOVER (West Street) ⇆ dep.	0624	0734			0911		1111		1311		1511		
ANDOVER (Bridge Street) dep.	0626	0736	0831		0913	1031	1113	1231	1313	1431	1513	1631	1735
London Road (Admirals Way)	0630	0740	0835		0917	1035	1117	1235	1317	1435	1517	1635	1739
Longparish (Station Hill)					0925		1125		1325		1525		1747
Longparish (Plough Inn)					0929		1129		1329		1529		1751
The Middleway	0634	0744	0839			1039		1239		1439		1639	
Hurstbourne Priors (Portsmouth Arms)	0641	0751	0846		0938	1046	1138	1246	1338	1446	1538	1646	1800
Whitchurch (Square)	0646	0756	0851		0943	1051	1143	1251	1343	1451	1543	1651	1805
Whitchurch (Bere Hill Estate) ⇆					0947		1147		1347		1547		1809
Whitchurch (Square)	0646	0756	0851	0851	0951	1051	1151	1251	1351	1451	1551	1651	1813
Laverstoke (Mill)	0653	0803	0858	0858	0958	1058	1158	1258	1358	1458	1558	1658	1820
Overton (Post Office) ⇆	0657	0807	0902	0902	1002	1102	1202	1302	1402	1502	1602	1702	1824
Deane Gate	0702	0812	0907	0907	1007	1107	1207	1307	1407	1507	1607	1707	1829
Newfound (Fox Inn)	0708	0818	0913	0913	1013	1113	1213	1313	1413	1513	1613	1713	1835
Worting (White Hart)	0712	0822	0917	0917	1017	1117	1217	1317	1417	1517	1617	1717	1839
Worting Road (South Ham)	0716	0826	0921	0921	1021	1121	1221	1321	1421	1521	1621	1721	1843
Basingstoke (Winton Square)	0720	0830	0925	0925	1025	1125	1225	1325	1425	1525	1625	1725	1847
BASINGSTOKE (Bus Station) ⇆	0725	0835	0930	0930	1030	1130	1230	1330	1430	1530	1630	1730	1852

1 Use the bus timetable to answer the following questions.

   a Mr Tully arrives at Basingstoke bus station at 10.15 am.
How long does he have to wait for a bus?

   b How many buses from Basingstoke stop at Longparish?

   c Miss Dawes catches the 0908 bus at Overton. To get to Salisbury she must change buses at Andover. The Salisbury bus leaves Andover at 1038.
How long does she have to wait at Andover?

   d Mrs Goff lives in South Ham and visits her mother in Whitchurch for at least 3 hours every Wednesday. If she catches the 1044 bus from Worting Road, which buses can she catch from The Square in order to be home before 5 o'clock?

2 Assume that the time in France and Belgium is 1 hour ahead of British time.

Dover/Boulogne [1¾ hours]	0030		0330		0630		0930		1230		1530		1830		2130		
Boulogne/Dover		0130		0430		0730		1030		1330		1630		1930		2230	2359

Dover/Calais [1¼ hours]		0200	0400	0600	0730	0900	1030	1200	1330	1500	1630	1800	1930	2100	2230
Calais/Dover	0015	0200	0400	0600	0730	0915	1045	1215	1345	1515	1645	1815	1945	2115	2245

Dover/Ostend [4 hours]	0015	0430		1000		1400	1630		1930	2130	
Ostend/Dover			0600		0945	1145	1345		1745	2100	2345

a How many ferries leave Dover in the evening between 7 o'clock and 10 o'clock?

b At what time does the 7.30 pm boat arrive in Ostend?

c The 1330 ferry from Dover arrives in Calais at 1610.
How many minutes late is it?

d The Carmichael family have hired a chalet in Boulogne, but it is not available until after 12 noon.
Assuming it takes 45 minutes to pass through customs and drive to the chalet, what is the earliest ferry they should catch from Dover?

e Mr and Mrs Davenport plan to return to England on the 0130 ferry from Boulogne but arrive just as the boat is leaving.
How much time will they save if they catch the next available ferry from Calais?
(Assume that it will take more than half an hour, but less than 2 hours to drive from Boulogne to Calais.)

f The 1215 ferry from Calais to Dover leaves 20 minutes late.
Because of heavy seas, the crossing takes 45 minutes longer than usual.
At what time does the ferry arrive in Dover?

EXERCISE 8.6

1 Paul and Catherine go to Portugal to buy cotton material for their company. The material costs 147 escudos per metre and the cost of printing the pattern is 74 escudos per pattern which is 662 cm in length. If the exchange rate is 305 escudos to the pound, how much are Paul and Catherine charged for 120 metres of the cotton material?

2 Paul and Catherine live in Southampton and decide to fly on the afternoon British Airways flight from Heathrow. The journey to Heathrow from Southampton takes 1 hour. Paul and Catherine want to allow 30 minutes to park their car, and intend to check in 50 minutes before the flight takes off. The flight timetable from Heathrow to Lisbon is shown below:

Heathrow	0825	1025	1350	1415	1830
Lisbon	1105	1305	1630	1650	2205
Airline	TAP	BA	TAP	BA	BA

Find:

a the latest time they should leave Southampton

b their time of arrival in Lisbon.

3 Enzo and Lucinda are going to a marketing conference in Naples, Florida. They consider two flights:
- American Airlines
departing London Heathrow at 0955, arriving Miami at 1440
- Virgin Atlantic
departing London Gatwick at 1115, arriving Miami at 1545.

The time in Miami is 5 hours behind Britain. Naples is a two-hour drive from Miami.

a Give two factors which could determine which airline Enzo and Lucinda use.

b Assuming that to pass through immigration control in Miami would take 11 hours and that collection of their hire car would take a further 40 minutes, what would be the time in Britain when they arrive in Naples if they use:
(i) American Airlines   (ii) Virgin Atlantic?

4 Enzo and Lucinda hire a 2-door full-size car in America. The cost is given in the table below. In addition, they must pay insurance (LDW) which is $11.95 per day. They arrive in Miami on Tuesday afternoon and, using the same airline, fly home on Friday afternoon. One day for the car hire is any 24-hour period. In addition they are charged $14.95 for a tank full of petrol. Using the exchange rate of $1.62 to the pound, calculate the total cost in pounds of hiring the car.

RENT A CAR RATES

	Economy		Compact		Intermediate				Full Size				Luxury		Minivan/ Convertible	
	2-Door (EXAR)		4-Door (CCAR)		2-Door (ICAR)		4-Door (IDAR)		2-Door (SCAR)		4-Door (FCAR)		(LCAR)		(MVAR/ STAR)	
EFFECTIVE 01 JAN 94–31 DEC 94	D	W	D	W	D	W	D	W	D	W	D	W	D	W	D	W
FLORIDA	£8	£29	£16	£55	£17	£59	£18	£65	£20	£79	£25	£85	£40	£169	£42	£175
NEW YORK CITY	......	......	£25	£139	£27	£155	£29	£159	£32	£165	£33	£169	......	......	......	......
NEW YORK/ILLINOIS*	£18	£115	£24	£130	£25	£140	£26	£143	£27	£155	£29	£159	£35	£200	£37	£209
CALIFORNIA	£12	£49	£13	£65	£15	£75	£17	£79	£18	£89	£19	£95	£22	£135	£25	£139
REST OF USA	£13	£63	£17	£79	£18	£89	£19	£95	£20	£105	£20	£109	£21	£155	£22	£159

5 A rest-home organises a day trip for its residents to France. The coach leaves Salisbury at 9 am and takes 3½ hours to travel to the Channel Tunnel. The shuttles leave at 5, 20, 35 and 55 minutes past each hour and 53 minutes after arriving at the terminal at Folkestone the coach is driven on to the French motorway.
At what time does this coach go on to the French motorway?

6 Six helpers and 34 residents have lunch and tea in France. Lunch with wine costs 44.2 francs each, and tea costs 500 francs for the whole party. At an exchange rate of 10.45 francs to the pound, find the total cost in pounds of their meals.

7 A travel company is pricing a holiday package to the Canary Islands. The flight will cost £11 000 and the company expects to fill 120 of the 150 seats on the plane. The hotel will charge 5400 pesetas per person per night. The travel company adds on 20% of the total costs for its profit and agent's commission. At 230 pesetas to the pound, what cost should the company price a one-week (7-night) holiday?

8 The data below shows the timetable of an airline between Boston and Dallas/Fort Worth and between Dallas/Fort Worth and Corpus Christi. Edward arrives at Boston at 10.30 am and catches the next flight. At what time should he arrive at Corpus Christi?

Boston Departure	Dallas/Fort Worth Arrival	Dallas/Fort Worth Departure	Corpus Christi Arrival
6.44 am	9.59 am	6.53 am	8.06 am
8.30 am	12.01 pm	8.10 am	9.45 am
11.48 am	3.15 pm	10.57 am	12.15 pm
2.10 pm	5.46 pm	12.52 pm	2.08 pm
		3.50 pm	5.09 pm
5.20 pm	9.03 pm	5.12 pm	6.50 pm
6.45 pm	11.49 pm	9.51 pm	11.05 pm

9   A manufacturer of navigational instruments sells instruments for cruisers. One instrument measuring sea depth is sold in the Caribbean for $84. In England it is sold for £34.

What is the percentage increase in cost in the Caribbean?

(Use $1.62 to the pound.)

10   A company exports its goods using the Portsmouth–Caen ferry. Frank knows that he must allow $3\frac{1}{4}$ hours to drive to Portsmouth and an additional hour for customs.

a   What time must he leave to catch the afternoon ferry on Tuesday 27 July?

JUL	T	F	S	S	M	T	W	T	F	S	S	M	T	W	T	F	S	S	M	T	W	T	F	S	S	M	T	W	T	F	S
	1	2	3	4	5	6	7	8	9	10	11	12	13	14	15	16	17	18	19	20	21	22	23	24	25	26	27	28	29	30	31
0800	E	E	D	E	E	E	E	E	E	D	E	E	E	E	E	C	C	D	E	E	D	D	C	C	D	D	D	D	D	C	C
1500	E	E	E	E	E	E		E	E	E	E	E	E			E	D	D	D	E	E		D	D	D	D	E	E		D	D
2330	E	D	E	E	E	E	E	E	D	E	E	E	E	E	E	C	C	D	E	E	D	D	C	C	D	D	D	D	D	C	C

C, D, E identify the tariff operating on that ferry.

The crossing time is 6 hours, except for the 2330 from Portsmouth which takes 7 hours.

b   When does he expect to arrive in Caen?

      Give your answer in British time.

9 *Statistical Terms*

In 1834, the Royal Statistical Society was founded, and defined statistics as 'using figures and tabular exhibitions to illustrate the conditions and prospects of society'. Statistics is now used to deal with the collection, classification, tabulation and analysis of information and opinions.

Data. Data is the information which has been collected or researched. The word 'data' is a plural and the singular is 'datum' (a single piece of information).

Variables. Information is collected about *variables* such as weights, numbers of clients, types of disease.

A *variable* is something which can change from one item to the next. It can be either **quantitative** (i.e. numerical like weight or number of clients) or *qualitative* (i.e. an attribute like car colour or type of disease).

There are two types of quantitative variables:

(i) *Continuous.* A continuous variable is a variable which could take all possible values within a given range, e.g. the height of a tree.

(ii) *Discrete.* A discrete variable is a variable which increases in steps (often whole numbers), e.g. the number of rooms in a building.

A discrete variable does not have to consist only of whole numbers. For example, the size of shoes is also a discrete variable, and the sizes go up in steps of a half (5, $5\frac{1}{2}$, 6, $6\frac{1}{2}$, etc.).

The number of steps climbed is a *discrete* variable.

The distance travelled on the escalator is a *continuous* variable.

Observation. An observation is the value taken by a variable. For example, an age of 17 years is an observation when the variable is age.

Population. The term '*population*' means everything (or everybody) in the category you are considering. For example, if you were making a study of cathedrals, the population could be all the cathedrals in Britain. If you were investigating what attracts people to certain types of holiday, the population would be all holiday-makers.

EXERCISE 9.1

For each population below, state whether the variable given is qualitative, discrete or continuous:

1   the numbers of employees in a county's factories

2   the weights of new born babies in Britain

3   the age at death in 1994 of a town's inhabitants

4   the lengths of bolts coming off a factory production line

5   the colour preferences of customers in a city's clothes shops

6   the acceleration rates of new models of motorbike in a given year

7   the time taken to complete a job by each employee of a firm

8   the brands of toothpaste sold by chemists

9   the number of passengers on flights to the Continent during one summer

10   the newspapers on sale at station kiosks

11   the number of cars parked each morning in a firm's car park over a period of time

12   the type of holiday accommodation available in a resort.

10 *Sampling, Surveys, Questionaires*

One of the problems with statistical surveys involving people is that, whatever your opinion, there are likely to be many other people with the same opinion. If you ask only these people, your opinion will be seen to be that of the whole population. If you ask only people with the opposite opinion, you will be seen to be in a minority. Therefore, you must ask a variety of people, so that you have a true picture of the population.

Remember, however, that in statistics, the term **population** does not necessarily refer to people. If you wish to survey the ages of cars on the road, your population might be all the cars in Britain.

10.1 *Surveys*

When you record any information – for example, about other people's opinions or numbers of surviving African elephants or types of road accidents – you are carrying out a **survey**. The survey results may be obtained by asking questions, by observation or by research.

To obtain completely accurate information, you would have to ask *everybody* (in your town or country or whatever), and receive answers from everybody, or observe *all* the elephants in Africa.

10.2 *Censuses*

When information is gathered about all the members of a population, the survey is called a **census**.

A national census is carried out every ten years, in years ending with 1 (e.g. 1991, 2001). Every adult in Britain is asked a large number of questions on mainly factual matters, for example the number of rooms in their house, their age, and the number of cars they possess.

A national census is a very large undertaking, and the results, though accurate, take a substantial length of time to be produced. Apart from the vast number of people to be asked, and the placing of their answers in computers, it is very difficult to ensure that every adult has in fact replied. It costs the country a great deal of money to complete a national census.

10.3 *Samples*

It is usually impossible for firms, newspapers, biologists, medical researchers, etc., to obtain information about the whole population, because the survey:

- may be expensive
- may take a long time

- may involve testing to destruction – e.g. if you wish to find out how long batteries last, you test them until they run out
- may be impossible to carry out for every member of the population – e.g. a survey to find the weights of trout in Scottish rivers.

A small part of the population is chosen for the survey and this is called a **sample**.

The statistician then assumes that the results for the sample are representative of the population as a whole. The larger the number of people asked, the more likely their response is to be a valid result for the whole population.

Clearly it is vital that for the survey to be accurate the sample you choose must be representative of the whole population.

To achieve this, every member of the population must have an equal chance of being chosen.

10.4 *Sampling methods*

Random sampling

A random sample is one in which every member has an equal chance of being selected.

Campaign groups for or against a particular issue (such as the possible siting of a new supermarket near a park) can often obtain a large majority for their point of view simply by selecting which passers-by to question (perhaps the people living near the park who will be worried about the possibility of noise). By careful selection, majorities as high as 70% can easily be obtained both for and against the same issue! (Some people may well want a supermarket behind their back garden.)

The simplest way to obtain a random sample is to give every member a number, and to select numbers from tickets in a box (as in a raffle), or (if there are too many for this method) to select numbers by computer. Random numbers can also be obtained by using the RAN button on some calculators.

It is common to use the electoral roll of a suitably sized area (on which every adult is listed) to obtain a numbered list from which to select a sample.

Periodic sampling

With periodic or systematic sampling, a regular pattern is used to pick the sample, for example, every hundredth firework on a production line. This can give a unrepresentative sample if there is a pattern to the list which is echoed by the sample.

Stratified random sampling

A stratified sample is more accurate than a random sample, and is used in opinion polls, when 1 or 2% accuracy is important. A stratified sample (or **strata sample**) is one in which the population is divided into categories. The sample should then be constructed to have the same categories in the same proportions.

Random sampling is then used to select the required numbers in each category.

For example, if you wished to find out about the earnings of students in a sixth-form college, it would be sensible to have both lower sixth and upper sixth students represented. You may also wish to make sure that one-year students, males and females, are fairly represented. Suppose there are 1000 students in college, of whom 220 are lower sixth one-year students, 420 are lower sixth two-year students and 360 are upper sixth students.

A sample of 50 would contain the following numbers:

LVI one-year students $= \dfrac{220}{1000} \times 50 = 11$

LVI two-year students $= \dfrac{420}{1000} \times 50 = 21$

UVI students $\qquad = \dfrac{360}{1000} \times 50 = 18$

The eleven LVI one-year students would be randomly chosen from the 220 students in college. The other two strata would be chosen in the same way.

Quota sampling

For a quota sample, a manufacturer may determine the proportions of each group to interview.

For example, if a manufacturer wishes to launch a new chocolate bar on the market, it may be more important to canvass the opinions of children and those who do the shopping than any other sector of the market.

A market researcher paid to survey a sample of 100 people could be instructed to ask, say, 20 people under the age of 18, 30 in the age range 19–40 who do the family shopping, 10 in the same age range who don't, 30 in the age range over 40 who do the family shopping, and 10 in this age range who don't. The researcher will probably use convenience sampling (see below) to choose who to ask, but once one of the quotas is filled, no more people in that category may be asked. The researcher will continue to ask people in the other categories until the sample of 100 has been surveyed.

This is a common method used for market research, but inexperienced (or lazy!) researchers may choose an unrepresentative sample.

Convenience sampling

The most convenient sample is chosen, which, for a sample of size fifty, usually means the first fifty people you meet. There is obviously no guarantee that this sample will be representative. In fact it is highly likely that it won't be.

10.5 *Bias*

The results of a survey are biased if the sample is not representative of the whole population.

Bias can be introduced if:

- the sample is unrepresentative. Even when using random sampling an unusual sample may be chosen, and this is just bad luck.

- an incorrect sampling method is used. Sampling methods, other than random, or stratified random sampling, are very likely to produce biased samples.

If you wanted to know people's views on drinking, a survey held outside a public house at closing time would clearly produce a different response from one held outside the office of the 'Teetotallers' League'! Neither would be representative of the complete population. Both of these samples would be biased.

- the questions asked in the survey are not clear or are leading questions (see section 10.6).

EXERCISE 10.1

In questions 1 to 8:

a identify the population

b criticise the method of obtaining the sample

c recommend an alternative way of obtaining a sample.

1 A journalist at a local newspaper wants to canvass popular opinion about plans for a new shopping centre in town. He goes into the High Street, and asks people, until he has asked 50.

2 Stephanie wishes to find out the earnings of college students. She goes into a college common room, and asks 40 girls.

3 The police wish to ascertain how many cars have a valid tax disc. One day, they set up a survey point on a road out of a town, between 5pm and 6pm. They stop a car and check its tax disc. As soon as it has left, they stop the next car.

4 A geography student needs to collect five soil samples from his garden for a project. He stands in the middle, and throws a coin in the air. Where it lands, he takes a sample.

5 For a survey into the smoking habits of teenagers, Carol went to a tobacconist's near a school at 3.30pm, which was when the school day ended. She asked everyone entering the shop how much they spent on cigarettes in a week.

6 To find out how many homes in a telephone area have central heating, a salesgirl telephones 100 people, picked at random from a telephone directory.

7 To find out the make of car that people in an area of town use, Peter went out after lunch and knocked on doors until he had one hundred responses. He was pleased with his efficiency, as he had finished by 4pm.

8 To investigate what influenced people in their decision on mode of transport to work, John went to the station just before the 8.15 train departed, and asked as many people as he could.

10.6 *Questionnaires*

If your questions are written down and given to people to complete, the list of questions is called a **questionnaire**. The questions you ask must be chosen with care. They must:

(i) **not give offence.** Some people do not wish to give their precise age, or social class, so you *either*: (*a*) find an alternative questions, (e.g. 'Which of these age ranges applies to you?'), *or* (*b*) fill in the information by using your own judgement.

(ii) **not be leading.** 'What do you think of the superb new facilities at . . .' will *lead* most people to agree they are better than the old facilities. People do not usually want to contradict the questioner. However, the point of the survey should not be to obtain agreement with your view, but to obtain other people's opinions.

(iii) **be able to be answered quickly.** The person answering the questions will often have only a small amount of time to spare and will not want you to write long sentences on their point of view. To obtain information easily from the survey it is helpful to have Yes/No answers or 'boxes' for the answers which are ticked. Here is an example:

How many different television sets does your household possess?

0	1	2	3	4	5	More
□	□	□	□	□	□	□

A questionnaire must also be easy for anyone to understand. The questions themselves must also be designed carefully. The question 'How much do you watch TV?' could result in the following types of response:

'A lot', 'Not much'
'Every night', 'twice a week'
'For two hours a night'
'Whenever there's sport, a film, . . .'

A better question is 'How many hours do you spend watching TV?', but this may encourage wild guesses because of poor memory.

An even better question to ask is 'How many hours did you watch TV *last* night?'. You can then offer a range of possible answers such as:

'Not at all'
'Up to $\frac{1}{2}$ hour'
'$\frac{1}{2}$ to 1 hour'
'1 to 2 hours'

and so on.

If you suspect different times are spent on different days, it is up to you, as a statistician, to ask a few people each day over a period of a week.

All surveys are open to error. The larger the sample, the more accurate the result.

10.7 *Pilot surveys*

It is common for companies to carry out an initial survey on a small area of the country in order to identify potential problems with the questions and to identify typical responses. This limits the errors in expensive large-scale surveys.

EXERCISE 10.2

Criticise the questions asked in this exercise and suggest questions which should be asked to find the information required.

1   What do you think of the improved checkout facilities?

2   Do you agree that BBC2 programmes are the best on TV?

3   What is your date of birth?

4   Sheepskin coats are made from sheep. Do you wear a sheepskin coat?

5   Dolphins are wild animals. Do you enjoy watching dolphins perform?

6   Sunbathing causes skin cancer. Do you sunbathe?

7   Vitamin D is obtained from sunlight. Do you sunbathe?

8   Is the new decor a major improvement on the old?

9   Would you rather use your local shops than a major supermarket miles away?

10.8 *Hypothesis testing*

A statistical survey should have a purpose. It may be used to find out people's opinions (e.g. an opinion poll) or to discover what the population requires of a new product (consumer research), but often it is used to test a theory. A statement is made about a population, or populations, which can be tested statistically. This statement is called a **hypothesis**.

For example:

1   'Women live longer than men.'
2   'You can't tell margarine from butter.'

3   'A new leisure centre would benefit the town.'
4   'The most popular colour of car is red.'

are four statements which are **hypotheses** (plural of 'hypothesis'). Each of these hypotheses can be investigated statistically.

To test the truth of the hypothesis someone must devise an appropriate method to collect data. This must then be analysed before a conclusion can be made, based on the results of the analysis.

The hypothesis can be tested by carrying out a survey or experiment, by observation, or by using published data (which is the result of someone else's survey).

For the four examples above:

1   To test the hypothesis that women live longer than men, government statistics published over several years could be used. Averages and measures of spread could be calculated (see Unit 13) and compared.

2   An experiment could test whether or not it was possible to tell the difference in taste between margarine and butter, perhaps by blindfolding people and seeing whether they can identify which is which.

3   A method for deciding if a new leisure centre is needed could be to devise a suitable questionnaire and survey a sample of the town population.
Among other things, the questionnaire would need to find out what facilities people required for sports, how their needs were being met at the present time, and whether they would consider using a new local leisure centre.

4   One method of testing the hypothesis that 'the most popular colour of car is red' would be to carry out a survey of cars on a busy stretch of road and record results taken at different times on different days on a survey sheet.

You will understand more about analysing data when you have worked through Units 13 (Averages) and *14 (Cumulative Frequency).

EXERCISE 10.3

1 State an appropriate method which could be used to test the following hypotheses:

   a If it rains on St Swithun's day, it will rain for the next forty days and forty nights.

   b Consumers prefer . . .
   (Choose any product or set of products which interests you).

2 Devise an experiment to test the hypothesis: 'Students studying Leisure and Tourism have quicker reactions than those studying Art and Design.'

3 An artist wants to find out the preferences of potential customers in their choice of paintings. How would he carry out a survey to discover these preferences?

4 A potter in Cornwall considers whether to produce coffee mugs or cups and saucers for his new hand-made range.
   How would he carry out a survey to test opinion on which holiday-makers would prefer to buy?

5 Design a questionnaire to test the hypothesis that most burglar alarms are sold to victims of a recent burglary.

6 An estate agent wants to carry out a survey to discover what incentives would make house sellers use his agency in preference to others. How would he do this?

7 One village has a high incidence of childhood leukaemia.
   How would you test the hypothesis that this is due to natural causes?

8 A student nurse decides to investigate differences in the occurrence of breast cancer in Europe. The rate in Southern France is very low. Design a questionnaire to test the hypothesis that this difference is due to diet rather than lifestyle.

9 A tour operator wonders whether it would be profitable to arrange flights between Exeter, the local airport, and Malaga, Spain.
   Construct three questions for a questionnaire designed to discover whether this would be profitable.

10 A doctor analyses sporting injuries in two neighbouring villages, Hartington and Easeham. Hartington shows a greater number than Easeham. The doctor believes that this is because the residents of Hartington are younger than those in Easeham.
   How would you design a questionnaire to test this hypothesis?

11 A company considers producing a cabriolet (open-top) version of a small car.
   Design a questionnaire to survey opinion and discover whether this would be a sensible decision.

12 A manufacturer makes fittings for front doors. The fittings are made in brass and chrome and the manufacturer is wondering whether to introduce a range in black matt finish.
   How would the company carry out a survey to find out whether the new range would be successful?

11 *Classification and Tabulation of Data*

11.1 *Tabulation*

The purpose of tabulation is to arrange information, after collection and classification, into a compact space so that it can be read easily and quickly. It then may be represented pictorially to enable relevant facts to be seen readily, as explained in the next chapter.

Tabulation consists of entering the data found in columns or rows.

EXAMPLE

The numbers of pensioners living in certain villages were:

Village	Number of pensioners
Ashurst	31
Botleigh	17
Crow	28
Downton	24
Eaglecliffe	19
Fillingdales	33
Total	152

It is important that the tables produced are neat, all rows and columns are clearly identified, and that units (where appropriate) are given.

11.2 *Classification of data*

Assuming that additional data had been collected, more detailed information could be given by subdividing the rows and/or columns.

EXAMPLE

Using the data from the Example above and subdividing the columns into male and female gives more information about the pensioners:

Village	Number of pensioners	
	Male	Female
Ashurst	12	19
Botleigh	5	12
Crow	10	18
Downton	11	13
Eaglecliffe	9	10
Fillingdales	15	18
Total	62	90

Note: It is essential that all the relevant information is collected during the survey.

It is not possible, for example, to determine a person's sex after the survey has been completed.

11.3 *Tally charts*

It is common to record the data by means of a **tally chart**.

Suppose a survey was being carried out to determine the popularity of the various activities offered at a local leisure centre. First a list would be drawn up of possible activities: swimming, badminton, fitness training, etc. Then each person entering the leisure centre would be asked which activity they were paying for and a tally mark (*I*) would be recorded against the chosen activity.

To enable the results to be totalled quickly, it is usual to tally in groups of five, the fifth stroke being drawn diagonally across the previous four: *JHT*.

A section of the results for this survey could look like this:

Activity	Tally	Total
Archery	JHT JHT I	11
Badminton	JHT JHT JHT JHT III	23
Bowls	JHT III	8
Fitness room	JHT JHT JHT IIII	19
Judo	JHT JHT JHT JHT	20

11.4 *Frequency tables*

A table which shows a set of variables and the number of times each variable occurs (its **frequency**) is called a **frequency table** or **frequency distribution table**.

If a large amount of quantitative data has been collected, it is generally convenient to record the information in a more compact form by combining variables into **groups** or **classes**. Continuous variables, such as time, length, speed, will normally be grouped before the information is collected.

Suppose the leisure centre survey is extended to find the amount of time people spend in the centre.

First the size of each class is decided (say 15 minutes).

Then a table is drawn up of all the classes.

The time each person in the survey has spent in the centre is tallied against the appropriate class and hence the frequencies are found.

Time spent (minutes)	Tally	Frequency
Less than 15	JHT I	6
15–29	JHT JHT	10
30–44	JHT JHT III	13
45–59	JHT JHT II	12
60–74	JHT JHT JHT I	16
75–89	JHT JHT JHT JHT	20
90–104	JHT JHT JHT JHT I	21
105–119	JHT JHT JHT II	17
120–134	JHT JHT IIII	14

EXERCISE 11.1

1 During a survey to find how knowledgeable the general public is about art, 40 people were asked to name as many artists as possible in one minute. The responses were:

1	5	3	5	1	8	15	1
2	2	1	3	4	4	1	2
13	11	8	6	1	2	5	2
3	4	9	2	3	10	1	6
2	7	1	4	6	4	5	3

Use a tally chart to draw up a frequency table for this data.

2 A textile mill spins yarn. The thickness of the yarn is measured at intervals, and the measurements, in millimetres, of a sample of 50 are given below.

0.72	0.98	0.81	0.96	0.91	0.90	0.76
0.92	0.95	0.91	0.83	0.91	0.89	0.86
0.93	0.94	0.78	0.93	0.83	0.86	0.91
0.78	0.92	0.88	1.03	1.04	1.01	0.94
1.03	0.90	0.85	0.85	0.91	0.82	0.88
0.95	1.02	0.99	0.97	0.92	0.82	0.90
1.03	0.93	0.94	0.96	0.87	0.93	0.89
0.92						

Using intervals of 0.70–0.74, 0.75–0.79, 0.80–0.84, etc., draw up a tally chart to obtain the frequency distribution.

3 A small business carried out a survey to find the number of days absence of the employees over one year. The results were:

3	1	4	2	1	15	20	5	15
0	17	26	0	11	1	3	10	8
15	10	17	10	6	13	12	10	14
5	8	3	21	0	3	18	3	18
3	42	9	18	10	21	10	5	6
14	1	5	5	0	5	7	30	9
0	5	6	25	23	6	4	11	12

Collect the information on a frequency table using intervals 0–4, 5–9, 10–14, 15–19, etc.

4 During a survey into changes in the conditions of work of clerical staff, 50 workers gave their present salaries (in £) as:

14030	12670	10180	11320	9870
10120	10130	15460	13680	9920
13830	11610	11880	14280	12200
11020	11570	10990	9700	11810
10880	11370	12090	9800	9670
12230	11680	8590	9680	10280
10420	12120	9330	10540	7490
9240	8990	7630	11010	9180
8320	8640	15200	8680	12040
8680	7480	7720	8290	8470

Organize the data on a frequency table using intervals £7000–£7999, £8000–£8999, etc.

5 The staff in a medical practice monitored the waiting times of patients from the time the patient sat down until called to see the doctor. The times, in minutes and seconds, were:

10:03	12:05	7:15	9:44	11:15
10:02	14:23	12:15	12:42	15:00
5:43	9:08	9:53	9:03	14:21
7:24	10:57	12:26	7:13	15:30
10:53	12:26	10:57	13:48	8:00
9:24	12:48	10:17	11:02	7:48
9:56	14:09	7:23	9:03	9:59
9:32	8:05	7:53	14:23	13:03

a Write each waiting time to the nearest minute and use a tally chart to obtain the frequencies.

b Summarise the given waiting times in a frequency table using intervals $5.00 \leqslant T < 7.00$, $7.00 \leqslant T < 9.00$, etc., where T is the waiting time.

6 The weights (in kg) of 63 male patients admitted to a ward were recorded as:

72.4	68.2	69.3	71.1	66.8	67.2	65.4
68.0	78.9	76.0	70.8	64.3	82.3	70.2
74.2	76.7	65.5	71.6	74.1	68.7	66.8
83.3	74.9	71.5	75.7	71.6	73.2	82.5
73.8	78.2	65.6	76.9	76.8	81.5	77.2
75.8	75.4	80.3	78.0	68.3	76.0	78.5
78.8	71.7	74.4	69.8	77.6	73.4	77.3
74.9	72.4	66.9	73.7	74.4	68.8	82.6
73.7	79.8	74.0	71.8	73.4	76.0	79.2

Using intervals 60–, 65–, 70–, etc., summarise the information in a frequency table.

7 An increasing number of couples are choosing to celebrate their wedding in an exotic location. A survey to find the most popular destinations produced the following data (A = Antigua, B = Barbados, F = Florida, J = Jamaica, K = Kenya, L = St Lucia, M = Mauritius, S = Seychelles):

```
B  J  L  S  S  L  K  A  K  B
M  A  A  J  L  L  L  L  B  S
K  J  F  F  B  L  K  K  L  A
M  K  J  J  K  L  B  S  J  K
L  B  J  K  K  L  M  A  L  J
```

Record the data on a frequency table.

8 The number of unoccupied seats on 80 transatlantic flights in one day were:

```
32   8   9   6  12  30   9  11   5  39
 6  25  26  42  33  16  13  30   5  29
43  34  11  26   2  39  35  19  20  40
15  11  20  34  31  17  23   2  17  15
32   3  44   6   1   7  26  35  18  25
37   4  39  37  34  26  33   7  21  16
18  15  29  35  21   6  40  39  13  12
 4   4  38  39  12   0   4  33  34  18
```

Summarise the information on a frequency table using class intervals 0–4, 5–9, 10–14, 15–19, etc.

9 The following data are the weights (w), in kilograms, of the luggage of 50 passengers boarding a charter flight to Europe. The luggage allowance was 20 kg per person.

```
18.04  22.32  18.02  20.16  20.50  15.18
13.48  19.90  17.98  19.76  17.12  22.00
21.44  20.04  17.30  16.30  20.24  18.76
17.24  19.96  16.72  15.92  19.66  17.94
18.70  19.94  15.02  17.58  16.80  17.52
17.10  19.82  22.44  15.80  19.02  18.82
15.76  19.46  18.29  20.23  17.78  15.82
15.90  16.46  16.72  18.22  19.00  20.50
17.62  20.44
```

Group the information into classes of width 2 kg using intervals $12.00 < w \leqslant 14.00$, $14.00 < w \leqslant 16.00$, $16.00 < w \leqslant 18.00$ etc. and display in a frequency table.

10 The number of faults found in a sample of 50 micro chips was:

```
1  0  0  0  2  0  0  0  1  0
0  0  1  1  0  1  0  0  2  0
0  0  0  0  1  0  0  0  0  0
2  0  0  1  0  1  1  0  3  0
1  1  0  0  2  0  2  1  0  1
```

Summarise the data on a frequency table.

11 A firm manufactures ball bearings for the motor and motorbike industries. In order to monitor accuracy, samples are taken at intervals from five machines and the diameters (d) of those bearings are measured in millimetres.

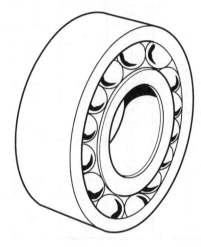

The results of one set of samples are given below:

```
49.46  50.15  51.15  51.36  49.72
50.41  50.03  48.16  50.26  49.43
49.66  49.31  50.32  49.76  46.78
50.16  50.98  51.15  49.40  48.88
48.90  50.47  49.33  50.08  48.20
49.76  49.67  50.05  50.70  49.46
50.14  49.39  52.63  49.93  49.19
50.09  49.27  49.63  51.09  48.21
```

Summarise the data on a frequency table using class intervals of 1 mm:

$46.00 \leqslant d < 47.00$, $47.00 \leqslant d < 48.00$, ..., $52.00 \leqslant d < 53.00$.

12 People leaving a department store were asked to take part in a survey on shopping habits. A section of the results is shown below:

Customer	Sex	Age			Time in shop			Amount spent		
		Under 20	20–40	Over 40	Under 5 min	5–20 min	Over 20 min	Nil	Up to £20	Over £20
1	M		✓			✓			✓	✓
2	F			✓			✓			✓
3	M	✓			✓			✓		
4	F	✓				✓			✓	
5	F		✓			✓			✓	
6	F	✓			✓			✓		
7	M			✓			✓		✓	
8	F			✓			✓			✓
9	M		✓			✓			✓	
10	M	✓			✓				✓	
11	F			✓		✓				✓
12	F		✓				✓		✓	
13	M		✓		✓				✓	
14	M	✓				✓				✓
15	F		✓			✓		✓		
16	M			✓		✓			✓	
17	F			✓	✓			✓		
18	F		✓				✓			✓
19	F	✓			✓			✓		
20	F	✓				✓			✓	

a Suggest a number of ways in which the data could be divided into two or more groups.

b Using two of your suggestions, display the relevant data on frequency tables.

12 *Statistics on Display*

12.1 *Pictorial representation of data*

The presentation of data in the form of tables has been considered in Unit 11. However, most people find that the presentation of data is more effective, and easier to understand, if the data is presented in a pictorial or diagrammatic form.

The pictorial presentation used must enable the data to be more effectively displayed and more easily understood. The diagrams must be fully labelled, clear and should not be capable of visual misrepresentation. Types of pictorial representation in common use are the pictogram, bar chart, pie chart and frequency polygon.

Statistical packages may also be used to present data in a variety of ways. You cannot, however, rely completely on a computer to produce your pie charts, pictographs, etc. You must also be able to carry out the necessary calculations yourself and draw the most appropriate diagrams for the given data.

There are many ways of presenting data in pictorial form. It is clearly necessary to be able to interpret correctly any diagrams given.

The general interpretation of statistical pictures and graphs is that the bigger the representation, the larger the population in that group. However, it is also possible to interpret statistical diagrams so as to be able to calculate the population of each group.

12.2 *Pictograms*

In a **pictogram** data is represented by the repeated use of a pictorial symbol. The example below shows how a pictogram works.

EXAMPLE

A survey of 1000 people living in Freeton was taken, to see what colour of cars they owned. Represent this data in the form of a pictogram. The results of the survey were:
Colour of cars Number of cars

Colour of cars	Number of cars
Red	60
White	200
Blue	100
Grey	80
Gold	50
Black	30

Key: 🚗 = 20 cars

Here is one possibility. A full car symbol represents 20 cars; half a car represents 10 cars. It is not possible to show small fractions of a symbol accurately, and the detail required should not normally be to more than half of a symbol (but certain symbols may allow for a quarter).

EXERCISE 12.1

1   The numbers of bottles of champagne sold in five villages is shown on the following pictogram:

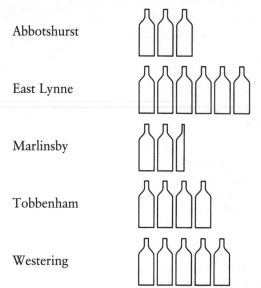

Abbotshurst

East Lynne

Marlinsby

Tobbenham

Westering

a   In which village were the most bottles sold?
b   How many bottles were sold in Martinsby?
c   How many bottles were sold in total?

2   The contents of a fruit bowl comprised:

Apples	7	Bananas	3
Pears	5	Peaches	7
Kiwi fruit	6	Oranges	2

Illustrate this data by means of a pictogram.

3   Students in a department of a college were asked about the type of accommodation in which they lived. The data was:

Flat	25	Semi-detached house	40
Maisonette	5	Detached house	30

Illustrate this data by means of a pictogram.

4   In a survey to find the most popular design on Christmas cards, 600 people were asked which animal they preferred. The results are shown on the pictogram.

Reindeer

Penguin

Robin

Polar bear

(A full picture represents 50 voters.)

a   How many people chose the polar bears design?
b   What percentage of people chose the reindeer?
c   Find the ratio of the votes for robins to the votes for penguins.

5   The number of people present in a Paris fashion show were:

Individual buyers	54
Store buyers	18
Celebrities	27
Photographers	45
Journalists	36

Illustrate this data by means of a pictogram.

6   The numbers of employees in four solicitors' offices were:

Archibald and Archibald	8
Dugdale, Wynne and Luff	10
JSC Weston-Hough	6
Mordecai and Sons	12

Draw a pictogram to represent this data.

7   A college canteen carried out a survey to decide which type of bread roll to serve. The answers are shown in the pictogram.

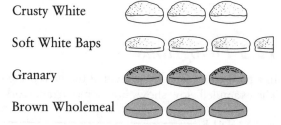

Crusty White

Soft White Baps

Granary

Brown Wholemeal

(One roll represents 4 votes.)

a   Which was the favourite type of roll?
b   How many customers preferred wholemeal rolls?
c   What percentage preferred white bread?

8   The number of patients on a register of six doctors in a group practice is:

Dr Smith	2400
Dr Rawlings	1800
Dr Wong	3000
Dr Payne	2700
Dr Williams	23100
Dr Fisher	1500

Show this information on a pictogram.

9 The number of residents in five rest-homes is shown on the pictogram.

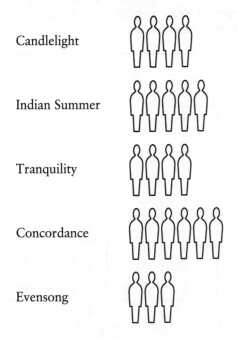

Candlelight

Indian Summer

Tranquility

Concordance

Evensong

(Each picture represents five residents.)

a How many residents are there in Candlelight?

b Which rest-home has the smallest number of residents?

c What is the total number of residents?

10 The number of flights for each airline out of Gatwick in a one-hour period was:

British Airways	8	Aer Lingus	2
Swissair	1	Britannia	6
Virgin Atlantic	1	Monarch	3

Illustrate this data on a pictogram.

11 One clock represents one hour on the following pictogram, which shows the time taken to cross the English Channel by different routes.

Dover–Calais

Dover–Ostend

Portsmouth–Caen

Portsmouth–Cherbourg

Plymouth–Roscoff

a Which route takes the longest time?

b How long does it take to go from Portsmouth to Cherbourg?

c What is the difference in the time taken to cross the Channel between the Dover-to-Calais route and the Dover-to-Ostend route?

12 The management of a car plant wanted to know how many of the workers used the cars produced by their company. They decided to carry out a survey of the cars parked in the factory's car park one day. The results were:

Ford	35	Citroen	20
Rover	30	Renault	10
BMW	5	Vauxhall	25

Construct a pictogram to illustrate the results.

13 The workforce of a factory were asked by which mode of transport they came to work. The results are shown in the following pictogram, each figure representing 10 workers:

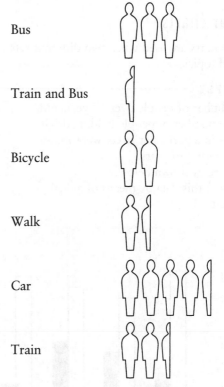

Bus

Train and Bus

Bicycle

Walk

Car

Train

a How many of the workers walk to work?

b Which form of transport is used least to get to work?

c What is the total work force of the factory?

12.3 *Bar charts*

A **bar chart** is a diagram consisting of columns (i.e. bars), the heights of which indicate
the frequencies. Bar charts may be used to display discrete or qualitative data.

---EXAMPLE---

Fifty households were surveyed,
and the number of children in
each family was recorded as
follows:

Children in family	Frequency
0	8
1	11
2	17
3	8
4	5
5	1

Represent this data by means
of a bar chart.

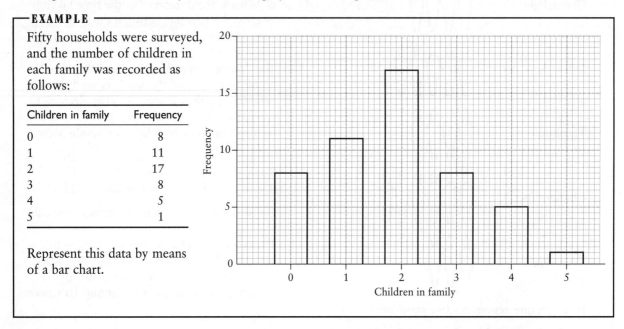

Dual bar charts

Dual bar charts are used when two different sets of information are given on
connected topics.

---EXAMPLE---

The number of people over 17 years old,
and the number of people holding driving
licences in a particular street were found
over a period of years.
These are as shown below.
Represent this data by means of a dual
bar chart.

Year	1995	1996	1997	1998	1999	2000
No. of people over 17	32	27	29	31	33	39
No. of people with driving licence	12	17	19	11	24	28

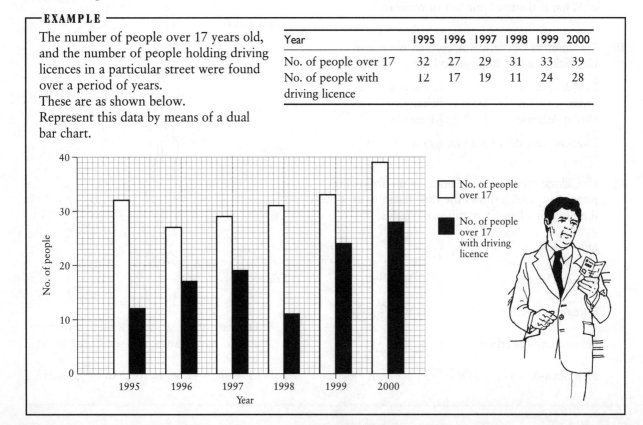

Sectional bar charts

Sectional bar charts, or **component bar charts**, are used when two, or more, different sets of information are given on the same topics. They are particularly useful when the *total* of the two or more bars is also of interest.

EXAMPLE

The numbers of saloons and hatchbacks sold by a garage were recorded.

Month	Jan	Feb	Mar	Apr	May	Jun
Saloons	18	7	8	12	10	13
Hatchbacks	16	12	9	7	9	8

Represent this data by means of a sectional bar chart.

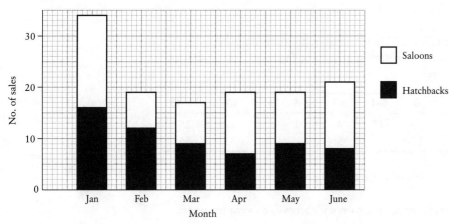

Note that each column gives:

 (i) the number of saloons sold,

 (ii) the number of hatchbacks sold, and

 (iii) the total number of cars sold during that month.

All three sets of information can rapidly be compared by using the same diagram.

EXERCISE 12.2

1   The bar chart shows the type of trees recorded during a survey of a section of a forest.

Oak
Elm
Chestnut
Beech
Conifer
Cedar

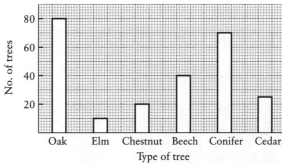

 a   Which tree was seen most frequently?

 b   Reconstruct the frequency table.

 c   What was the total number of trees growing in this area?

2   Twenty people noted the television channel they were watching at
    8.15pm on two successive nights. The results were:

	First night	Second night
BBC 1	6	7
BBC 2	4	1
ITV	6	6
CHANNEL 4	3	4
SATELLITE	1	2

Draw a suitable bar chart to illustrate this data.

3   Thirty students designed ball gowns. The colours of the gowns were
    12 black, 5 gold, 10 red, 2 blue, and 1 green.

    Illustrate this information by means of a bar chart.

4   A graphics company investigated how many hours their employees
    actually worked on a computer during a week in January 1998 and again
    in 1999. The results were:

Time per week (hours):	0	0–1	1–2	2–4	4–10	10–20	20–40
1998	32	17	4	10	2	1	25
1999	17	2	5	11	12	21	34

Represent this data by means of a dual bar chart.

5   The number of students in an art class on six successive evenings were:

	Eve 1	Eve 2	Eve 3	Eve 4	Eve 5	Eve 6
Male	11	9	8	9	7	6
Female	7	8	9	10	11	13

Illustrate this information by means of a section bar chart.

6   In a three-month period, the number of days in which different products
    were advertised on two hoardings were compared. These are shown in
    the dual bar charts below.

    a   One hoarding was in an inner city, and the other one was in a
        suburban area.
        Which hoarding was in the inner city?

    b   How many more days did Hoarding A advertise alcohol than
        Hoarding B?

    c   Which products were advertised only on Hoarding A?

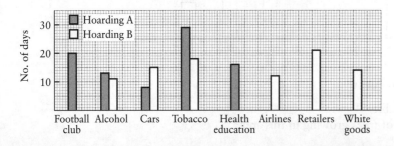

7   The numbers of large appliances sold by an electrical retailer during one day were:

Washing machines	35	Cookers	28
Televisions	38	Video Recorders	12
Refrigerators	21		

Illustrate this data by means of a bar chart.

8   An insurance company keeps records of life endowment policies sold by its representatives. In a six-month period the number of policies sold by their top salesmen were:

	With Profits	Without Profits
January	11	21
February	15	12
March	28	13
April	21	20
May	18	27
June	16	30

Represent this data by means of a section bar chart.

9   The number of houses sold by four agents in the first six months of 1998 and 1999 were:

	1998	1999
John	27	29
Mary	15	24
Carl	28	19
Latha	22	32

Represent this data by means of a dual bar chart.

10 Peter and Frances Mead decide to apply for a franchise. They investigate the possible companies selling fast food and the results of their investigations are shown on the bar chart below.

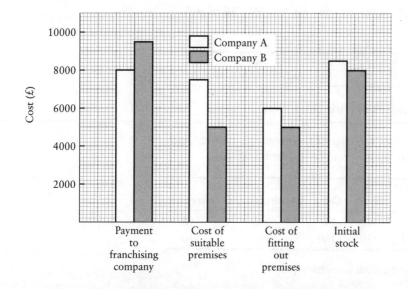

   a What is the total cost of franchising with Company A?

   b What is the total cost for franchising with Company B?

   c How much greater is the payment to franchising Company A than to Company B?

   d If Peter and Frances franchise with Company A, they would expect to have double the profits than if they had franchised with Company B. What other information would they need to know before they chose which company to franchise with?

11   The numbers of patients in six wards of a general hospital were:

Children	32	Cardiac	16
Orthopaedic	17	Surgical	28
Gynaecological	24	Geriatric	36

Represent this data by means of a bar chart.

12   The numbers of residents, and the numbers of staff employed at nursing homes in a small town were:

Nursing home	Residents	Staff
Golden Memories	45	28
Peacehaven	21	16
Autumn Leaves	41	24
Silver Threads	31	19

Represent this data by means of a sectional bar chart.

13   The birth rate per 1000 of population and the infant mortality rate per 1000 live births were found for a number of countries:

	The Gambia	Hungary	Italy	Samoa	UK
Birth rate	47.5	12.2	10.1	39.1	13.3
Infant mortality rate	174	20.4	10.9	4.4	9.4

Construct a dual bar chart to represent this data.

14   The goals scored in 42 football league matches on Saturday 26 March 2000 were:

Number of goals in match	0	1	2	3	4	5	6
Number of matches	1	9	10	12	6	3	1

Illustrate this information by means of a bar chart.

15   Jean-Paul and Michelle noted how the cost of their summer holiday had varied in the last two years. The money had been spent as shown:

	Travel	Rent of Villa	Food	Drink	Entertainment	Insurance
Cost 1998 (£)	720	820	550	140	250	110
Cost 1999 (£)	650	920	480	160	150	120

Represent this data by means of a dual bar chart.

16 The holiday destinations of 100 people entering an airport were:

	France	Spain	Greece	Italy	Morocco	USA
Male passengers	3	18	9	8	5	9
Female passengers	4	11	15	2	6	10

Draw a sectional bar chart to illustrate this data.

17 The bar chart below shows the results of a survey of socio-economic groups which was conducted in two housing estates in the same town. For each household, the occupation of the head of the house was used to determine the appropriate group.

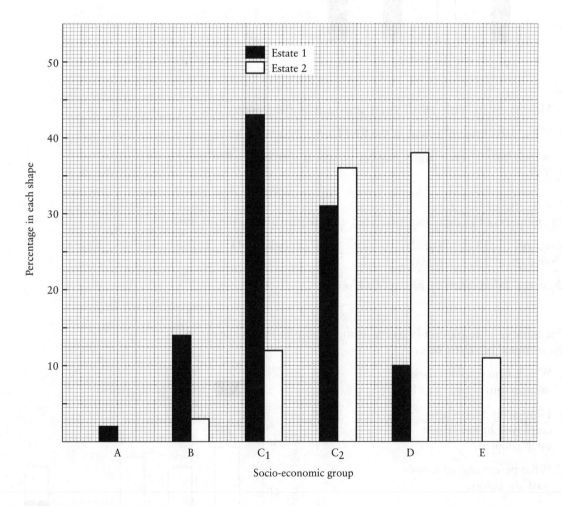

a What can you deduce about the two housing estates?

b What percentage of households belong to group D in:
(i) Estate 1, (ii) Estate 2?

c If 215 households were surveyed in Estate 1, how many are in Group B?
(Give your answer to the nearest whole number.)

18 A researcher for a guide to good, small hotels collects data on the facilities offered by each establishment. The data obtained is represented in the sectional bar chart shown.

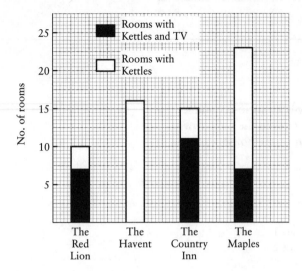

a How many (i) kettles, (ii) TVs are provided by the Country Inn?

b What percentage of rooms at the Red Lion have not a TV?

c Which hotel has the largest number of rooms with both a kettle and a TV?

19 The numbers of kitchen units produced each day by one workman were:

Monday   38   Tuesday   29   Wednesday   41
Thursday   35   Friday   27

Show this information by means of a bar chart.

20 The number of employees in five tailoring establishments is shown on the sectional bar chart below.

a Which firm employs most salespersons?

b How many tailors are employed by the largest establishment?

c What percentage of Jones's staff are tailors?

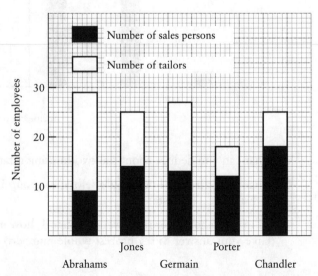

21 The percentage of trade of certain countries with the UK and the USA was calculated in 1996 to be as follows:

	Barbados	Canada	Hong Kong	Ireland	Luxembourg	Sweden
% trade with E.C.	16.8	1.4	5.0	25.7	3.1	9.6
% trade with USA	13.5	82.3	25.4	8.2	6.3	8.3

Illustrate this information by means of a dual bar chart.

22 The number of employees in five small printing companies were:

Firm A	6 secretaries	and 17 other staff
Firm B	8 secretaries	and 14 other staff
Firm C	11 secretaries	and 10 other staff
Firm D	5 secretaries	and 12 other staff
Firm E	7 secretaries	and 6 other staff

Represent this data by means of a sectional bar chart.

12.4 *Pie charts*

A **pie chart** is another type of diagram for displaying information. It is particularly suitable if you want to illustrate how a population is divided up into different parts and what proportion of the whole each part represents. The bigger the proportion, the bigger the slice (or 'sector').

EXAMPLE

Represent by a pie chart the following data.

The mode of transport of 90 students into college was found to be:

Walking	12
Cycling	8
Bus	26
Train	33
Car	11
Total	**90**

Represent this data by means of a pie chart.

A circle has 360°. Divide this by 90 to give 4°. This is then the angle of the pie chart that represents each individual person.

Since 12 people walk to college, they will be represented by $12 \times 4° = 48.°$

Similarly for the others:

	Angle in pie chart
Walking	$12 \times 4 = 48°$
Cycling	$8 \times 4 = 32°$
Bus	$26 \times 4 = 104°$
Train	$33 \times 4 = 132°$
Car	$11 \times 4 = 44°$
	Total = 360°

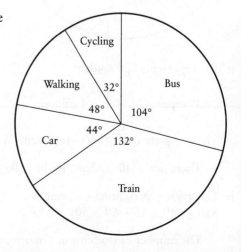

Method for calculating the angles on a pie chart

Here is a summary of how to work out the size of each bite of 'pie'.

(i) Add up the frequencies. This will give you the total population (call it p) to be represented by the pie.

(ii) Divide this number into 360.

(iii) Multiply each individual frequency by this result. This will give you the angle for each section of the pie chart.

Interpreting pie charts

The initial interpretation is the fact that the largest portion of a pie chart relates to the largest group, and the smallest portion to the smallest group. However, if any of the data is known, the rest of the data can be calculated.

EXAMPLE 1

The pie chart below shows the number of students in different sections of a college. 220 students are in the Construction department.

a How many students are there in the college?

b How many students are there in Catering?

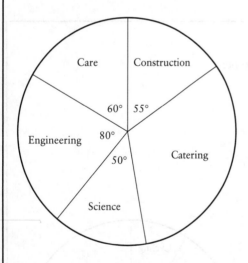

a 55° represents 220 students.

$\therefore$ 1° represents $\dfrac{220}{55} = 4$ students.

The complete circle (360°) represents $4 \times 360 = 1440$ students.

$\therefore$ There are 1440 students in the college.

b The angle representing Catering is
$360 - (80 + 55 + 60 + 50) = 115°$.

$\therefore$ The number of students in Catering is $4 \times 115 = 460$.

EXERCISE 12.3

Illustrate the data given in questions 1, 2 and 3 below by means of a pie chart.

1 The types of central heating used by households in a village were:

Solid fuel	14
Gas	105
Electricity	41
None	20

2 240 students were asked what they were intending to do during next year. The results were:

80 going to university
86 staying at college
64 going into employment
10 with no firm intention.

3 The numbers of bedrooms in 720 houses recorded as:

1 bedroom	80
2 bedrooms	235
3 bedrooms	364
4 bedrooms	39
5 bedrooms	2

4 The pie chart shows the different drinks sold at lunchtime in a college. 720 drinks were sold in total.
Find the number of each different drink sold during lunchtime:

a Coke

b Orange

c Coffee

d Chocolate

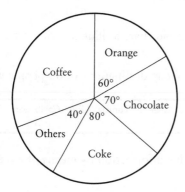

5 The number of special birthday cards sold by a newsagents in a week were:

Mum	42
Dad	34
Grandad	18
Granny	16
Brother	25
Sister	17
Son	15
Daughter	13

Illustrate this information on a pie chart.

6 An artist designed book jackets for 225 books during a five-year period with one publishing house. The books were classified as Thriller, Romance, Travel, Hobby and Science.

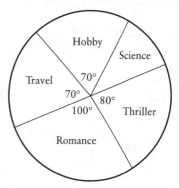

a What size angle represents science books?
b How many jacket designs did the artist create for science books?
c How many jacket designs were created for thrillers?
d What fraction of the designs were for romances? (Give your answer in its lowest terms.)

7 Each pound spent at the Winchester Theatre Royal box-office is used to meet the theatre's expenses as follows:

Performance fees	60p
Salaries	17p
Premises and depreciation	10p
Administration	5p
Publicity	5p
Equipment	3p

Draw a pie chart to show how each pound is spent.

8   The number of clients of each of the partners in a business were:

Kerry   43
Michell   22
Owen   18
Richard   7

Illustrate this information on a pie chart.

9   The proportion of the cost of manufacturing a dinner service was:

Raw material   5%
Manufacture cost   28%
Hand painting cost 51%
Overheads   5%
Profit   11%

Represent this data on a pie chart.

10 The pie chart shows the different types of petrol which a garage sold in one week. The garage sold 25 000 gallons of diesel.

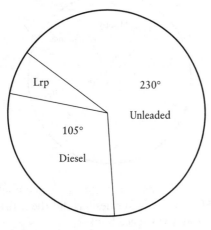

a   How much unleaded petrol was sold?
b   How much lead replacement petrol was sold?
c   What were the total sales?

11 A health centre calculated the distance patients from one practice lived from their GP's surgery:

Under 1 mile: 510 patients
Between 1 and 2 miles: 1230 patients
Between 2 and 3 miles: 140 patients
Over 3 miles: 280 patients.

Illustrate this information on a pie chart.

12 The pie chart shows the type of dwellings in which people in a village live. There are 720 dwellings in the village. By measuring the angles, find how many are:

a   detached houses
b   bungalows
c   semi-detached houses

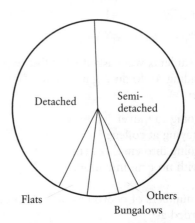

13 The number of villagers undertaking an activity to ensure 'active living' were:

Swimming   1020
Walking   3580
Jogging   105
Keep fit centre   85
Other   610

Draw a pie chart to illustrate this data.

14 The holiday destinations of 60 people were:

France	Spain	Greece	Tunisia	USA	Caribbean	Portugal
21	15	6	3	8	5	2

Represent this information by means of a pie chart.

15 At a sports centre, the ages of 100 people were recorded as follows:

Under 20 years   30
20 to 29 years   15
30 to 39 years   12
40 to 59 years   14
60 years and over   29

Construct a pie chart to illustrate this data.

16 The pie chart shows the number of passengers flying from London to Miami on one afternoon. 1800 passengers in total flew this route on that afternoon.

Find the number flying:

a Virgin

b American Airlines

c British Airways

The plane used by Virgin is a Boeing 747 seating 370 passengers.

d What percentage of the Virgin seats were occupied?

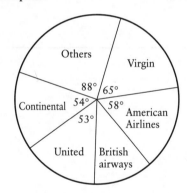

17 Out of 90 employees in a manufacturing company, there were 10 managers, 15 salesmen, 52 production line workers, 4 typists, and 9 quality controllers.
Illustrate this information on a pie chart.

18 A manufacturer of combined harvesters commissioned a survey on the use of agricultural land in South Australia. The result is shown in the pie chart.

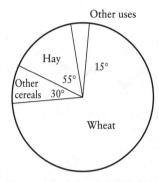

a Find the percentage of land use for wheat.

b The total acreage is 3 000 000 acres. What area was used for hay?

19 In 1984, in the UK, there were 4 500 000 people employed in manufacturing. Of these, 600 000 were in the food industry, 659 000 were in mechanical engineering, 500 000 in electronic engineering and 400 000 in printing. Identify the remainder as 'other industries', and draw a pie chart to represent this information.

12.5 *Line graphs*

A bar chart can be replaced by a line graph, provided that the quantity on the horizontal axis is continuous, e.g. age, temperature or time.

In this case the data is plotted as a series of points which are joined by straight lines.

Line graphs associated with time are called **time-series graphs**.

They are used, for example, by geographers to illustrate monthly rainfall or yearly crop yield, etc., and by businesses to display information about profits or production over a period of time.

They show trends and have the advantage that they can be easily extended.

---EXAMPLE---

The temperatures, recorded every six hours, of a patient in a hospital ward are given on the table:

Time (hours)		Mon.			Tues.					Wed.
	06	12	18	00	06	12	18	00	06	12
Temperature (°F)	99.0	99.12	99.12	99.2	99.2	98.99	98.68	98.6	98.6	

Represent this data by means of a line graph.

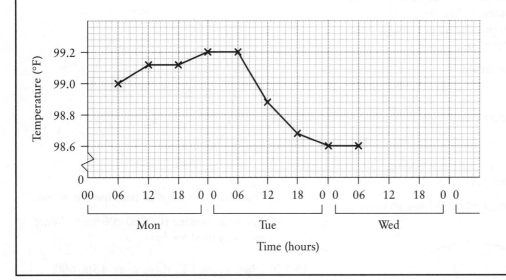

EXERCISE 12.4

Illustrate the data given in questions 1, 2 and 3, using a line graph.

1 The rainfall during a period of six months was:

Month	Jan	Feb	Mar	Apr	May	Jun
Rainfall (mm)	75	192	86	89	25	19

2 The maximum temperatures for six successive months at Sunbourne were:

Month	Apr	May	Jun	Jul	Aug	Sep
Temperature (°C)	61	74	72	91	85	56

3 The girth of a tree was:

Age (years)	10	20	30	40	50	60
Girth (cm)	25	63	98	135	170	210

4 In an art class, students were asked to draw a bowl of fruit. The number of grapes drawn by the students were:

Number of grapes	0	1	2	3	4	5
Number of students	2	7	6	3	2	1

Construct a line to show this information.

5 The graph below shows the number of births (measured along a vertical axis) in a given year (measured along a horizontal axis).
Answer the questions below by reading off the values from the graph.

a Estimate the number of children born in 1915.

b In which years were approximately 825 000 children born?

c Which year had the lowest number of births?

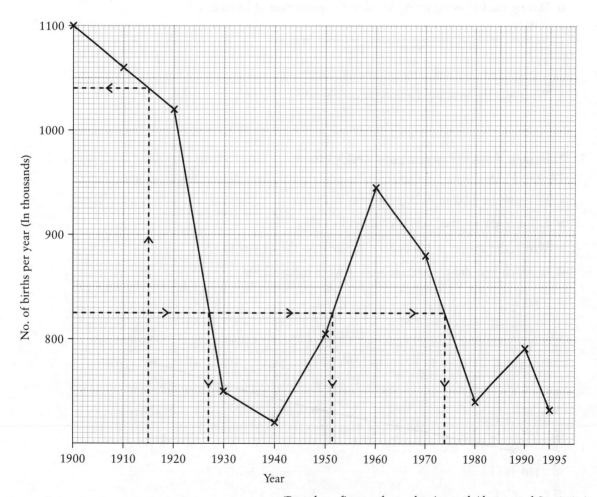

(Based on figures from the *Annual Abstract* of *Statistics*)

6   Mordecai makes cuddly toys. The number of koala he made in one week
    is shown on the line graph below:

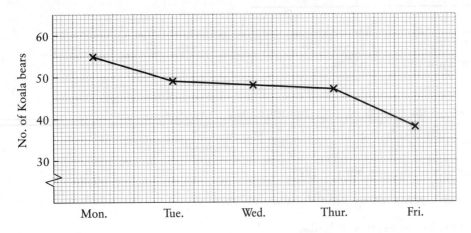

a   The trend of this graph is downwards. Give a possible reason for this.

b   During the following week, Mordecai's production of koala bears
    was:

Mon	Tue	Wed	Thur	Fri
41	46	49	48	42

What was the total production for each week?

7   The graph shows the median gross weekly earnings of women from
    1976 to 1994.

a   Estimate the median weekly earnings in 1981.

b   Estimate the median weekly earnings in 1993.

c   Why is the answer to **b** a better estimate than the answer to **a**?

d   In which year did the average weekly wage reach £200?

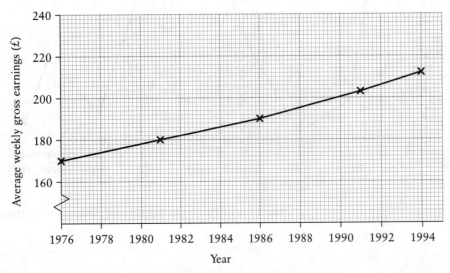

(Based on figures from *Social Trends*, 1998.)

8 The temperature of an office in degrees Fahrenheit, was recorded on a day in winter as:

8 a.m.	9 a.m.	10 a.m.	11 a.m.	12 noon	1 p.m.	2 p.m.	3 p.m.
56	66	68	69	70	71	70	69

a Draw the information on a line graph.

b Between which times was the temperature change greatest?
   Give a possible reason for this change.

c The recommended temperature for an office is between 61 and 80.
   Estimate for how long the temperature was at the recommended level.

9 Mark's height was recorded each year on his birthday; the result for every second year is shown on the line graph.

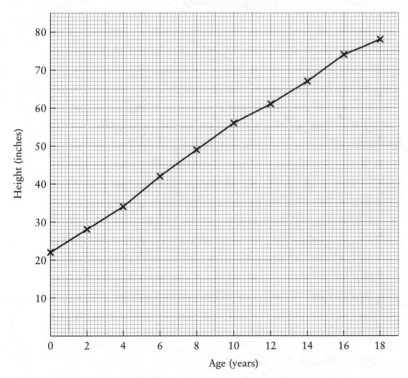

a Estimate Mark's height on his ninth birthday.

b During which two years was his rate of growth the greatest?

c What do you think will happen to his growth rate after his eighteenth birthday?

10 The numbers of children with mumps registering at a health centre were:

Monday	Tuesday	Wednesday	Thursday	Friday
18	7	8	9	6

Show this information on a line graph.

11 The line graphs below compare the number of set days during the year in London and Nice.

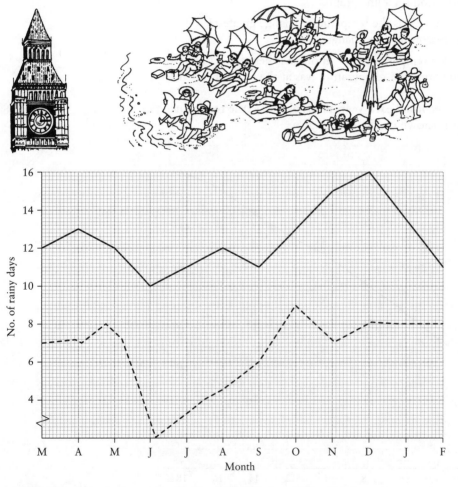

a Which graph represents the number of rainy days in London?

b Which is the wettest month for each city?

c Which month is the driest for each city?

d In which month does the smallest difference in the number of wet days occur?

12 The numbers of passengers carried by an airline (in thousands) were as follows (Sp = spring, Su = summer, etc.):

1997				1998				1999			
Sp	Su	Au	Wi	Sp	Su	Au	Wi	Sp	Su	Au	Wi
21	48	31	17	22	49	29	18	23	41	24	25

  a Plot this information on a line graph.
  b State any trends which the data suggests.

13 The numbers (in thousands) of steel pipes made by a company were:

Jan	Feb	Mar	Apr	May
24	23	18	14	27

Illustrate this information by means of a line graph.

14 The graph below shows the number of cars supplied per month by a car manufacturer to a garage's sales section:

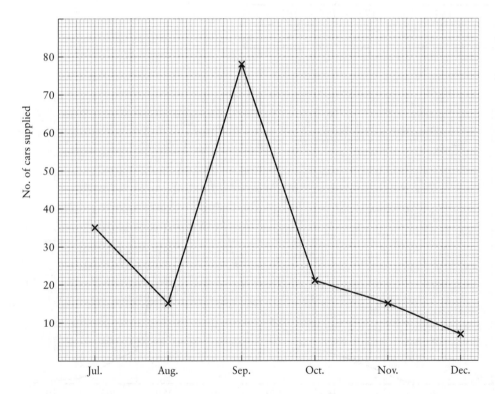

  a In which month were most cars supplied?
  Give a possible reason for this large amount.

  b How many cars were supplied in November?

  c What was the total number of cars supplied during the six months?

  d What was the average number of cars supplied per month during this period?

12.6 *Frequency polygons*

A method of presenting data which is an alternative to a histogram is the **frequency polygon**. They are often used to compare frequency distributions, i.e. to compare the 'shapes' of the histograms, because it is possible to draw more than one frequency polygon on the same graph. It is easier to make comparisons using frequency polygons than using histograms.

For ungrouped data, the frequencies are plotted as points. For grouped data, which is more usual, the frequencies are plotted against the mid-point of the class interval. In both cases the points are joined with straight lines.

EXAMPLE 1

The heights of 80 students were recorded. The data was:

Height (cm)	150–160	160–170	170–180	180–190	190–200	200–210
No. of students	4	7	15	47	6	1

Represent this data by means of a frequency polygon.

The new table is:

Mid-point of class	155	165	175	185	195	205
Frequency density	4	7	15	47	6	1

Frequency polygon

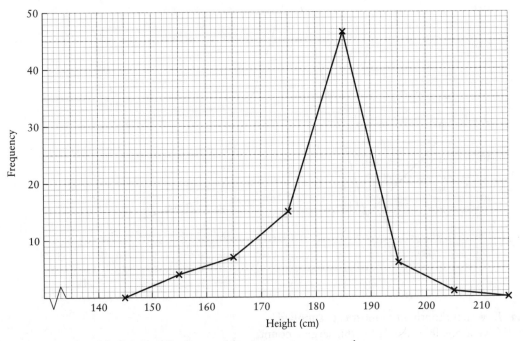

The polygon is completed by joining the first and last points to zero at the mid-point of the next bar.

When frequency polygons are used to compare two sets of data, it is the shapes of the distribution which are important. For this reason, the mid-points of the classes are often plotted against the actual frequencies, rather than the frequency densities which would be used for a histogram.

EXAMPLE 2

The mock examination results in Mathematics for two successive GCSE groups are recorded on the table below.

Mark	1–20	21–40	41–60	61–80	81–100
Group 1 % frequency	5	12	35	28	20
Group 2 % frequency	7	26	48	9	10

a Draw the frequency polygon for each group.

b Assuming the ability of the pupils was the same in each year, comment on the mock examination papers.

a In this example, the percentage frequencies are plotted against the class mid-points, which are 10.5, 30.5, 50.5, 70.5 and 90.5.

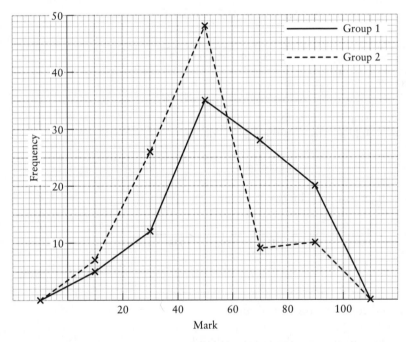

b Group 2 appear to have been given a more difficult examination paper than Group 1.

EXERCISE 12.5

1   Draw the frequency polygon for the data given below.

The speeds of 100 cars on a motorway were recorded.
The data found was:

Speed (mph)	30–40	40–50	50–60	60–70	70–80	80–90
Number of cars	2	11	35	42	9	1

2   A teacher noted the rates of absence from her Maths class on Mondays
    and Fridays. The results are given on the table below.

Number absent from class	0	1	2	3	4	5	6	7	8	9	10	11
Monday frequency	3	6	6	7	4	4	3	0	0	0	0	0
Friday frequency	0	2	2	3	4	5	2	0	6	3	2	1

   a Draw the frequency polygon for each day, using the same axes.
   b Comment on the absence rates for the two days.

3   The table below shows the number of letters per word in 100 words of
    two books.

No. of letters	1	2	3	4	5	6	7	8	9	10	11	12
Frequency, Book A	3	12	28	7	14	11	6	6	7	4	1	1
Frequency, Book B	6	8	37	22	7	11	6	0	1	2	0	0

   a Draw the frequency polygons using the same axes.
   b One extract was taken from a child's story and the other from an
      adult science fiction story.
      State which is which, giving reasons for your decision.

4   The number of new designs being introduced by two furniture
    manufacturers was:

	1994	1995	1996	1997	1998	1999
Modern Design	8	7	8	5	2	1
Traditional Style	4	4	3	4	6	7

Draw the frequency polygons and comment on your results.

5   Choose two daily newspapers, one full size and the other a tabloid.
    Compare them by drawing frequency polygons of the number of words
    per sentence in one hundred sentences taken from similar sections in
    each newspaper.
    (If you keep these results, they could be used in future work to calculate
    means, medians, and standard deviations.)

6   The table below shows the population of males and females in 1993 in
    the UK.

Age	0–4	5–15	16–44	45–59	60–64	65–79	80+
Male population (thousands)	1929	4276	12258	5270	1355	3042	726
Female population (thousands)	1834	4059	11840	5312	1418	3840	1643

(Source: *The Office of Population Censuses and Surveys*)
Draw the frequency of polygons and comment on your results.

7   A casino carried out an experiment using eight dice to find the number
of sixes in each throw of the dice.
The objective was to see if the experimental results matched the
expected theoretical calculations.
The frequency polygon shows the expected results.

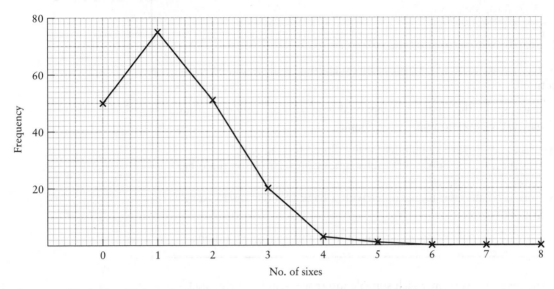

The experimental results were:

Number of sixes	0	1	2	3	4	5	6	7	8
Frequency	50	75	51	20	3	1	0	0	0

a   Copy the given graph and plot the frequency polygon for the
experimental results of the same axes.

b   Comment on the two sets of results.

8   The number of faults on a car production line in two successive months,
before and after a new model was introduced, was:

Number of faults	0	1	2	3	4	5	6	7	8	9	10
Frequency (old models)	0	0	1	4	5	8	8	2	1	0	2
Frequency (new model)	4	8	5	11	1	0	2	0	1	0	0

Draw the frequency polygons and comment on your results.

12.7 *Drawing inferences from diagrams*

When you can readily transfer data to pictorial form, and can convert
pictorial representation back into numerical data, you can start to draw
inferences from the data given in either form.

Drawing inferences from statistical data is not an exact science. There is rarely
a correct, precise answer. If some of the data does not fit the overall pattern,
this should be noted. Then, the reasons for the apparent contradiction should
be considered.

We can illustrate this by an example.

> **EXAMPLE**
>
> The number of people each day visiting an open-air swimming pool in August were
>
> ---
>
> 341, 352, 347, 355, 361, 341, 344, 352, 344, 360, 371, 347, 329, 351, 621, 357, 348, 359, 354, 172, ...
>
> ---
>
> What can be inferred from this data?
>
> The 15 August figure of 621 is clearly exceptional and should be easily identified.
>
> The reasons why this figure is exceptional would be unlikely to be found without further questioning – for example:
>
> (i)   was an alternative swimming facility closed for the day?
> (ii) was the weather on the 15th substantially hotter than on the other days?
> (iii) does the data refer to a country with a Bank Holiday on 15 August (e.g. France)?
>
> These are all possible reasons and you may be able to suggest others.

Some data give results from which suitable inferences can be fairly quickly drawn. Here is an example.

> **EXAMPLE**
>
> A men's clothes shop has two branches: one in a city centre, and one at an out-of-town shopping complex. The weekly sales of the two shops over a period of three months are given below:
>
> | Date (week | commencing) | December | | | | January | | | | February | | | March | |
> |---|---|---|---|---|---|---|---|---|---|---|---|---|---|---|
> | | | 7 | 14 | 21 | 28 | 5 | 12 | 19 | 26 | 2 | 9 | 16 | 23 | 2 | 9 |
> | Sales in | City shop | 18 | 21 | 23 | 14 | 29 | 31 | 28 | 7 | 5 | 8 | 6 | 4 | 5 | 8 |
> | thousands | Out-of-town | 22 | 27 | 52 | 15 | 4 | 5 | 6 | 8 | 9 | 8 | 10 | 9 | 7 | 8 |
> | of pounds | shop | | | | | | | | | | | | | | |
>
> What can be inferred from this data?
>
> From the above data, the following inferences could be made:
>
> (i)   Sales immediately prior to Christmas are higher than at other times in the three-month period.
> (ii) Sales in the out-of-town complex are generally higher than those in the city shop.
> (iii) The city shop had a 'sale' during the first three weeks of January.
> (iv) During the 'sale' the trade at the out-of-town shop was reduced.
>
> In reality, the firm could well investigate the types of garments sold over the year to decide whether or not to promote the same articles in both shops at the same or different times. Computerisation of sales enables shops to keep far better checks on stock sold. This enables them to react more quickly to consumer demand and to supply each individual shop with the goods which its specific customers require.

13 *Averages and Range*

Frequency distributions and graphs, such as dual bar charts and frequency polygons may be used to compare sets of data. It is also very useful to be able to compare a single, 'typical', statistic from one set of data with a single, 'typical', statistic from another set of data.

This statistic must be representative of the distribution. For this reason it is usually located at or near the centre of the distribution and is called a **measure of central location** or **average**.

The most commonly used averages are the **mean**, **mode** and **median**.

13.1 *The arithmetic mean*

The **arithmetic mean**, which is usually just referred to as the mean, is the most widely used average.

To calculate the mean, the total of the values is found and this is 'shared out' equally by dividing by the total number of values.

EXAMPLE

A company owns five nursing homes. The number of residents in the five homes is 45, 21, 41, 31 and 38.
What is the mean number of residents per home?

$$\text{Total number of residents} = 45 + 21 + 41 + 31 + 38$$
$$= 176$$

$$\text{Number of homes} = 5$$

$$\therefore \text{ Mean number of residents} = \frac{176}{5} = 35.2$$

This means that, if the five homes had the same number of residents, each home would cater for approximately 35.

Note. Although it is impossible to have 35.2 residents, it is usual to leave a mean as a decimal answer to show that it is a calculated value and to allow more accurate comparisons to be made.

The mean is often denoted by the symbol $\bar{x}$ and given in formula form as

Mean $= \dfrac{\Sigma x}{n}$

Σ is a capital Greek letter (sigma). $\sum x$ means the sum of all the terms and n is the number of terms.

EXERCISE 13.1

1   The weekly wages of ten workers were:

£110, £115, £135, £141, £119, £152, £144, £128, £117, £139.

Find the mean wage.

2   The wind speed (in mph) at 8 am on a particular day, was recorded at a number of measuring stations as:

88, 74, 61, 92, 48, 59, 71, 80, 70, 51, 48, 45, 75, 80, 82.

Find the mean wind speed.

3   A rugby team scores 37, 21, 64, 0, 18, 7, 35, 49, 28, 51, 82, 71 points in 12 successive matches. What is its mean score?

4   Eight people were asked their ages, and the replies were 37, 41, 29, 17, 15, 21, 32, 38. John claims that their average age is over 29. Why is he correct?

5   Five men have a mean height of 1.95 m.

Four women have a mean height of 1.72 m.

What is the mean height of the nine people?

6   The attendances at an art exhibition on six successive days were 130, 97, 110, 78, 64 and 150.

What was the mean daily attendance?

7   A quilter bought eight odd lengths of material from the ends of rolls to use for patchwork. She was charged for eight metres.

The actual length of the pieces were 1.50 m, 0.75 m, 1.20 m, 0.90 m, 1.30 m, 1.25 m, 1.55 m and 1.90 m.

a   What was the mean length of a piece of material?

b   Did she make a 'good buy'?

8   A secretary typed four documents in one hour. The numbers of words (to the nearest 10 words) were 1200, 850, 1570 and 880.

a   What was the average number of words per document?

b   What was the secretary's average typing speed in words per minute (w.p.m.)?

9   A canteen's food bills for one week were £498, £529, £384, £366, £620, £591, £485.

a   What was the mean cost per day?

The number of employees served on each day was 109, 110, 84, 88, 122, 14, 82.

b   What was the average cost per head?

10 In six successive weeks, the number of cases dealt with by a probation officer was 12, 15, 13, 11, 14, 16.

What was the mean number of cases per week?

11 Five overweight people volunteered to go on a sponsored diet. Their initial weights were 183 lb, 227 lb, 138 lb, 199 lb and 150 lb.

After three months, their weights were 141 lb, 180 lb, 126 lb, 146 lb and 150 lb.

a   What was the total weight loss?

b   What was the mean weight loss per person?

c   What was the mean weight loss per week? (Assume 1 month = 4 weeks)

12 The map shows the temperatures in various parts of Britain on a given day.

a   What was the mean temperature?

b   What was the mean temperature for:
    (i) the North?
    (ii) the South?

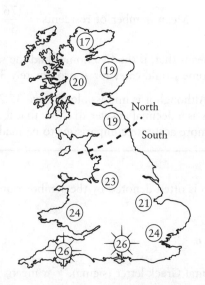

13 In an athletic match, in 1988, the winning distances for the discus were 52.78 m, 51.78 m, 50.77 m.

In 1998 the winning distances were 58.82 m, 57.48 m, 57.38 m.

a What was the mean distance in 1988?

b What was the mean distance in 1998?

c Comment on the results.

14 Twelve cars of the same model were fuelled with exactly one gallon of petrol. The cars were then driven over the same course at a steady speed of 56 m.p.h. until the petrol ran out. The number of miles travelled by each car was recorded:

38, 41, 44, 38, 35, 42, 41, 39, 44, 43, 46 and 40.

Is the manufacturer justified in claiming that the number of miles per gallon, at 56 m.p.h., is 41 for this model of car?

15 A time study was carried out at a factory to find the times taken for each process. Six fitters were timed assembling a piece of machinery. Their times (in minutes and seconds) were:

6:50, 5:35, 7:05, 5:10, 6:20 and 5:30.

What was the mean time for the job?

13.2 *The mode*

The **mode** is the number which occurs most frequently. Suppose seven students scored as follows in a test:

$$2, 3, 6, 7, 7, 8, 9$$

The mean score here is $\dfrac{42}{7} = 6$.

The **mode**, the number which occurs most frequently, is 7.

Some distributions can have more than one mode. For example, the numbers of people hiring a firm's mini bus were:

3, 3, 4, 5, 7, 8, 8, 8, 10, 11, 13, 13, 14, 15, 15, 15.

Both 8 and 15 are modes.

This distribution is said to be **bimodal**.

EXAMPLE 1

The number of days spent in hospital by patients on a surgical ward were 2, 3, 3, 2, 4, 4, 3, 5, 10, 3, 2, 4, 3, 4.
Find the mode.

When the numbers of days are written in ascending order:
2, 2, 2, 3, 3, 3, 3, 3, 4, 4, 4, 4, 5, 10
it can be seen that the number occurring most often is 3.
This means that the mode or modal number of days is 3.

Modal class

When the values are grouped the mode is replaced by a **modal class**, which is the group of values occurring most frequently.

EXAMPLE 2

What is the modal class in the following table, which shows the time spent by customers in a leisure centre.

Time spent (minutes)	Frequency
Less than 15	6
15 –	10
30 –	13
45 –	12
60 –	16
75 –	20
90 –	21
105 –	17
120 – 135	14

There are 21 people who spent between 90 and 105 minutes in the leisure centre.
This is the highest frequency.
∴ The class 90 – 105 is the modal class.

13.3 *The median*

The **median** is the value of the 'middle' observation when the observations are placed in numerical order.

To calculate the median, list all the observations given in numerical order (usually ascending), and the median is the value of the middle one.

A median cannot, therefore, be found for qualitative data.

EXAMPLE 1

The cost of diesel fuel (per litre) at five garages is 76.8p, 74.2p, 82.9p, 83.7p and 78.9p.
What is the median cost?

Write the costs in ascending order:

        74.2   76.8   78.9   82.9   83.7

Find the cost in the middle position:

        74.2   76.8   (78.9)   82.9   83.7

∴ The median cost is 78.9p per litre.

EXAMPLE 2

A sixth garage charges 76.9p per litre for diesel. The costs are now
76.8p, 74.2p, 82.9p, 83.7p, 78.9p and 76.9p.
What is the median cost?

Because there is an even number of costs, there are *two* costs in the
'middle':
74.2   76.8   (76.9   78.9)   82.9   83.7

The convention is to average these two 'middle' values.

The average (mean) of 76.9 and 78.9 $= \dfrac{76.9 + 78.9}{2} = 77.9$

$\therefore$ The median cost is 77.9p per litre.

EXERCISE 13.2

1 A die was thrown 12 times, and the scores were
2, 4, 1, 3, 4, 1, 5, 6, 6, 4, 2, 5.

  a What was the modal score?

  b What was the median score?

2 Eleven cars have the following colours: blue,
black, red, white, silver, blue, red, grey, black,
blue, green.

  What is the modal colour?

3 The IQs of 70 students were recorded, to the
nearest integer, as:

IQ	Frequency
95 – 99	5
100 – 104	7
105 – 109	18
110 – 114	21
115 – 119	7
120 – 124	4
125 – 129	5
130 – 134	1
135 – 140	2

  What is the modal class?

4 The number of cars per hour on a country road
during the hours of daylight were recorded as 11,
13, 15, 11, 17, 12, 18, 14, 7, 9, 14, 16, 7, 11.

  a Find the mean number of cars.

  b Find the modal number of cars.

5 The weights of parcels (in kg) delivered to a
library were:

7.4, 8.2, 11.1, 7.8, 2.5, 5.6, 7.1, 8.9, 2.3, 2.7,
2.9, 4.1.

Find the median weight.

6 What was the modal number of artists named by
the general public in question 1 of Exercise 11.1
(p. 82)?

7 A photographer arranges a family group with
the tallest members of the family in the centre
and the smallest on the outside:

Alec 4′ 6″   James 5′ 1″   Mrs Lee 5′ 8″   Me Lee 5′ 11″   Linda 5′ 4″   Eric 4′ 6″

For his next photograph, he arranges the family
in ascending order of height.

  a Who are now in the centre of the line?

  b What is the median height of the family?

  c Which average is not a representative value?

8   The price of a loaf of bread (in pence) at 10 shops was found to be:

44, 49, 51, 68, 62, 44, 69, 51, 44, 47.

a   What was the median price?

b   What was the modal price?

9   Five managerial staff have car allowances of £35 000, £23 000, £21 000, £18 000, £28 000. Six office staff each have a car allowance of £10 000.

a   What is the median allowance?

b   What is the modal allowance?

c   What is the mean allowance?

d   Which average best represents the allowances?

10   What was the modal class in:

a   Question 5

b   Question 6

of Exercise 11.1 (p. 82)?

11   The ages at which eleven patients were first diagnosed as diabetic were:

5, 12, 16, 18, 25, 16, 17, 57, 32, 60, 61

a   What was the median age?

b   What was the modal age?

12   In question 7 of Exercise 11.1 (p. 83), what was the modal holiday destination for a wedding?

13   The cost of a ski lift pass in seven popular ski resorts is:

£112, £160, £134, £100, £88, £112, £120

a   What is the modal cost?

b   What is the median cost?

14   The number of missing parts in packs of kitchen units was recorded for a sample of 10 packs as:

4, 3, 6, 4, 1, 0, 1, 2, 0, 4

a   Find the modal number of missing parts.

b   Find the median number of missing parts.

15   The time taken (in minutes and seconds) to carry out the test on packs of kitchen units was recorded for six quality controllers as:

5:20, 6:40, 5:30, 4:24, 3:58, 4:30

Find the median time taken.

13.4 *The use of mean, mode and median*

The three averages are useful in different contexts.

- If you were an employer considering the production capacity of your works, it would be helpful to use the *mean* of past production, as this would give you a good idea of the number of goods you can produce.

- If you were a shopkeeper wanting to keep a minimum stock of shirts to sell, the *mode* would be the best to use, as this will tell you which shirts you are most likely to sell.

- If you were a union wage negotiator, the *median* salary would be appropriate to use, because the few high wage earners would not then affect your 'average' of the wages paid.

EXERCISE 13.3

In each of the following situations, decide which of the mode, the median and the mean would be the most appropriate to use. (You are not required to find any values.)

1   A group of artists working on a sculpture each suggested how it should be positioned.

   A typical value is required.

2   Students in an art class were asked how long they had spent on their last project.

   The replies (in hours) were:
   3, 4, 3, 5, 10, 4, 4, 3

3   Witnesses to a shoplifting incident were asked how many thieves were involved.

   Their answers were:
   1, 2, 2, 3, 3, 3, 3, 4

4   A student tries to decide if he is fairly paid for his part-time job.

   He asks some friends how much per hour they are paid for similar work.

5   The electricity consumption for a dental practice is noted for the months from October to March.

   A typical value is required.

6   Witnesses to a heart attack were asked to estimate how long the sufferer was unconscious. The answers (in minutes) were:
   $8 \quad 8\frac{1}{2} \quad 7\frac{1}{2} \quad 9 \quad 9\frac{1}{2}$

   The time needs to be determined as accurately as possible.

7   Ten students were asked how much they spent on their last year's holiday.

   The answers were:
   £250, £162, £340, £140, £860, £300, £98, £380, £970 and £105

8   Caravaners returning from Europe on a cross-channel ferry were asked what distance they had travelled during their holiday.

   A typical value was required.

9   A manager and his deputy managers were asked to estimate the cost of installing a new production process.

   The average of the estimates is to be taken as a working value.

10   Matches are packed into boxes on which is written 'average contents 280 matches'.

*13.5 *The mean and median of a frequency distribution*

In this example the data is recorded in a frequency table:

EXAMPLE 1

Find the mean and mode of the following scores:

Score	Frequency
1	3
2	5
3	11
4	1
5	5

The score of 2, for example, occurred five times, but instead of totalling $2 + 2 + 2 + 2 + 2$, it is quicker to multiply 2 by 5. Similarly, instead of totalling $3 + 3 + 3 + \ldots$ eleven times, it is quicker to calculate 3×11.

The table can be extended like this:

Score x	Frequency f	Score × Frequency xf
1	3	3
2	5	10
3	11	33
4	1	4
5	5	25
Totals:	$\Sigma f = 25$ *(Total frequency)*	$\Sigma xf = 75$ *(Total of 25 scores)*

Mean score $= \dfrac{\sum xf}{\sum f} \left(\text{i.e. } \dfrac{\text{Total of 25 scores}}{\text{Total frequency}}\right) = \dfrac{75}{25} = 3$

The highest frequency is 11.

∴ The mode is 3.

EXAMPLE 2

Thirty households were surveyed, and the number of children in each household was recorded. Find the mean and the mode.

No. of children in each family	0	1	2	3	4	5
Frequency	4	6	13	4	2	1

No. of children in each family x	Frequency f	xf
0	4	0
1	6	6
2	13	26
3	4	12
4	2	8
5	1	5
Totals:	30	57

$$\text{Mean} = \frac{\Sigma xf}{\Sigma f}$$

$$= \frac{57}{30}$$

$$= 1.9 \text{ children}$$

There were 30 households. Therefore the median number of children is between the numbers in the 15th and 16th households. The cumulative frequencies (see Unit 14) are 4, 10, 23, ..., i.e., both the 15th and 16th households contained 2 children.

∴ The median is 2 children.

EXERCISE 13.4

1 An agricultural researcher counted the numbers of peas in a pod in a certain strain as follows:

No. of peas	3	4	5	6	7	8
No. of pods	5	5	20	35	25	10

Find the mean number of peas per pod.

2 The Ace Bus Company went through a bad patch when its buses always left the city centre late. This grouped distribution table shows how late:

Minutes late	0–10	10–20	20–30	30–40	40–60
Frequency	5	8	21	14	5

Find the mean number of minutes late.

3 The numbers of words per sentence on a page of a book were:

No. of words	1–3	4–6	7–9	10–12	13–15
Frequency	3	38	59	27	4

Find the mean length of a sentence.

4 The numbers of faults found by a potter in glazed pots after being fired in the kiln were:

No. of faults	0	1	2	3	4	5
Frequency	15	8	7	6	3	1

a What was the mean number of faults?

b What was the median number of faults?

c What was the modal number of faults?

d Which average best represents the data?

5 The number of weddings per week attended by a photographer was:

No. of weddings	0	1	2	3	4	5	6	7	8
No. of weeks	2	8	3	5	10	7	9	5	3

a What was the mean number of weddings attended per week?

b What was the median number of weddings attended per week?

6 The numbers of times the photocopier was used on one day by the staff in an office were recorded:

No. of times used	2	5	6	7	8	9	10
Frequency	1	3	3	2	4	4	1

Find **a** the median, **b** the mean number of times the photocopier was used on this day.

7 The manager of an electrical business recorded the number of TV sets brought in for repair each week day over a three-month period. The results of the survey were:

No. of TV sets	0	1	2	3	4	5	6
Frequency	5	7	12	15	19	16	4

a What was the median number of TV sets?

b What was the mean number of TV sets?

8 The numbers of children per family on a housing estate were recorded as follows:

No. of children	0	1	2	3	4
No. of families	12	15	5	2	1

Find **a** the mean, **b** the median number of children per family.

9 At a research centre for the common cold, 25 volunteers were exposed to the cold virus under controlled conditions. The time taken (in days) for the first symptoms of a cold to appear were (one person did not catch a cold):

No. of days	2	3	4	5	6
Frequency	2	5	8	7	2

a Find the mean number of days.

b Find the median number of days.

c If the person who did not catch cold were included in the data, which average would not be changed?

10 The goals scored in 42 football league matches on Saturday 26 March 2000 were:

No. of goals per match	0	1	2	3	4	5	6
No. of matches		1	9	10	12	6	3	1

a Find the mean number of goals per match.

b Find the median number of goals per match.

11 The numbers of injuries per week sustained at a dry-ski school were:

No. of injuries	0	1	2	3	4	5	6	7
No. of weeks	3	10	9	13	5	7	4	1

a Find the mean number of injuries per week.

b Find the median number of injuries per week.

12 Find **a** the mean, **b** the median number of faults in the micro chips (see question 10, Exercise 11.1, p. 83).

No. of faults	0	1	2	3
Frequency	31	13	5	1

c Which average should be used to compare this data with a similar set?

13 During a survey into the ages of employees in a factory, the ages of the apprentice tool makers were recorded as:

Age (years)	17	18	19	20	21	22	23
Frequency	4	4	5	2	3	2	1

a Find the median age.

b Find the mean age.

c Comment on your results.

13.6 *Range*

Averages are used to represent sets of data or to compare them, but an average on its own does not give sufficient information about the distributions.

Suppose we are comparing the climate of two places in Turkey. Town A has an average yearly temperature of about 12°C and town Z has an average yearly temperature of about 13°C. From this we might suppose that the climates are similar and that town Z possibly lies south of town A.

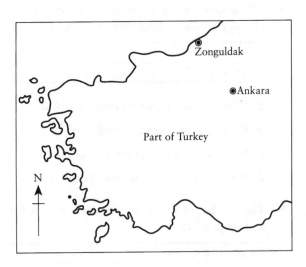

In fact, town Z is Zonguldak, which is on the Black Sea coast, and town A is Ankara, which is further south in the interior of Turkey.

The monthly temperature distributions for the two towns are:

Month	J	F	M	A	M	J	J	A	S	O	N	D
Temperature in Ankara (°C)	−0.2	1.2	4.9	11.0	16.1	20.0	23.3	23.4	18.4	12.9	7.3	2.1
Temperature in Zonguldak (°C)	6.0	6.3	7.0	10.5	15.0	19.2	21.7	21.6	18.4	15.0	11.5	8.5

We can see that the climate in Ankara is more variable than in Zonguldak. There is a larger difference between summer and winter temperatures, whereas in Zonguldak there is a smaller spread of temperatures and a more equable climate.

We need a statistic which will measure this spread of values. The term we use to describe spread is **dispersion**, and there are several ways of measuring it.

The simplest measure of spread is the **range**, which is the difference between the lowest and the highest values.

The range of temperatures for each town is

Ankara: Range = 23.4 − (−0.2) = 23.6°C
Zonguldak: Range = 21.7 − 6.0 = 15.7°C

There is a problem with using the range because it uses only two values and so it can be distorted by a very high of low value.

EXERCISE 13.5

1   A fashion designer makes a particular style of skirt in various lengths:

   16", 19", 24", 28", 32", 34" and 36".

   What is the range of lengths?

2   Five bank clerks took a 'tea break' at 10.30 am. They returned to their desks at the following times:

   1038, 1040, 1042, 1045 and 1048

   a   Find the time taken for each 'tea break' and calculate the mean.

   b   Find the range of the times.

3   Eight patients suffering from lung cancer were asked how many cigarettes per day they smoked. The replies were:

   40, 44, 25, 0, 50, 30, 35, 30.

   Calculate (i) including the non-smoker, (ii) excluding the non-smoker:

   a   the mean number of cigarettes smoked per day.

   b   the range of the number of cigarettes smoked per day.

4   The numbers of cars on a hovercraft in one day were:

   37, 28, 8, 5, 17, 39, 22, 10.

   Find the range.

5   The number of cars produced per year per employee by nine manufacturers in England were:

   7.1, 12.1, 8.1, 4.7, 11.6, 9.4, 3.6, 12.5, 3.9.

   Find the range.

6   Two designers collect shells, fossils, small stones, etc., with which to make jewellery and to decorate their designs.

   They collect from two beaches early in the morning. The numbers of items collected each day for a week are recorded below:

Day	Mon	Tue	Wed	Thu	Fri	Sat	Sun
Beach 1	20	27	49	71	62	24	15
Beach 2	43	39	29	46	51	37	42

a Calculate the mean of each distribution.

b Calculate the range of each distribution.

c Which beach is the best for beach combing and why?

7 Two book clubs offer 'mystery parcels' of books for £8.50, stating that the minimum value of the contents is £15.

A survey of eight such parcels from each of the two clubs found that the actual value of the contents was:

Club 1 Value (£)	16.00	15.80	16.85	15.80	17.85	15.30	15.75	15.45
Club 2 Value (£)	15.95	16.90	16.85	17.85	15.25	17.50	17.00	17.25

a Calculate the mean and range of the data and comment on your results.

b Find the median value of the contents for each club.

c By comparing the mean and median, describe the distribution of each set of data.

8 A patient's blood pressures were recorded on 10 successive days.

Systolic blood pressure	118	126	119	125	127	126	120	136	120	106
Diastolic blood pressure	78	80	80	82	88	87	87	96	81	66

a Calculate the mean systolic and diastolic blood pressures.

b Find the range of:
(i) the systolic blood pressures   (ii) the diastolic blood pressures.
Normal levels are 110–140 for systolic and 70–90 for diastolic pressure.

c What can you conclude about this patient's blood pressure?

9 Two archers each shot six arrows at similar targets. The distance, in centimetres, of each shot from the centre of the target was measured and recorded:

Shot	1	2	3	4	5	6
1st archer	89	53	45	54	56	38
2nd archer	120	112	10	26	59	6

a Calculate the mean distance from the centre for each archer.

b Calculate the range for each archer.

c Which archer was the better shot?

10 The diameters (in millimetres) of ball bearings should be 50 mm.
Two samples of eight bearings, produced by two of the machines in question 11, Exercise 11.1 (p. 81), had diameters as given below:

Machine 3	51.15	48.16	50.32	51.15	49.33	50.05	52.63	49.63
Machine 5	49.72	49.43	46.78	48.88	48.20	49.46	49.19	48.21

a Calculate the mean diameter for each machine.

b Calculate the range for each machine.

c Comment on the performances of the two machines.

13.7 *Cumulative frequency*

The cumulative frequency is the total frequency up to a particular class boundary. It is a 'running total', and the cumulative frequency is found by adding each frequency to the sum of the previous ones.

The cumulative frequency curve (or ogive)

Virtually all cumulative frequency curves (or ogives) have an 'S' shape. How an ogive is built up will be seen in the following example.

EXAMPLE

The marks obtained by 100 students in an examination were as shown below.

Marks	No. of students (frequency)
0–10	1
11–20	2
21–30	13
31–40	24
41–50	32
51–60	16
61–70	11
71–80	1

Draw the cumulative frequency curve for this data.

First, we construct a new table. This keeps a running total of the frequencies in the second column.

Marks	Cumulative frequency
0–10	1
0–20	$1 + 2 = 3$
0–30	$3 + 13 = 16$
0–40	$16 + 24 = 40$
0–50	$40 + 32 = 72$
0–60	$72 + 16 = 88$
0–70	$88 + 11 = 99$
0–80	$99 + 1 = 100$

From the cumulative frequency column we can see that one student has 10 marks or less, three students have 20 marks or less, sixteen students have 30 marks or less, and so on.

Next we plot the cumulative frequencies against the **upper class boundaries**. For example, we plot 3 (students) against 20 (marks) and 16 (students) against 30 (marks). The completed graph then looks like this:

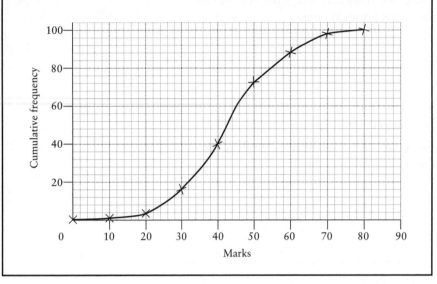

The median

The median mark is the mark obtained by the middle student. For example, if there are 100 students, the median student is the 50th (half-way point). (The strict definition would of course be the $50\frac{1}{2}$th student, but this accuracy cannot be obtained from a graph, and it is unnecessary at this stage.)

Suppose we wanted to find out the median mark in the example on page 123. We would look across from the 50 on the cumulative frequency axis to the curve, then read down vertically to the number of marks. In this case the median is 43 marks. This is illustrated below:

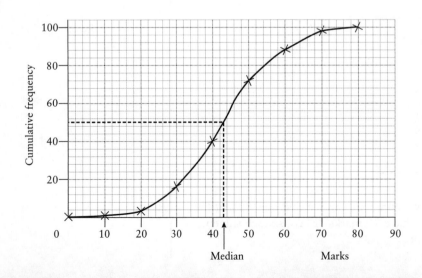

The interquartile range

(i) The **lower quartile** is the mark obtained by the student $\frac{1}{4}$ of the way along the distribution.

There are 100 students in the example on page 196, so the 25th student is $\frac{1}{4}$ of the way up the cumulative frequency axis. From the graph, the 25th student has 35 marks, so the lower quartile is 35.

(ii) The **upper quartile** is the mark obtained by the student $\frac{3}{4}$ of the way up the cumulative frequency axis. This is the 75th student, whose mark is 52, so the upper quartile is 52.

The upper and lower quartiles are illustrated below:

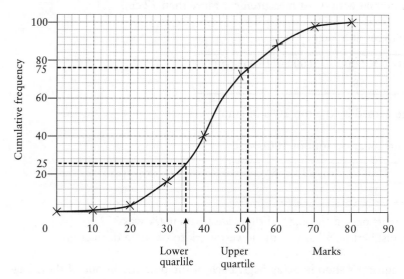

(iii) The **interquartile range** is the difference between the upper quartile and the lower quartile.
In our example, the interquartile range is:

$$52 - 35 = 17 \text{ marks.}$$

The **semi-interquartile range** is half the interquartile range, 8.5 in our example.

Note. Half the students have a mark between the lower and upper quartiles. Hence the interquartile range of 17 shows that half the marks obtained lie in an interval of 17. The semi-interquartile range of 8.5 shows that half the population lie (roughly) within 8.5 marks of the median mark.

EXERCISE 13.6

In questions 1–4, calculate the cumulative frequencies, and draw the cumulative frequency curve. Hence find:

a the median

b the lower quartile

c the upper quartile

d the interquartile range.

Part **e** is given separately for each question.

1 The times taken for students to complete two questions were recorded as:

Time in minutes	0–20	20–25	25–30	30–35	35–40	40–45	45–50
No. of students	3	12	25	49	21	7	3

e Estimate the number of students who took more than 41 minutes.

2 The waist measurements of 100 people were recorded. The data found were:

Waist (cm)	40–50	50–60	60–70	70–80	80–90	90–100
Frequency	2	11	25	41	20	1

e (i) Estimate the number of people with waist measurement less than 53 cm.
(ii) Estimate the number of people with waist measurement more than 72 cm.

3 The annual gross wage of employees at a factory were:

Wage (£)	0–	8000–	10 000–	12 000–	14 000–	16 000–18 000
Frequency	1	15	34	58	27	3

e Estimate the minimum wage earned by the top 20% of employees.

4 The marks gained by 90 students on a test (out of 100) were:

Marks	0–20	21–40	41–60	61–80	81–100
Frequency	2	15	32	33	8

e (i) What percentage of students passed the exam if the lowest pass mark was 37?
(ii) Six students are given a distinction. What was the lowest mark to obtain a distinction?

5 Potatoes are supplied to a greengrocer's shop in 50 kg bags. Each of the potatoes in one of these bags was weighed to the nearest gram, and the following table was drawn up:

Mass (g)	50–99	100–149	150–199	200–249	250–299	300–349
No. of potatoes	5	53	87	73	33	3

a (i) Complete the cumulative frequency for these potatoes.
(ii) Draw the cumulative frequency graph.

b From your graph, estimate:
(i) the median mass
(ii) the number of potatoes weighing at least 225 g each.

c For a party, Harry requires 50 baking potatoes, each weighing at least 225 g. The greengrocer sells the potatoes without special selection.
(i) Use your answer to b(ii) to estimate how many kilograms Harry will have to buy.
(ii) Taking the mean mass of the 50 baking potatoes to be 260 g, estimate how many kilograms of potatoes he will have left over.

14 *Algebra*

14.1 *The basics of algebra*

From words to symbols

Every Saturday the milkman delivers the following to 16 Cromarty Street:
3 loaves of bread, 4 pints of milk and a dozen eggs.

He then presents his bill.

A sentences such as 'the cost of three loaves of bread, four pints of milk and a dozen eggs' is difficult to deal with mathematically.

Algebra is a mathematical language which enables us to deal with problems more easily.

Suppose we let:

b stand for 'the cost of a loaf of bread'
m stand for 'the cost of a pint of milk'
and e stand for 'the cost of a dozen eggs'.

The milkman's bill for 3 loaves of bread, 4 pints of milk and 1 dozen eggs becomes

$$3b + 4m + 1e \text{ or } 3b + 4m + e$$

where $3b$ means 3 times b (or $3 \times b$).
We can miss out the 1 in front of the e
(e means $1 \times e$).

The foundation of algebra, as a science of equations, was laid down in the year 825 by an Islamic mathematician, Muhammad Ibn Musa al-Khwarizmi.

EXAMPLE 1

Don thinks of a number, multiplies it by 3, adds 4 and then divides this answer by the original number.
Write his final number in algebraic terms.

Let his first number be	n
Multiply by 3:	$3n$
Add 4:	$3n + 4$
Divide by the original number:	$\dfrac{3n + 4}{n}$

Final number $= \dfrac{3n + 4}{n}$

EXAMPLE 2

A holiday has two prices, one for adults and the other for children.
Write down an algebraic expression for the cost of a holiday for two adults and three children.

Let the cost for one adult be £A and the cost for one child be £C:

Cost for 2 adults $=$ £$2A$

Cost for 3 children $=$ £$3C$

Cost of the holiday $=$ £$2A +$ £$3C =$ £$(2A + 3C)$

EXERCISE 14.1

Simplify the following phrases and sentences by translating them into algebraic expressions:

1   The sum of seven times x and five times y.

2   The difference between q and twice p.

3   Double the number a and divide by the number b.

4   A number is formed by multiplying a number x by five and then subtracting eight.

5   A number is formed by dividing a number y by four and then adding six.

6   The cost of admission to an art exhibition for 4 adults and 3 children.

7   To make purple paint, an artist mixes 4 cl of blue paint, 6 cl of red paint and 2 cl of white paint.

8   The cost of 4 reams of paper, 3 packs of pens and 2 bottles of Tipp-ex®.

9   The charge levied by a tax adviser who on your behalf writes 6 letters, makes 8 phone calls and has 2 interviews with you.

10   The number of beds in a hospital that has 22 NHS wards and 3 private wards.

11   The time spent by a social worker whose case-load is 4 teenagers, 5 retired couples and 3 single mothers.

12   The entrance fee to a leisure centre for 3 adults and 5 children.

13   The total paid in deposits to a travel agent who has taken 15 bookings in a day: 7 for a flight package, 5 for a ferry crossing to France, and the remainder for holidays in England.

14   The cost of fitting a door in a house for which a carpenter needs 2 handles, 3 hinges, and 22 screws.

15   Owen's commission if he sells 55 appliances of which 28 are fridges, 12 are microwaves, and the rest are washing machines.

Collecting like terms

Mrs Goodman empties her son's pockets on washing day and finds two sweets, one dirty hanky, two pencils, two more sweets and another pencil.

The contents of the pocket can be listed in algebraic terms as

$$2s + 1h + 2p + 2s + 1p$$

The list can be simplified if articles of the same kind are added together. This is called **collecting like terms**. If we collect the like terms from Master Goodman's pocket, the list becomes $h + 3p + 4s$ (which cannot be simplified further as each term is different).

Addition and subtraction

Only like terms may be added or subtracted.

Like terms are those which are multiples of the same algebraic variable.

For example, $3a$, $7a$ and $-8a$ are all like terms.

The expression $3a + 7a - 8a$ can be simplified to $2a$.

The terms $7a$, $3b$ and $4c$ are unlike terms and the expression $7a + 3b + 4c$ cannot be simplified any further.

EXAMPLE 1

Simplify the following expression:

$$2a + 3c + a + 4b + 2c + b$$

$$2a + 3c + a + 4b + 2c + b = (2a + a) + (4b + b) + (3c + 2c)$$
$$= 3a + 5b + 5c$$

EXAMPLE 2

Simplify the following by collecting like terms:

$$5x + 2y - 4z + 3x - y + z$$

$$5x + 2y - 4z + 3x - y + z = (5x + 3x) + (2y - y) + (z - 4z)$$
$$= 8x + y - 3z$$

EXERCISE 14.2

Simplify the following by collecting terms:

1 $2x + 3x$

2 $8n - n$

3 $3a - a + 6a$

4 $5y - 6y + 3y$

5 $3a + 2a + c + b + 2a + 3c + 5b$

6 $x + 2y + z + 3y + 8z$

7 $5p + 3q + 2r - q + 7p - 3p - r$

8 $2x - y + 3x - 2y + z$

9 $a + b - 2a + c - 2b + 3c$

10 $3x - y + \frac{1}{2}y - 2\frac{1}{2}y + 8y$

Substitution

The letters in an algebraic expression stand for numbers or amounts.

For example, in the expression $3b + 4m + e$, b stands for the cost of a loaf of bread, m for the cost of a pint of milk and e for the cost of a dozen eggs.

The advantage of the letters is that the amounts are not fixed, they can change or vary.

The letters are called **variables**. The numbers, which are constant, are called **coefficients**.

If a loaf of bread costs 54p, a pint of milk 39p and a box of eggs 63p
(i.e. $b = 54$, $m = 39$, $e = 63$), then

Weekly bill $= 3b + 4m + e$

$\qquad = (3 \times 54) + (4 \times 39) + 63$

$\qquad = 381$ pence

If, however, prices rise and $b = 56$, $m = 41$, $e = 66$, then

Weekly bill $= 3b + 4m + e$

$\qquad = (3 \times 56) + (4 \times 41) + 66$

$\qquad = 398$ pence

EXAMPLE 1

Evaluate $\dfrac{3x - y}{x + y}$ when $x = 3$, $y = -1$

$$\frac{3x - y}{x + y} = \frac{(3 \times 3) - (-1)}{3 + (-1)} = \frac{9 + 1}{3 - 1} = \frac{10}{2} = 5$$

EXERCISE 14.3

1   Evaluate the following expressions when $x = 3$, $y = 5$, $z = 2$.

   a $2x + y$ **c** $y + 4z$ **e** $\dfrac{y}{10}$ **g** $3z - 12x$ **i** $x + y - 4z$ **k** $y - xz$

   b $3x - 2y$ **d** $\dfrac{12}{z}$ **f** $4z - 6$ **h** $2x - 5z$ **j** $xy + z$ **l** $yz - 4x$

2   Evaluate each of the expressions in question 1 when $x = -1$, $y = 3$, $z = -2$.

3   Evaluate the following expressions if $x = 4$, $y = 3$, $z = -2$:

   a y^2 **c** $2z^2$ **e** $xz + y$ **g** $2x^2 - yz$ **i** $x(x + y)$ **k** $\dfrac{x + 2z}{y}$

   b xyz **d** $\dfrac{x}{y}$ **f** $\dfrac{y}{2z}$ **h** $\dfrac{x + y}{x - y}$ **j** $\dfrac{2y}{x - z}$ **l** $(x + y)(x + z)$

4   Evaluate each of the expressions in question 3 when $x = -2$, $y = \frac{1}{2}$, $z = -1$.

Multiplication and division

Multiplication of algebraic terms is usually easier than multiplication in
arithmetic. For example:

$$a \text{ multiplied by } 4 = a \times 4 = 4a$$

$$p \text{ multiplied by } q = p \times q = pq$$

$$x \text{ divided by } y = x \div y = \frac{x}{y}$$

$$a \text{ multiplied by } a = a \times a = a^2$$

Algebraic terms are usually listed in alphabetical order with the constant first.

The rules for directed numbers are the same as on pp. 6–7. For example:

$$(+x) \times (+y) = xy$$

$$(-x) \times (+y) = -xy$$

$$(+x) \div (-y) = -\frac{x}{y}$$

$$(-x) \div (-y) = \frac{x}{y}$$

EXAMPLE 1

Simplify $5 \times p \times 6 \times q \div 3 \div r$

Collect numbers and letters separately:

$$5 \times p \times 6 \times q \div 3 \div r = (5 \times 6 \div 3) \times (p \times q \div r)$$

$$= \frac{10pq}{r}$$

EXAMPLE 2

Simplify $(3x) \times (-2y) \times (-z)$

$$(3x) \times (-2y) \times (-z) = (3 \times -2 \times -1) \times (x \times y \times z)$$

$$= 6xyz$$

EXAMPLE 3

Simplify $3a \times (2b)^2 \times (-a^2)$

$$3a \times (2b)^2 \times (-a^2) = (3 \times 2^2 \times -1) \times a \times b^2 \times a^2$$

$$= -12a^3b^2$$

EXERCISE 14.4

Simplify:

1 $5 \times x$	6 $c \div 2d \times 8b$	11 $a \times a \times b \times b$	16 $(-3a)^2 \times b$
2 $3 \times m \times n$	7 $(-2x) \times (-3y)$	12 $3a^2 \times a^2$	17 $(-2ab) \times (3b)^2$
3 $2 \times y \div z$	8 $(4p) \div (-2q)$	13 $3a \times b^2 \times a^2$	18 $(-2a) \times (-b) \div (-b)$
4 $a \times c \times b$	9 $(6x) \times (-3y) \div (-2z)$	14 $2a^2b \times -3bc$	19 $x^2y \times xy^2$
5 $2 \times p \times 3 \times r \times q$	10 $a \times a \times a$	15 $3ab^2 \times 2ab \times bc^2$	20 $12ab \div (-4c^2) \times (3ac)$

14.2 *Indices*

$$a \times a \times a = a^3$$

The number 3 is called an **index**. It shows, or indicates, the number of *a*s which have been multiplied together to give the third power of *a*.

$$a^1 \times a^2 = a \times a \times a \qquad = a^3 \quad \text{i.e.} \quad a^{(1+2)}$$

$$a^3 \times a^2 = a \times a \times a \times a \times a = a^5 \quad \text{i.e.} \quad a^{(3+2)}$$

In general: $\quad a^x \times a^y = a^{(x+y)}$

$$a^3 \div a^2 = \frac{a \times a \times a}{a \times a} = a \quad \text{i.e.} \quad a^{(3-2)}$$

$$a^5 \div a^3 = \frac{a \times a \times a \times a \times a}{a \times a \times a} = a \times a = a^2 \quad \text{i.e.} \quad a^{(5-3)}$$

In general: $\quad a^x \div a^y = a^{x-y}$

$$a^3 \div a^5 = \frac{a \times a \times a}{a \times a \times a \times a \times a} = \frac{1}{a \times a} = \frac{1}{a^2}$$

but $\quad a^3 \div a^5 = a^{(3-5)} = a^{-2} \qquad \text{i.e.} \frac{1}{a^2} = a^{-2}$

In general: $\quad a^{-x} = \dfrac{1}{a^x}$

$$a^3 \div a^3 = \frac{a \times a \times a}{a \times a \times a} = 1$$

but $\quad a^3 \div a^3 = a^{(3-3)} = a^0$

In general: $\quad \mathbf{a^0 = 1}$

The rules for indices can be summarised as follows:

$$a^x \times a^y = a^{(x+y)}$$

$$a^x \div a^y = a^{(x-y)}$$

$$a^{-x} = \frac{1}{a^x}$$

$$a^0 = 1$$

EXAMPLE

Simplify $x^5 \div x^3 \times x^2$

$$x^5 \div x^3 \times x^2 = \frac{x \times x \times x \times x \times x \times x \times x}{x \times x \times x \times x} = x^4$$

or $\quad x^5 \div x^3 \times x^2 = x^{(5-3+2)} = x^4$

EXERCISE 14.5

Simplify the following expressions:

1 $\quad x^5 \times x^3$	3 $\quad x^7 \div x^4$	5 $\quad x^4 \div x^4$	7 $\quad x^0$
2 $\quad x^3 \times x \times x^2$	4 $\quad x^4 \div x^5$	6 $\quad x^{-2}$	8 $\quad 3x^3 \times 2x \div 4x^2$

14.3 *Equations*

Forming equations

Many problems are solved more quickly if they are first written in algebraic terms.

An equation is, in algebra, the equivalent of a sentence. All equations must contain an equals sign.

The following problem is solved by first translating into algebra.

EXAMPLE 1

My brother is twice as old as I am and the sum of our ages is 42. How old am I?

English	Algebra
My age	x (years)
My brother's age	$2x$
The sum of our ages	$x + 2x$
The sum of our ages is forty-two	$x + 2x = 42$

In algebra the problem becomes: $x + 2x = 42$
$$3x = 42 \text{ (collecting like terms)}$$
$$x = 14 \text{ (dividing by 3)}$$

This translates back into English as:
My age is 14 years.

EXAMPLE 2

I think of a number, treble it, add seven and the answer is 19. Form an equation using this information.

Let the number thought of be n.
Then

treble the number add seven is nineteen becomes
$$3n \quad + \quad 7 \quad = \quad 19$$

EXERCISE 14.6

For each of the following, rewrite the problem as an algebraic equation:

1 Five added to a number gives the answer twelve.

2 Seven subtracted from a number leaves thirteen.

3 If 4 is added to twice a number, the answer is equal to 10.

4 Seven times a number is twenty-one.

5 Six subtracted from five times a number gives the answer twenty-nine.

6 Ten added to half of a number gives the answer twenty-two.

7 Think of a number, double it, subtract three and the answer is three.

8 Think of a number, divide by four, subtract three and the answer is three.

9 A rectangular tile has a length which is double its width. The perimeter of the tile is 18 cm.

10 The earring shown is made of strands of silver wire. The middle strand is 2 cm longer than the smallest strand and the largest strand is 5 cm longer than the middle strand. The total length of the wire is 27 cm.
Let x be the length of the middle strand.

11 In an office, the number of phones is three times the number of faxes. The total number of phones and faxes is twenty.

12 An office stocks three sizes of envelopes: foolscap, A5, and A4. The business uses twice as many A5 envelopes as A4, and uses 20 more foolscap envelopes than A5. In one day the business uses 135 envelopes.

13 The length of a desk is double its width. The perimeter of the desk is 12.6 feet.

14 The number of pills prescribed by a paediatrician varies according to the child's weight. Those heavier than average receive 6 more than the norm, whereas those lighter than average receive 4 less than the norm. The paediatrician sees 30 children of whom 10 are overweight and 6 are underweight, and he prescribes 906 pills.

15 In a step aerobics class, teenagers achieve twice as many steps as senior citizens. The number of steps completed by two teenagers and three senior citizens is 77.

16 In a theme park, the number of rides which may be taken depends on the child's height. There are only two rides on which a child under 3 ft is *allowed*, but there are only three rides which a bigger child up to 4 ft 6 in is *prohibited* from taking. The total number of rides possible for a family of two adults, one child between 3 ft and 4 ft 6 in, and two children under 3 ft is 37.

17 A parts supplier to the motor industry provides wheel hubcaps, headlight housings and rear fog-light housings. The number of parts supplied to a car manufacturer, for one day's production of cars, is 1750. Each car has one rear fog-light. Let x be the number of cars produced on that day.

18 The parts supplier provides similar parts for two cars made by another manufacturer. For every car made with one rear fog light, two are made with two rear fog lights. The manufacturers uses 10 350 parts from the supplier in a day. Let x be the number of cars produced with one fog light.

Solving equations

Once a problem has been written as an algebraic equation, the problem can be solved by solving the equation.

To solve $3n + 7 = 19$ means finding the value of n which makes the equation true.

To do this, the 7 and 3 must be eliminated from the LHS (left-hand side) of the equation to leave $n =$ the solution.

An equation must always be balanced,
i.e. the LHS must always equal the RHS (right-hand side).

In the equation above

$3n + 7$ balances 19

If 7 is deducted from the LHS, the equation will no longer be balanced.

To maintain the balance, 7 must also be deducted from the RHS, giving $3n = 12$.

$3n$ must now be reduced to $1n$ by dividing both sides by 3, giving $n = 4$.

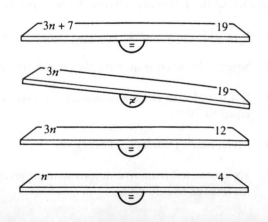

The stages are: $3n + 7 = 19$
Subtract 7 from both sides: $3n + 7 - 7 = 19 - 7$
giving $3n = 12$
Divide both sides by 3: $\dfrac{3n}{3} = \dfrac{12}{3}$
giving $n = 4$

$\therefore$ The number was 4.

EXAMPLE 1

Solve the equation $\frac{1}{2}x - 1 = 6$.

$$\frac{1}{2}x - 1 = 6$$

Multiply through by 2 to remove fraction: $x - 2 = 12$
Add 2 to each side: $x - 2 + 2 = 12 + 2$
                                           $x = 14$

EXAMPLE 2

Solve the equation $2(x - 3) = 5$.

$$2(x - 3) = 5$$

Multiply out the bracket: $2x - 6 = 5$
Add 6 to each side: $2x = 11$
Halve each side: $x = 5\frac{1}{2}$

EXERCISE 14.7

1–8 Solve the equations formed in questions 1–8 of Exercise 14.6 to find the number.

Similarly, for each of the questions 9–18, solve the equations formed in questions 9–18 of Exercise 14.6 to find:

9 the width of the tile.

10 the length of the longest strand of silver wire

11 the number of faxes

12 the number of foolscap envelopes

13 the length of the desk

14 the number of pills given to an overweight child

15 the number of steps taken by a teenager

16 the number of rides a child between 3 ft and 4 ft 6 in can take

17 the number of cars made in one day

18 the number of cars made in one day.

In the following questions, solve the equations to find the value of x:

19 $x + 7 = 11$

20 $4x = 15$

21 $4x - 5 = 19$

22 $\dfrac{3x}{4} = 6$

23 $12 - x = 9$

24 $17 - 2x = 5$

25 $2(x - 6) = 8$

26 $\dfrac{x}{2} + 3 = 7$

27 $\dfrac{x}{3} - 2 = 1$

28 $\dfrac{2x}{5} + 2 = 10$

14.4 *Harder equations*

The method used above can be very time-consuming and, when solving more difficult equations, a quicker method is used.

For the equation

$$3n + 7 = 19$$

when 7 is subtracted from both sides, we know it will disappear from the LHS; therefore it is only necessary to write it on the RHS:

$$3n = 19 - 7$$

i.e. the 7 has *changed sides* and has *changed sign* from $+$ to $-$.

We now have:

$$3n = 12$$

Similarly, when both sides are divided by 3 we know that the LHS will be reduced to n.

Showing the division on the RHS only we have:

$$n = \frac{12}{3} = 4$$

i.e. the 3 has *changed sides* and *changed sign* from $\times$ to $\div$.

The rule for eliminating a quantity from one side of an equation is

change to the opposite side and change to the opposite sign.

This process is called **transposing**.

EXAMPLE 1

Solve the equation $5x - 4 = 3x + 12$

In this type of equation, the x terms should be collected on one side of the equation and the numerical terms on the other, i.e. $3x$ must be eliminated from the RHS and -4 from the LHS.

$$5x - 4 = 3x + 12$$

Transposing $3x$ and -4 gives: $5x - 3x = 12 + 4$

$$2x = 16$$

$$x = 8$$

Answers to algebraic equations should *always* be checked by substituting back into the LHS and RHS of the original equation, as shown below:

$$\text{LHS} = 5x - 4 = 5 \times 8 - 4 = 36$$
$$\text{RHS} = 3x + 12 = 3 \times 8 + 12 = 36$$
$$\text{LHS} = \text{RHS, so the solution is correct.}$$

EXAMPLE 2

Solve $2(2x - 5) = 3(x - 4)$

$$2(2x - 5) = 3(x - 4)$$

Multiply out the brackets: $4x - 10 = 3x - 12$

Transpose $3x$ and -10: $4x - 3x = 10 - 12$

$$x = -2$$

EXAMPLE 3

Solve $4(x + 3) - 2(x - 5) = 46$

$$4(x + 3) - 2(x - 5) = 46$$

Multiply out the brackets: $\quad 4x + 12 - 2x + 10 = 46$

Collect terms: $\quad\quad\quad\quad\quad\quad 2x + 22 = 46$

Transpose 22: $\quad\quad\quad\quad\quad\quad\quad\quad 2x = 24$

Divide by 2: $\quad\quad\quad\quad\quad\quad\quad\quad\quad x = 12$

EXERCISE 14.8

Solve the following equations to find the value of x:

1   $7x + 3 = 5x + 11$ 4 $3 - 2x = 4 - 5x$ 7 $2(x + 7) + 4 = 18$ 10 $(x + 5) + 2(3x - 2) = 8$

2   $5x - 2 = 2x + 7$ 5 $3(x - 5) = 12$ 8 $2(x - 4) = (x + 2)$ 11 $4(x + 2) + 2(x + 3) = 32$

3   $6x - 4 = 10 - x$ 6 $5 + 2(x + 1) = 11$ 9 $3(2x - 1) = 7(x - 1)$ 12 $2(2x + 1) - 3(3x - 4) = 40$

Further problems

EXAMPLE 1

I buy a pizza and cut it into three pieces. When I weigh the pieces, I find that one piece is 8 g lighter than the largest piece and 5 g heavier than the smallest piece.

If the whole pizza weighs 360 g, how much does the smallest piece weigh?

Let the weight of the smallest piece be x grams

The weights of the other two pieces are $(x + 5)$ grams

and $(x + 5 + 8)$ grams

Total weight of the three pieces $= x + (x + 5) + (x + 13)$

$$\therefore x + (x + 5) + (x + 13) = 360$$
$$3x + 18 = 360$$
$$3x = 342$$
$$x = 114$$

The weight of the smallest piece is 114 grams.

EXAMPLE 2

This year, Dawn is three times as old as her brother Marcus, but in four years' time she will be twice as old. How old are Dawn and Marcus now?

Let Marcus' age now be x years

Then Dawn's age now is $3x$ years

In four years' time:

     Marcus will be $(x + 4)$ years

     Dawn will be $(3x + 4)$ years

Dawn will then be twice as old as Marcus

$$\therefore (3x + 4) = 2(x + 4)$$
$$3x + 4 = 2x + 8$$
$$3x - 2x = 8 - 4$$
$$x = 4$$

Marcus is 4 years old and Dawn is 12 years old.

EXERCISE 14.9

1 A rubber costs 25p more than a pencil. Twelve pencils and ten rubbers are bought for a bran tub. The cost of a pencil is x pence.

  a Write down, in terms of x:
    (i) the cost of a rubber
    (ii) the cost of 12 pencils
    (iii) the cost of 10 rubbers.

  b The total cost of the 12 pencils and 10 rubbers is £6.90. Using this information:
    (i) write down an equation in terms of x
    (ii) solve the equation to find x
    (iii) find the cost of one rubber.

2 A shop assistant accepts a £5 note from a customer and, in return, hands the customer two boxes of paper hankies and £2.50 change.

  a If x is the cost of one box of hankies, write down an expression for what the customer receives.

  b Write down an equation and solve it to find the cost of one box of hankies.

3 A pound of apples costs 5p more than a pound of pears. The cost of 5 pounds of apples and 3 pounds of pears is £4.65.
What is the cost of one pound of pears?

4 An unframed picture costs £x. The cost of framing a picture is £2.20. Ian buys three pictures and frames two of them. He is given £7.50 change from a £50 note.

  a Write down an equation in terms of x.

  b Find the cost of an unframed picture.

5 The cost of a 'Monchique' tile is £x. The cost of a 'Penina' tile is 30p more.

  a Write down the cost in pounds of a 'Penina' tile.

  Janice buys 4 'Monchique' tiles and 7 'Penina' tiles for £19.70.

  b Write down an equation in x.

  c Find the cost of a 'Monchique' tile.

6 Postage on a sale leaflet is x pence and postage for a brochure is 26 pence greater. An estate agent posts 8 leaflets and 5 brochures for £6.63.

  a Write down an equation in x.

  b Find the cost of posting a leaflet.

7 An office operates a fax and photocopying service. The cost of a fax is 6 times the price of a photocopy. Marcus sends 4 faxes and makes 12 photocopies. He is charged £7.20.
Find the cost of a fax.

8 Alan weighs 3 kg less than Barry who weighs 4 kg less than Colin.

  Barry weighs x kilograms and the total weight of the three boys is 193 kg.
How much does Colin weigh?

9 Walking to college takes me twice as long as cycling. Taking a bus takes me 25 minutes longer than cycling. One week I walked five times, and next week I cycled twice and took the bus three times. The total times for travelling to college were the same for the two weeks.
How long does it take me to cycle to college?

10 Mr Wilson regularly attends football matches when his team plays at home.

  a For x number of games he buys a seat in the stands. Each seat costs £9.
Write down an expression for the cost of these x games.

  b For the remaining matches he buys a ticket for the terraces. Each ticket costs £5.
If he attends 20 games in a season, write down an expression in x for the cost of tickets for the terraces.

  c Using your answers to **a** and **b**, write down and simplify an expression for the total cost for the season.

  d The cost for the season was £148. Write down an equation in terms of x.

  e Solve the equation to find the number of matches he watched from the stands.

11 At Gatwick airport 80 families were asked their destination by an interviewer. Five more were flying to Spain than Turkey. Twice as many were flying to Spain as were flying to the USA. Six were flying to Portugal, and nine gave a different country from these. Let x be the number flying to the USA.

  a In terms of x, write down:
    (i) how many were flying to Spain
    (ii) how many were flying to Turkey.

b Write down an equation in x. Hence find the number flying to Turkey.

12 There are x people at a double-glazing firm making phone sales. This is 4 more than the number of secretaries but 6 less than the number of travelling sales people. The total number of these employees is 35.

    a Write down an equation in x.

    b Find the number of secretaries.

13 A manufacturer sells a particular model of car with three different engine sizes: 1.3 litres, 1.6 litres and 1.9 litres. One garage finds that the 1.3 litre car sells least well. Twice as many 1.9 litre engine cars are sold as 1.3 litre and, in a three month period, the garage sells 20 more 1.6 litre cars than 1.9 litre. Let x be the number of 1.3 litre cars sold.

    a In terms of x, write down:
     (i) the number of 1.9 litre engine cars sold
     (ii) the number of 1.6 litre engine cars sold.

    b The garage sells 110 cars in the three month period.
    Form an equation in x and solve it to find the number of 1.6 litre cars sold.

14.5 *Flow diagrams*

Frequently in Mathematics, the hardest part of solving a problem is deciding how to do it. For example:

$y = 3x + 11$. Find y when $x = 4$.

The calculation is simple, once you realise that you multiply 3 by 4 then add 11 to the answer.

This method can be shown in a diagram:

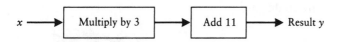

This diagram is called a **flow diagram** or **flow chart**.

A flow diagram does not have to refer to a numerical problem:

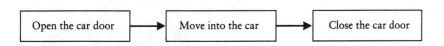

This is the normal way of getting into a car.

EXAMPLE

Find the relationship between x and y shown in the flow diagram below:

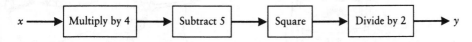

The results after each step will be:

$$x \qquad 4x \qquad 4x - 5 \qquad (4x-5)^2 \qquad \tfrac{1}{2}(4x-5)^2$$

$$y = \tfrac{1}{2}(4x-5)^2$$

EXERCISE 14.10

1 Draw a flow chart to represent each of these equations:

   a $y = 7x + 5$

   b $y = 3x - 11$

   c $y = 3x^2 + 5$

   d $y = (2x + 1)^2$.

2 Find the relationship between x and y shown in the flow chart:

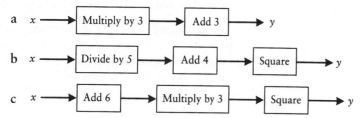

   a $x \longrightarrow$ Multiply by 3 $\longrightarrow$ Add 3 $\longrightarrow y$

   b $x \longrightarrow$ Divide by 5 $\longrightarrow$ Add 4 $\longrightarrow$ Square $\longrightarrow y$

   c $x \longrightarrow$ Add 6 $\longrightarrow$ Multiply by 3 $\longrightarrow$ Square $\longrightarrow y$

3 Draw a flow chart for each of these operations:

   a boiling a kettle

   b opening a door with a key

   c making a telephone call with a card

   d taking a photograph

   e making a plaster of Paris model with a mould

   f sending a fax

   g accepting payment from a customer by credit card

   h cleaning your teeth

   i putting someone in the recovery position after an accident

   j checking into an airport

   k going for a swim

   l fitting a new hinge to a door

   m changing a fuse in a plug.

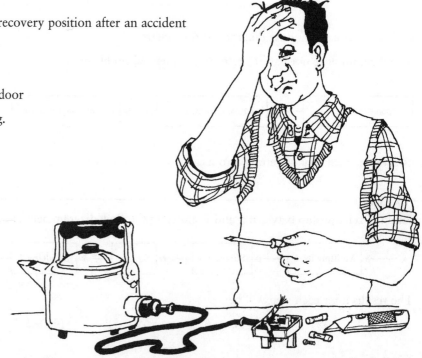

14.6 *Formulae*

Substitution in formulae

A second important use of algebra is to enable a relationship between two or more quantities to be expressed in a short but easily understood form. This is called a **formula**.

The volume of a cylinder is found by multiplying the area of the circular cross-section of the cylinder by its height. This is more neatly expressed by the formula

$$V = \pi r^2 h$$

In order to calculate the volume, the given values of r (radius) and h (height) are substituted into the formula.

EXAMPLE

The distance travelled by a vehicle in a given time can be found by using the formula:

$$s = ut + \tfrac{1}{2}at^2$$

where s is the distance travelled in metres, u is the starting velocity in metres per second, a is the acceleration in metres per second, and t is the time in seconds.

Find the distance travelled by a sports car:

a in 4 s if $u = 20$m/s and $a = 2.5$m/s^2

b in 10 s starting from rest with an acceleration of 3 m/s^2.

a $t = 4$, $u = 20$, $a = 2.5$

Substituting in $s = ut + \tfrac{1}{2}at^2$

gives $s = (20 \times 4) + (\tfrac{1}{2} \times 2.5 \times 4^2)$
$= 80 + 20$
$= 100$

The distance travelled was 100 m.

b $t = 10$, $u = 0$, $a = 3$

Substituting in $s = ut + \tfrac{1}{2}at^2$

gives $s = 0 + \tfrac{1}{2} \times 3 \times 10^2$
$= 150$

The distance travelled was 150 m.

EXERCISE 14.11

1 a The speed, or velocity, at which the sports car in the example above is travelling after a certain time, is given by the formula

$$v = u + at$$

Calculate the speed, in m/s, when
(i) $t = 4$, $u = 20$, $a = 2.5$
(ii) $t = 10$, $u = 0$, $a = 3.6$.

b The formula $V = 2.25v$ converts v m/s to V mph.
Calculate the sports car's speed in miles per hour for each of parts (i) and (ii) in **a**.

2 The formula for a straight line graph is

$$y = mx + c$$

Find the value of y if $m = 2$, $c = -3$ and $x = 4$.

3 To convert degrees Fahrenheit F to degrees Celsius C, the following formula is used:

$$C = \frac{5}{9}(F - 32)$$

Convert to degrees Celsius:

a 50°F, **b** 77°F, **c** 14°F.

4 The focal length of a lens is given by

$$\frac{1}{f} = \frac{1}{v} + \frac{1}{u}$$

Find f when: **a** $u = 12$, $v = 18$

b $u = 10.5$, $v = 7$.

5

A wedding dress is to be finished with an embroidered front bodice, decorated with pearls. The cost £C of the embroidered section is given by $C = h(2b + 3a)/20$, where h cm is the depth of the embroidered panel, a cm is the minimum width and b cm is the maximum width, as shown in the diagram.

Find the cost of the embroidery when

a $h = 25$, $a = 20$ and $b = 25$

b $h = 18$, $a = 18$ and $b = 19$.

6 When an amount of money, £P, is invested at a compound interest rate of $r\%$ per annum, the amount in the account after 2 years is given by

$$A = P\left(1 + \frac{r}{100}\right)^2$$

Find the amount in an account after 2 years if £1600 was invested at 9.5% per annum.

7 The cost, £C, of printing n posters for a concert is given by $C = 5.2 + 0.11n$.

a Find the cost of printing:
  (i) 100 posters (ii) 1000 posters.

b Find the cost per poster when 400 are printed.

8 The number of bacteria, n, in a piece of meat t hours after it is taken out of a fridge is given by $n = 800 \times 2^{20t}$.
Find the number of bacteria after:

a 1 hour **b** 3 hours **c** 30 minutes.

9 The volume of medicine, V cm³, in a bottle of height h cm is given by: $V = 8(h - 0.7)^2$.

Find the volume in a bottle of height:

a 8 cm **b** 9 cm.

10 300 lockers are being painted at a leisure centre. The surface area (S sq in) of each locker is given by $S = 2h(18 + w) + 36w$, where h inches is the height and w inches is the width. Find the surface area of a locker 6 feet high and 18 inches wide.

11 The volume of water, V cubic metres, in a swimming pool is given by $V = 30w(a + b)$, where a metres and b metres are the depths at the two ends and w metres is its width.

Find the volume of water when

a $a = 3$, $b = 2$ and $w = 20$

b $a = 4$, $b = 1.5$ and $w = 15$.

12 The combined resistance when three resistors are joined together in parallel is given by:

$$\frac{1}{r} = \frac{1}{r_1} + \frac{1}{r_2} + \frac{1}{r_3}.$$

Find r, when $r_1 = 7$ ohms, $r_2 = 8$ ohms and $r_3 = 11$ ohms.

13 The cost, £C, of transporting a yacht from a manufacturer to a purchaser is estimated to be given by $C = 80 + 0.76m + 0.2s$, where m miles is the distance to be travelled by road and s miles is the distance to be travelled by sea. The purchaser wants the yacht delivered to Cherbourg. Delivery will involve a road distance of 50 miles and a sea distance of 120 miles.

Find the cost.

14.7 *Rearranging formulae*

The formula which converts degrees Fahrenheit to degrees Celsius is

$$C = \frac{5}{9}(F - 32)$$

It may, however, be necessary to convert degrees Celsius to degrees Fahrenheit. In this case, the formula needs to be **rearranged**, or **transposed**, to give F in terms of C, i.e. F is made the subject of the formula.

EXAMPLE 1

a Rearrange the formula $C = \frac{5}{9}(F - 32)$ to give F in terms of C.

b Use the transposed formula to convert 15°C to °F.

a The method is the same as for solving equations.

$$C = \frac{5}{9}(F - 32)$$

(i) Multiply through by 9: $\qquad 9C = 5(F - 32)$

(ii) Remove the bracket: $\qquad 9C = 5F - 160$

(iii) Transpose 160: $\qquad 9C + 160 = 5F$

(iv) Dividing through by 5 gives the formula for F: $\qquad F = \dfrac{9C + 160}{5}$

b When $C = 15$ $\qquad F = \dfrac{9 \times 15 + 160}{5}$

$$= \frac{135 + 160}{5}$$

$$= \frac{295}{5}$$

$$= 59$$

$$\left(\text{Check.} \quad C = \frac{5}{9}(F - 32) = \frac{5}{9}(59 - 32) = \frac{5}{9} \times 27 = 15\right)$$

EXAMPLE 2

The profit (£P) made when an article is sold for a price £S with a percentage profit of $x\%$, can be calculated from the formula:

$$P = \frac{Sx}{100 + x}$$

a Find P when $x = 12$ and $S = 392$.

b Rearrange the formula to make x the subject.

c Find the percentage profit if a profit £33 is made when an article is sold for £253.

a
$$P = \frac{392 \times 12}{100 + 12} = \frac{4704}{112} = £42$$

b
$$P = \frac{Sx}{100 + x}$$

(i) Deal with the fraction by multiplying each side by $(100 + x)$:

$$P(100 + x) = Sx$$

(ii) Multiply out the bracket:

$$100P + Px = Sx$$

(iii) Collect x terms on one side, other terms on the opposite side (in this case, it is easier to collect x terms on RHS to avoid a negative sign for $100P$):

$$100P = Sx - Px$$

(iv) Take out a common factor of x:

$$100P = x(S - P)$$

(v) Divide each side by $(S - P)$ to find the value of x:

$$\frac{100P}{S - P} = x$$

c $P = £33$, $S = £253$

$$\text{Profit \%} = x = \frac{100P}{S - P} = \frac{100 \times 33}{253 - 33} = 15\%$$

EXERCISE 14.12

1 A silversmith makes jewellery by setting stones into silver. The stones are surrounded by a bezel of silver as shown:

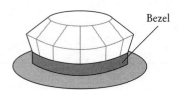

Bezel

The length of the bezel (L) is the circumference of the stone (C) plus one and a half times the thickness of the silver (T),

i.e. $L = C + 1\frac{1}{2}T$

or $L = \pi D + 1\frac{1}{2}T$

where D is the diameter of the stone.

a Find the length of the bezel needed for a stone of diameter 8 mm using silver of thickness 0.6 mm.

b Rearrange the equation to give T in terms of L and C.

c An oval stone has a circumference of 30.35 mm and a bezel length of 30.47 mm. What was the thickness of the silver used?

2 The number of mosaic tiles, 1 cm square, needed to surround rectangular mirrors with dimensions x cm by y cm, is

$$N = 2(x + y) + 4$$

a How many tiles are needed for a mirror which is 14 cm by 20 cm?

Glass for a mirror is 30 cm wide and there are 170 tiles left.

b Rearrange the formula to give y in terms of N and x.

c Use your formula to find the length of glass which should be cut to use up all the tiles.

The craftsman decides to make some of the mirrors square.

d Adapt the original formula and find the number of tiles needed for a mirror which is 30 cm square.

e Rearrange the formula to give x in terms of N.

f What should the dimensions of a mirror be if there are 150 tiles available for the surround?

3 The total cost £T of legal action is given by

$$T = 1200b + 350s + 50c$$

where b is the number of days a barrister is used, s is the number of days a solicitor is used and c is the number of days a clerk is used.

a Find the total cost if the barrister works for 4 days, the solicitor works for 10 days and the clerk works for 28 days.

b (i) Rearrange the formula to find the number of days the barrister works in terms of s, c and T.
 (ii) If $T = 3950$, $s = 3$ and $c = 10$, find b.

c (i) Rearrange the formula to find the number of days the clerk works in terms of b, s and T.
 (ii) If the total cost was £10 900, the barrister worked for 5 days, and the solicitor worked for 11 days, for how many days was the clerk employed?

4 The return on capital employed (ROCE) is calculated using the formula:

$$\text{ROCE} = \frac{\text{Net profit}}{\text{Capital}} \times 100$$

or $R = \dfrac{P}{C} \times 100$

a What is the return if $P = £2520$ and $C = £8000$?

b Rearrange the formula to give P in terms of R and C.

c What was the net profit if $C = £6500$ and $R = 26\%$?

5 The cardiac output C of a person is given by

$$C = HS$$

where C is the heartbeat rate and S the volume of each stroke.

Sally is an athlete. When at rest, she has a heartbeat of 35 beats per minute and a stroke volume of 130 cm^3.

a Find Sally's cardiac output.

b (i) Rearrange the formula to find Sally's heartbeat rate in terms of C and S.

Sally's friend, Gillian, is not an athlete, but she has the same cardiac output as Sally.

 (ii) Find Gillian's heartbeat rate if her stroke volume is 60 cm^3.

6 Every chocolate bar I eat will be a gain of 230 calories. If I then walk briskly, I will lose 6 calories per minute.

The excess calories which I have eaten are given by:

$$c = 230b - 6t$$

where c is the number of calories, b is the number of chocolate bars, and t is the time in minutes.

a Calculate the excess number of calories if I eat two chocolate bars and then walk briskly for 20 minutes.

b Rearrange the formula to give t in terms of c and b.

c If I eat three chocolate bars, for how long will I need to walk to use up all the extra calories?

7 Naismith's rule for hill walking is to allow 1 hour for every 4 km walked plus 1 minute for every 10 m climbed.

The formula is:

$$t = \frac{d}{4} + \frac{h}{600}$$

where t is the time in hours, d is the distance walked in kilometres and h is the height climbed in metres.

a Calculate the time which should be allowed for a walk which covers a distance of 8 km and a climb of 900 m.

b Rearrange the formula to give d in terms of T and h.

c Find an estimate for the distance walked if the time taken was 6 hours and the height climbed was 1050 m.

8   The deposit required when hiring a self-catering apartment is 10% of the cost per person hiring the apartment plus a charge of £50, which is returnable if no damage is caused, i.e.

$$D = \frac{CN}{10} + 50$$

where D is the deposit, C is the cost per person and N is the number of people hiring the apartment.

a   Calculate the deposit for 4 people on a holiday which costs £220 per person.

b   Rearrange the formula to give N in terms of C and D.

c   How many people occupy an apartment on a holiday costing £180 per person if the deposit is £158?

9   The power, P watts, of a battery source, is given by:

$$P = \frac{V^2}{R}$$

where V volts is the voltage and R ohms is the resistance.

a   Find P when $V = 240$ and $R = 70$.

b   (i)   Rearrange the formula to find R in terms of V and P.
    (ii) Find the resistance when the voltage is 240 volts and the power is 3000 watts.

c   (i)   Rearrange the formula to find V in terms of P and R.
    (ii) Find the voltage when the power is 2000 watts and the resistance is 90 ohms.

15 *Graphs*

15.1 *Graphs and curves*

This unit deals with line graphs. The lines may be straight or curved, but they illustrate a relationship between two quantities. This relationship must be clear to anyone looking at the graph.

Graphs are used by many bodies to convey information quickly and with impact!

For example, these graphs were used by:

a holiday company

a Government department

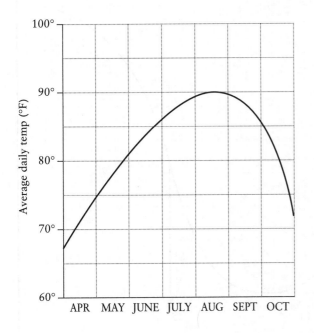

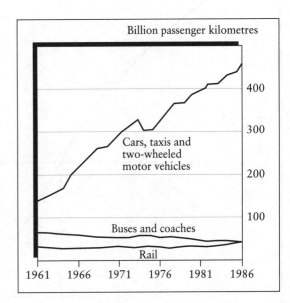

(Source: Department of Transport)

Many graphs involve time, which is always measured along the horizontal axis. The vertical axis then provides a measure of something that changes with time.

Whenever one measurable quantity changes as a result of another quantity changing it will be possible to draw a graph.

15.2 *The interpretation of graphs*

Once a graph has been drawn, information can be found from it very quickly.

EXAMPLE 1

The graph shows a cross-section through a river bed. The distance from point A on one bank of the river to point B, directly opposite on the other bank is 20 m.

Soundings were taken of the depth of the water at various points and plotted against the distance from A.

Find, from the graph:

a the depth of the river at a distance of 12 m from A

b the distances from A at which the depth of the river is 2.8 m.

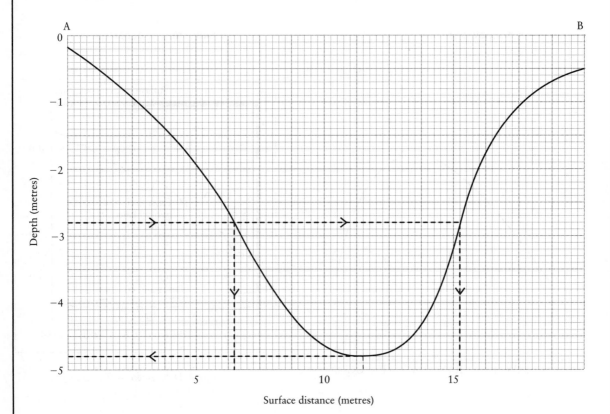

a The distance 12 m is located on the horizontal axis and a vertical line is drawn from this point to meet the graph. A horizontal line is then drawn across to the vertical axis and the distance is read off.
The distance is -4.8 m, i.e. the depth of the water is 4.8 m.

b The depth of 2.8 metres is located on the vertical axis at the point −2.8 and a horizontal line is drawn from this point which meets the curve at two points.
Vertical lines are drawn down to the horizontal axis and the two distances are read off.

The distances from A are 6.50 m and 15.25 m.

If a connection between two variables can be expressed algebraically, i.e. by an equation, then every point lies on the line or curve. If one value is known, the other can be found exactly, or as accurately as the scale of the graph allows.

For example, using the graph which shows the depth of a river (Example 1 above) the depth of the river can be given correct to the nearest 10 cm.

Often, however, the connection is not exact (as in Example 2 below) and, given one variable, only a rough estimate of the other variable can be found.

EXAMPLE 2

Each year thousands of tourists visit Britain, and the money which they spend here is a very welcome addition to the British economy. The larger the number of tourists staying in Britain, the larger the amount of money spent will be. However, the relationship between the number of tourists and the amount of money spent is not an exact linear relationship. For example, double the number of tourists will not necessarily spend double the amount of money.

The line drawn in the graph below is the one which best represents the relationship between the number of tourists and the money they spend.

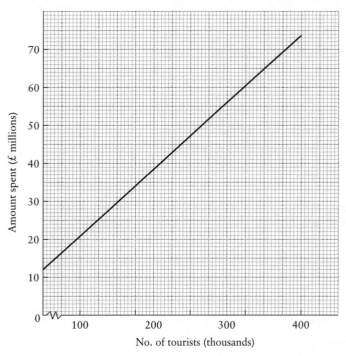

Values read from the graph are likely to be approximate, but the graph could be used to make predictions.

a Approximately how much money is spent by 250 thousand tourists?

b Predict the number of tourists needed to produce an income of £60 million.

From the graph:

a The amount of money spent is £47.5 million.

b The number of tourists required is 320 000.

EXERCISE 15.1

In the following questions state whether the answer found from the graph is exact, within the limits of the graph's accuracy, or whether it is a rough estimate.

1   The graph shows the relationship between the percentage of rejected mugs found by different potteries and the selling price of the mug.

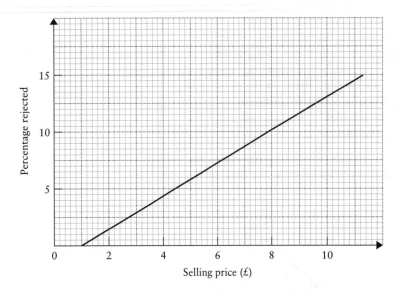

a   if the mugs sell at £5 each, what percentage is rejected?

b   If 13% of the mugs are rejected, what is the selling price?

2   The graph shows the number of complete patterns in a roll of dress material against the length of material bought.

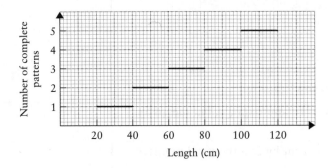

a   If 1.2 m of material is bought, how many complete patterns will there be?

b   A skirt is to be made with 3 complete patterns plus an allowance of 12 cm for hem and waist band.
What is the shortest length of material which could be bought?

3   The time a company allows its employees for lunch depends on their position in the company. The graph shows the amount of time allowed according to monthly salary.

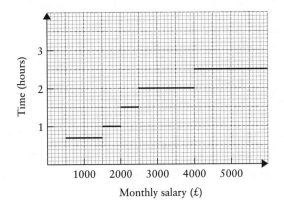

a   How long would the company allow an employee earning £2400 per month?

b   An employee is allowed a lunch break of 2 hours. What is the minimum salary earned?

4   The cost of sending an international fax, according to the time taken, is shown on the graph below.

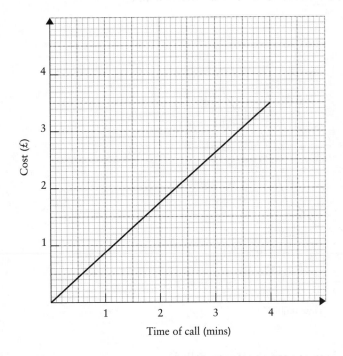

a   What is the cost of sending a fax which takes $2\frac{1}{2}$ minutes?

b   If a fax cost £1.10 to send, how long did it take?

5   The length of time for which a chicken should be cooked depends on the weight of the chicken, as shown on the graph below.

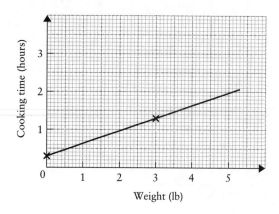

a   For how long should a chicken weighing 4 lb be cooked?

b   A chicken weighing $2\frac{3}{4}$ lb was cooked for 50 minutes. Was this long enough?

c   Why is it important to cook chickens for the correct length of time?

6   A pharmaceutical company delivers medicines to chemists. The distance travelled by the delivery vans against the time taken was recorded and the results plotted on a graph.

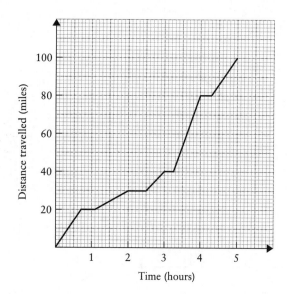

a   If the time taken was 2 hours, how far had the van travelled?

b   One driver had to travel a distance of 70 miles. How long did the journey take?

7 A leisure centre's income depends on the number of visitors, as shown
   on the graph below.

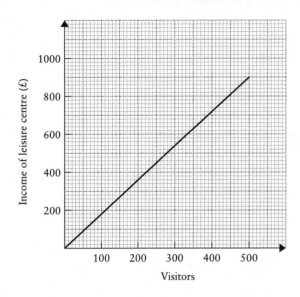

   a How much is the income if the number of visitors is 300?

   b If the income was £810, how many people visited the centre?

8 In a ladies hairdressers, the more skilled the stylist is, the more customers
   she tends to have and the more she is paid.
   The number of customers against weekly pay is shown on the graph
   below.

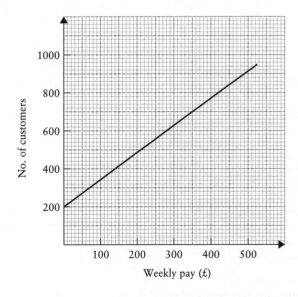

   a One week one of the hairdressers was paid £260. How many
       customers did she have?

   b If a stylist attended to 700 customers, what was her weekly pay, to the
       nearest £10?

9   Generally, the more a customer pays a building firm for the flat roof on an extension, the longer the roof lasts.
The graph shows the expected life of a roof according to the price paid.

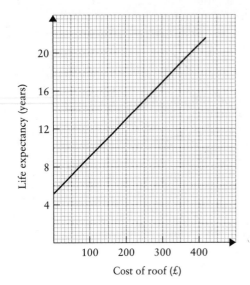

a   For how long might a roof costing £250 be expected to last?

b   For how long might a roof costing £350 be expected to last?

10   The depth of tread on a vehicle's tyres depends on the mileage covered.
A firm regularly checks the tyres of its vehicles and notes the mileage.
The results are shown on the following graph.

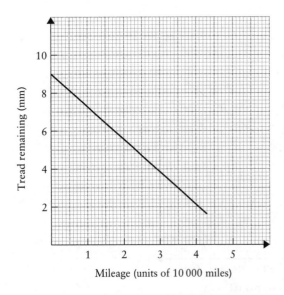

a   If the mileage was 36 000 miles, what was the depth of tread on the tyres?

b   If the depth of tread was 5 mm, what was the mileage covered, to the nearest 1000 miles?

15.3 *Graph plotting*

When plotting graphs a certain procedure should be followed.

1   Choose the scales.   4   Plot the points.

2   Draw the axes.   5   Join the points.

3   Scale the axes.

The information from which the graph is to be drawn is usually given in a table.

EXAMPLE

£1000 is invested in a savings account for 5 years. The amount in the account at the end of each year is shown on the table:

Number of years (x)	0	1	2	3	4	5
Amount in £ (y)	1000	1100	1210	1331	1464	1610

Plot the graph and find

a   the amount in the account after $2\frac{1}{2}$ years

b   the length of time for which the money must be invested to amount to £1500.

1   Choose the scales:

 (i)   Find the range of values for each axis.

    On the horizontal axis the range is 5.
    On the vertical axis the values range from 1000 to 1610, i.e. the range is 610.

 (ii)   Count the number of large squares in each direction on the graph paper.

    The graph paper provided here has 18 large squares in both directions and a grid with five small divisions in each large division.

    The aim is to draw as large a graph as possible, but the scale must be easy to read.

    Taking the 18 large division width for the horizontal axis, the range of 5 does not divide exactly into 18.

    A convenient scale would be 2 large divisions representing 1 year. On the vertical axis, a range of 610 does not divide into 18 large divisions, but 14 cm is divisible by 700. There will be little wastage of space if a scale of 2 large divisions representing £100 is chosen. The axis is scaled from £1000 to £1700.

2   Draw the axes.

Once the scales have been chosen, there is no problem in placing the axes.

The origin can be placed 2 large divisions from the left and 2 large divisions from the bottom edges of the graph paper.

This allows space for labelling the axes. Label the origin O.

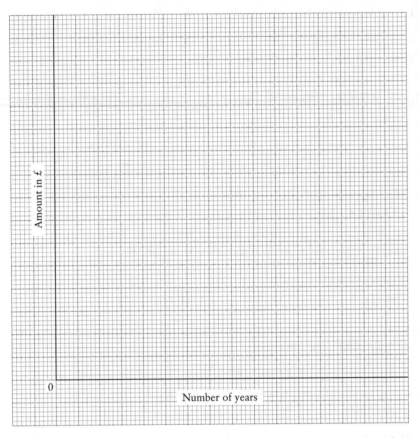

3   Scale the axes: ·

Mark the position of each year along the horizontal axis as shown on the following graph.

Mark the position of each £100 along the vertical axis as shown.

4 Plot the points.

Plot the six points given as explained on p. 144.

5 Join the points.

The points are joined with a **smooth** curve.

Trace through the points with a pencil, but without touching the paper, to find the shape of the curve. When you are satisfied that the path of the curve is smooth, draw the curve through the points in one movement.

If the values of the coordinates have been rounded, the line may not pass exactly through each point.

6 To find the required information draw appropriate lines on the graph (see p. 144) and read off the values:

a £1270   **b** 4.3 years

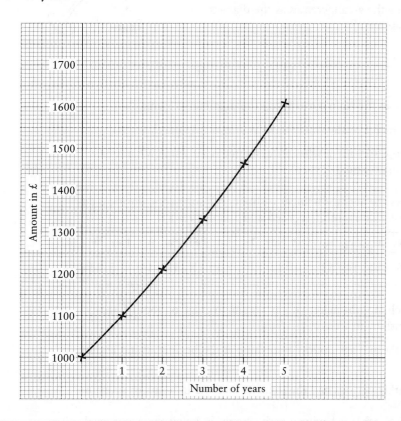

EXERCISE 15.2

In the following questions, you are given the information connecting the two variables in a table. In each case plot the points and join them with a smooth curve.

1 Mrs Lister weighed herself now and again through the year. After one Christmas she found her weight was over $10\frac{1}{2}$ stone.

She joined Weightwatchers and was determined to reach her target weight of $8\frac{1}{2}$ stone before the next Christmas.

The table shows her weight in stones and pounds at the beginning of each given month (1 stone = 14 lb.)

Month/year	Jan/98	May/98	Sep/98	Jan/99	May/99	Sep/99
Weight in st–lb	9–2	9–12$\frac{1}{2}$	10–6	10–8	10–4	9–6

a What weight was Mrs Lister in August 1998?

b What was the heaviest weight she reached?

c During which months did she weigh 9 stone 7 lb?

d Do you think she would have reached her target weight before Christmas 1999?

2   While at a party, William spills a glass of red wine over the table cloth.

The stain spreads rapidly in a circular shape and the table shows how the area increases as the diameter of the stain increases.

Diameter (cm)	0	2	4	6	8	10
Area (cm²)	0	3	12	27	48	75

a   What area does the stain cover when the diameter is 9 cm?

b   What is the radius of the stain when its area is 50 sq cm?

c   The stain stops spreading when its diameter is 10.9 cm. What area does the stain eventually cover?

3   The table shows the average number of hours the sun shone during a day in the middle of each month, recorded at a Spanish resort.

	Jun	Jul	Aug	Sep	Oct	Nov	Dec	Jan	Feb	Mar	Apr	May	Jun
Hours of sunshine	16	15.5	14	12	10	8.5	8	8.5	10	12	14	15.5	16

a   During which months might you expect an average of about $10\frac{1}{2}$ hours of sunshine in a day?

b   What were the average hours of sunshine at the beginning and end of May?

c   Which monthly periods had the smallest increase in hours of sunshine?

4   One day when Heather is having a bath, she notices that the water level is gradually decreasing and realises that the plug is leaking. When she started her bath the depth of water was 300 mm. Plot the points given in the table below to show the depth of water remaining at a given time.

Time (in minutes)	0	1	2	3	4	5
Depth of water (in mm)	300	110	41	15	5.5	2.0

a   What was the depth of the water after $2\frac{1}{2}$ min?

b   After how long was the bath half empty?

c   What was the drop in water level after $1\frac{1}{2}$ min?

5   Two young children have a swing in the garden. On one particular day it is Lucy's turn on the swing and Tony pulls the swing back through an arc of 100 cm and then releases it.

100cm

The table shows the position of the swing (distances are measured along the arc of the swing) at different times during its motion.

Time (in seconds)	0	0.2	0.4	0.6	0.8	1.0	1.2	1.4
Distance (in cm)	100	89	57	13	−34	−74	−97	−98
Time (in seconds)	1.6	1.8	2.0	2.2	2.4	2.6	2.8	3.0
Distance (in cm)	−77	−38	9	54	87	100	91	61

a How long does it take for one complete swing?

b In what position is the swing after 0.7 seconds?

c How long does it take to travel through 50 cm?

d How long does it take to travel through 250 cm?

15.4 *Conversion graphs*

A graph is a very useful means of converting quickly from one quantity to another.

Ranjit is planning a summer holiday in France. He sees in the newspaper that the exchange rate is 10.2 FF = £1, but he wants to be able to compare French prices with prices at home quickly and easily. Before he goes he draws a pocket-size conversion graph which he can keep handy while on holiday.

He knows that:

- A conversion graph is a straight line, so he only needs to plot two points (though a third point is useful as a check).
- Most conversion graphs go through the point (0,0).
- Either variable can be measured along the vertical or horizontal axis.

As Ranjit will mainly be changing from francs to pounds he measures francs along the horizontal axis.

He knows that £1 = 10.2FF and that the graph goes through the origin. He plots these two points. They are very close together so he finds another point further from the origin.

£10 = 102 FF is an easy one to calculate.

He then draws a straight line through the three points.
(If the line does not pass through all the points there is a mistake and the calculations must be checked.)

This is what his graph looks like:

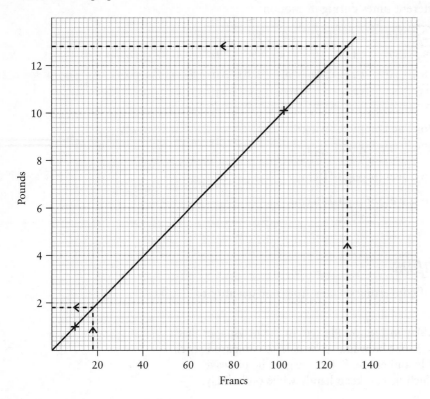

From the graph he can see than a 18-franc bottle of French wine is cheap at less than £1.80 and a meal for two costing 130 francs is about £12.80.

EXERCISE 15.3

1 The equation $F = 1.8C + 32$ converts degrees Celsius to degrees Fahrenheit.
Draw a graph of F against C for values of C up to 40°.

Use your graph to answer the following:

a The temperature of the solution for processing black and white film should be 20 °C. What is this in degrees Fahrenheit?

b The temperature of an office should be between 19.4 °C and 22.8 °C.
Does a temperature of 64 °F comply with the regulations?

c People begin to suffer from hypothermia when the body temperature drops below 95 °F. What is this temperature in °C?

d The temperature on a very hot day in August reached 32 °C.
What was the temperature in °F?

e The factory act requires the temperature of a working area where heavy work is done to be between 12.8 °C and 15.6 °C.

Would the employees be comfortable if the temperature was 58 °F?

2 An artist draws a design for a poster on A4 paper and then enlarges it to A3 size.

Length on A3 = 1.41 × Length on A4

Draw a graph of A3 sizes against A4 for values up to 30 cm.

a The A4 size poster measures 20.7 cm × 29.7cm. What is the size of the A3 poster?

b The caption is to be in letters 2.5 cm high. What height should the letters be in A4 format?

3 An international business which trades with Japan needs to convert from pounds to yen and vice versa.
Draw a conversion graph given that the exchange rate is £1 = 170 yen.

Use your graph to convert:

a 3500 yen to pounds   b £11 to yen.

4 Since 1977, hospitals have recorded weights of babies in kilograms. However, many parents prefer the imperial units of pounds and ounces. Draw a graph to convert kilograms to pounds and ounces and use your graph to find the weight, in pounds and ounces, of a baby weighing:

a 4 kg   **b** 2.75 kg.

5 Five miles is approximately equal to eight kilometres.
Draw a graph to give a rough conversion between miles and kilometres.

a A family on holiday in France sees a sign board on the A10. Convert the distances given on the sign board to miles.

A10	
ORLEANS	106
TOURS	245
POITIERS	350
BORDEAUX	560

b A French family on holiday in Britain travels 64 miles.
How far have they travelled in kilometres?

6 Goods are sent from a factory in Britain to the Gulf. During the journey, the driver discovers that the vehicle's fuel gauge is faulty. He knows how many miles he can travel on a litre of fuel, but in Saudi Arabia the fuel is sold in US gallons. Draw a graph to convert US gallons to litres. (1 US gallon = 3.79 litres.)

a If he puts 25 gallons into the tank, how many litres is this?

b His petrol consumption is 3 miles per litre. How many miles can he expect to travel before he needs more fuel?

15.5 *Cartesian coordinates*

In the early seventeenth century, the French mathematician René Descartes introduced the idea of a grid for locating and plotting points.

Onto this grid, called a **cartesian** graph, are drawn two straight lines at right angles to one another, called the **rectangular axes**.

Usually the axes cross at the **origin**, O, or starting point. The axes are scaled as number lines with positive numbers to the right and above the origin and negative numbers to the left and below the origin.

The position of any point (A, say) can then be described by two numbers: one referring to the horizontal axis *x* and one to the vertical axis *y*.

The two numbers are called the **cartesian coordinates**, after Descartes.

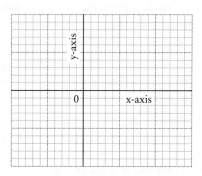

In general, the coordinates are called *x*- and *y*-coordinates, written as (x, y), and are plotted by first counting along the horizontal or *x*-axis and then along the vertical or *y*-axis.

In the diagram opposite A is at the point $(3, -2)$.

It is usual to plot a point on a graph using a cross (+ or ×) or a dot (·).

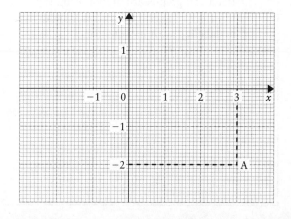

15.6 *Straight-line graphs*

Drawing straight-line graphs

An equation of the form $y = mx + c$ can be represented graphically by a straight line.

To draw a straight line requires **two** points, but it is better to find **three** points as a check.

EXAMPLE

Draw a graph to represent the line $y = 3x - 2$ for values of x from -3 to 3.

1   Choose the scales.

     Choose three values for x between -3 and 3, e.g. -3, 0, 3.
     Calculate the corresponding y-values and write the three pairs of coordinates in a table:

x	-3	0	3
y	-11	-2	7

     The range for y is 18 and for x is 6.
     Suitable scales are 1 large division to 1 unit on the x-axis
                       and 1 large division to 2 units on the y-axis.

2, 3   Draw and scale the axes.

     As the negative values of x equal the positive values, set the y-axis near the centre of the graph paper.

     The x-axis must be drawn above the halfway mark to allow for more negative values of y.

     The axes are scaled in both positive and negative directions.

4, 5   Plot and join the points.

     If several graphs are drawn using the same set of axes, each graph should be labelled with its equation.

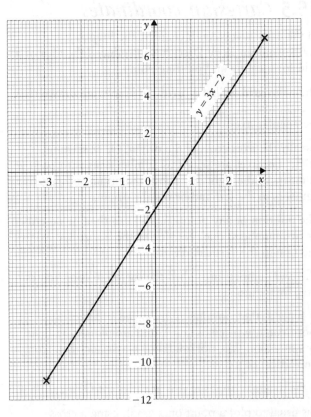

EXERCISE 15.4

Calculate and plot three points for each of the following lines.

Draw the graphs of each set of equations using the same axes.

1 $y = x$
   $y = x + 3$
   $y = x - 1$
   $y = x - 2$

2 $y = 2x$
   $y = 2x + 3$
   $y = 2x - 1$
   $y = 2x - 2$

3 $y = -x$
   $y = -x + 3$
   $y = -x - 1$
   $y = -x - 2$

4 $y = -3x$
   $y = -3x + 2$
   $y = -3x - 1$
   $y = -3x - 3$

5 $y = \frac{1}{2}x$
   $y = \frac{1}{2}x + 2$
   $y = \frac{1}{2}x - 1$
   $y = \frac{1}{2}x - 3$

6 $y = -\frac{1}{2}x$
   $y = -\frac{1}{2}x + 2$
   $y = -\frac{1}{2}x - 1$
   $y = -\frac{1}{2}x - 3$

7 a What do the equations in each set have in common:
      (i) in their algebraic form,
      (ii) in their graphical form?

   b What conclusion can you draw from this?

8 a What do the equations $y = x$, $y = 2x$, $y = -x$, $y = -3x$, $y = \frac{1}{2}x$, and $y = -\frac{1}{2}x$ have in common?

   b What conclusion can you draw from this?

9 What does the constant term on the RHS of an equation tell you about the graph of that line?

10 Compare the graphs in questions 3, 4 and 6. What does a negative coefficient of x tell you about the graph of that line?
   (See p. 125 if you need a reminder about what a 'coefficient' is.)

EXERCISE 15.5

1 An art student needs to frame a series of pictures and photographs for an exhibition. He calculates that, if the framing costs £1.50 per foot, the cost of framing (£C) is given by:

   $$8C = P + 8$$

   where P is the perimeter of a picture in inches. Draw a graph of C against P and use it to find:

   a the cost of framing three pictures with perimeters 28″, 50″ and 42″

   b the size of picture which could be framed for £5.25.

2 The 'golden section' is used in architecture and painting where perfect proportions are required. It is the division of a line so that the ratio of one part of the whole is the same as the ratio of the parts:

   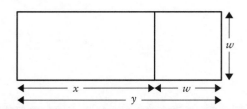

   i.e. $y : x$ is the same as $x : w$.
   An approximate relationship between x and y is given by $y = 1.618x$.
   Draw a graph of this relationship for values of x from 0 to 10, and use it to find approximate values of y, x and w when:

   a $x = 6.2$ cm   b $y = 6.5$ cm.

3 A firm measures the effectiveness of its advertising campaign by calculating the return on money invested as:

   $$\text{Return} = \frac{\text{Increase in profit} - \text{Investment}}{\text{Investment}} \times 100$$

   If the money invested was £5000, then

   $$R = \frac{P}{50} - 100$$

   Draw a graph of R against P for values of P up to 5000.

   a What is the return if the profits increased by:
      (i) £7500   (ii) £3000?

   b If a return of 25% is required, what increase in profit must be made?

4   For incomes between £4385 and £5905, the amount of income tax paid per year at single person's rate, is given by:

$$T = \tfrac{1}{10}I - 438.5$$

where T is the tax and I is the annual income. Draw a graph of T against I and find:

a   the amount of tax paid by a clerk whose annual income was £5695

b   the amount earned if the tax paid was £150.

5   Estimates of a person's height as an adult can be made from their height at 3 years of age.

If H = adult height, h = height at age 3,

for women $H = 1.73 \times h$
for men $\quad H = 1.87 \times h$

Draw graphs of both lines on the same axes and use your graphs to find:

a   an estimated full height for a woman and a man who were both 95 cm tall at 3 years of age

b   the probable height at 3 years of a man who is 168 cm tall.

6   If I take vigorous exercise, the number of calories I will 'burn up' is given by:

$$C = 59 \times T$$

where C is the number of calories and T(min) is the time.

Draw a graph of C against T and find for how long I will need to exercise if I wish to use up:

a   500 calories   b   250 calories.

7   Delays in aircraft take off times cost travel firms money. A company estimates that an average cost per head for delays is given by:

$$C = 2T - 2$$

where C is the cost per head (£) and T is the time delay (hours).
Draw a graph and estimate:

a   the cost per head for a delay of $7\tfrac{1}{2}$ hours

b   the cost for a party of 250 if the delay is $5\tfrac{1}{4}$ hours

c   the delay if the cost per head has reached £10.

8   An estimate of the taxi fare from an Australian airport into town can be calculated by:

$$C = 2D - 6$$

where C is the cost in \$A and D is the distance in miles.

Draw a graph of C against D for values of D from 0 to 20.

a   Find an estimate of the fare if the distance into town is 14 miles.

b   If the taxi fare was \$A9, find an estimate for the distance to town from the airport.

9   In a factory, iron is smelted and made into nuts, bolts, hinges, etc. The weight of iron produced is related to the volume by:

$$W = 7.9 \times V$$

where W is the weight in kg and V is the volume in litres.

Draw a graph connecting weight and volume and find:

a   the weight of iron products made from a volume of 2500 cc

b   the volume required to produce 10 kg of iron products.

10   In a quality control experiment increasingly heavy weights were hung on springs to test their elasticity.

For springs of the correct elasticity

$$L = 2.5W + 300$$

where L (mm) is the stretched length of a spring and W (kg) is the weight hung on the spring. Draw a graph of L against W and find:

a   the length when the weight is 55 kg

b   the weight which should stretch a spring to a length of 45 cm

c   the unstretched length of a spring.

15.7 *Gradients and intercepts*

All linear (straight-line) equations are of the general form:

$$y = mx + c$$

where m is the gradient of the line and c is the intercept along the y-axis, providing the origin O is at the intersection of the axes.

The **gradient** of a line is the increase in the vertical value for every unit (i.e. 1) increase in the horizontal value.

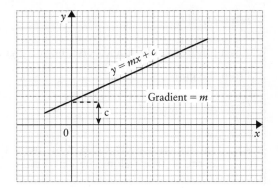

EXAMPLE 1

Find the gradient of the straight line shown on the graph.

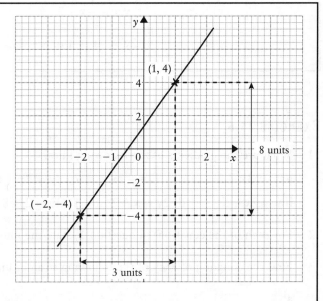

To calculate the gradient of a line:

1 Find two convenient points on the graph (i.e. the x-values should be integers). Convenient points on the graph given would be $(-2, -4)$ and $(1, 4)$.

2 Find the horizontal and vertical differences between the two points.

Horizontal difference $= 1 - (-2)$
$\qquad\qquad\qquad\quad = 3$

Vertical difference $\;\; = 4 - (-4)$
$\qquad\qquad\qquad\quad = 8$

3 Calculate the gradient by $m = \dfrac{\text{Increase in } y\text{-value}}{\text{Increase in } x\text{-value}}$

$\qquad\qquad\qquad\quad = \dfrac{8}{3}$

EXAMPLE 2

Find the equation of the line shown.

1 Gradient of line $= m = \dfrac{\text{Increase in } y\text{-value}}{\text{Increase in } x\text{-value}}$

$\qquad\qquad\quad = \dfrac{1 - 3}{2 - (-2)}$

$\qquad\qquad\quad = \dfrac{-2}{4} = \dfrac{-1}{2}$

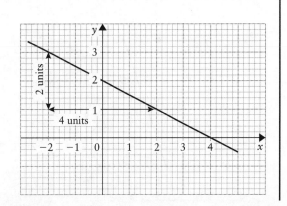

Alternatively,

╱ is a positive gradient and ╲ is a negative gradient

From the graph:

Gradient of line $= m = \dfrac{-2}{4} = \dfrac{-1}{2}$ or -0.5

2   The line crosses the y-axis at the point $(0, 2)$,
     i.e. the intercept along the y-axis is $c = 2$

3   The equation of the line is $y = mx + c$

$$\therefore y = \dfrac{-1}{2}x + 2$$

$$2y = -x + 4 \text{ or } x + 2y = 4$$

EXERCISE 15.6

1   What are the gradients of the following lines?

     a $y = 3x + 2$ **c** $y = 4 - 2x$ **e** $3y = 2x + 6$ **g** $x + y = -2$ **i** $x + 3y = 6$

     b $y = 2x - 5$ **d** $2y = x - 2$ **f** $4y = 2 - 8x$ **h** $2x + y + 4 = 0$

2   For each of the equations in question 1, state the intercept along the y-axis.

3   Find the equation of each of the following straight line graphs:

a

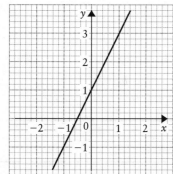

c

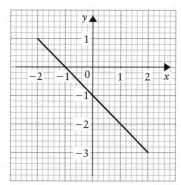

b

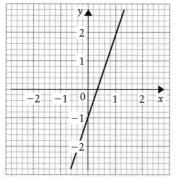

d

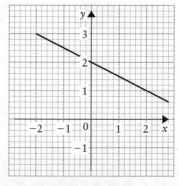

4 Each of the following sketch graphs represents one of the equations:

   a $y = 2x + 1$ **c** $y = 3 - x$ **e** $x = -1$

   b $2y = x$ **d** $y = 2$ **f** $x + y = -1$

   Which is which?

   (i)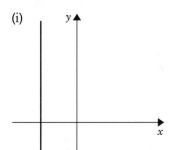

   (iii)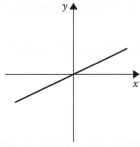

   (v)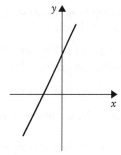

   (ii)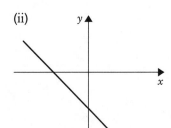

   (iv)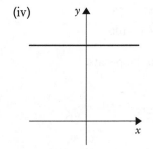

   (vi)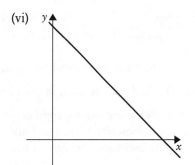

5 The amount of light entering a camera is controlled by the shutter speed and the aperture.

   The table below shows shutter speeds and aperture settings which allow equal amounts of light to the film.

Aperture (A)	$f22$	$f11$	$f5.6$	$f2.8$
Shutter speed (S)	1/66	1/125	1/250	1/500

   Plot the points (A, S) and draw a line to fit the points.

   a What is the equation of your line?

   b What should the shutter speed be for an aperture setting of $f8$?

6 When a retailer tries to sell large amounts of a particular item, the price per item will generally affect the demand, i.e. a lower unit price will often result in an increased demand.
   Plot the points (x, y) given in the table below:

Price per unit (x)	20	15	10
Demand per week (y) (in thousands)	6	10	15

   Draw a line to fit the points.

   a Find an equation for your line.

   b Use your line to predict the demand if the price dropped to 5p.

   c At 5p per item the demand was actually 23 000. Comment on this result.

7 Patietns who cannot take food by mouth are fed by intravenous drips which the nurse sets to deliver the required number of drips per minute. The doctor's prescription states the quantity
(Q ml) to be given per hour.

The setting for the drip feed (D) is 15 drops per minute when the prescription requires 60 ml per hour.
The drip is set at 20 drops per minute when the quantity prescribed is 80 ml per hour.

Draw axes of D against Q and plot two points to represent the information given.

Draw a line through the points.

What is the equation of your line?

8 The table below shows the pulse rates for healthy people of different ages taking exercise.

Age	20	25	30	35	40	45	50
Pulse rate	120	117	115	110	108	105	100

a Plot the points and fit a straight line to the points.

b Find the equation of your line.

c What are the appropriate pulse rates for:
   (i) someone 55 years of age
   (ii) someone 18 years of age?

9 If you screw through thin sheet metal, a pilot hole is required. (A pilot hole is an initial hole which is smaller than the diameter of the screw.) The drill size required for the pilot hole is given on the table below for different screw sizes.

Screw gauge	4	6	8	10
Pilot drill size (mm)	2.0	2.5	3.0	3.5

Draw a graph of drill size against screw size.

a Find the equation of your line.

b Use your equation to find the drill size for a pilot hole for a screw of size 12.

16 *Geometrical Shapes*

Geometry is one of the oldest branches of mathematics. The name is derived from the Greek words 'ge', meaning earth, and 'metrein', the verb to measure. The Ancient Babylonians, Egyptians and Greeks all contributed to the development of geometry.

16.1 *Lines and angles*

Lines

Lines can be curved or straight.

There are very few straight lines in nature, but much of geometry is concerned with straight lines.

On a flat surface – and most ancient civilisations believed the earth to be flat – a straight line is the shortest distance between two points.

A point marks a position and has no size.

The line below joins the two points A and B:

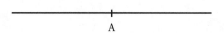

To indicate a point in a line, it is usual to mark the point with a small 'dash':

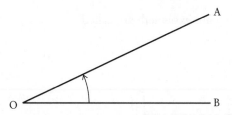

Straight lines are drawn using a ruler, a rule or a straight edge.

Angles

When two straight lines meet they form an angle. The angle between AO and OB is called the angle AOB (or it could be called BOA).

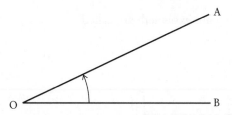

The size of the angle AOB is a measure of how far the line OA has been rotated from a starting position along OB. If we continue to rotate OA in a clockwise direction until it once again lies along OB, it will have been rotated through a full circle or **360 degrees** (also written as **360°**).

The reason there are 360 degrees in a full circle is because the Babylonians believed there were 360 days in the year. An angular measure was derived in order to chart the movements of the stars, which took one year for a full rotation about the earth.

A rotation through half of a circle, or half-turn, is a turn through 180°.

A rotation through a quarter of a circle, or a quarter-turn, is a turn through 90°.

An angle of 90° is usually called a **right angle**.

Right angles occur a great deal in the man-made world. If you look around any room, you will see many examples of right angles.

Draughtsmen use a set square for drawing and checking right angles.

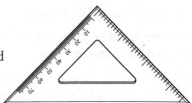

Two lines which intersect at right angles are called **perpendicular lines**. The diagram on the right shows two perpendicular lines.

The special symbol for a right angle has been used in the diagram.

Other types of angle are:

acute angles, of size between 0° and 90°

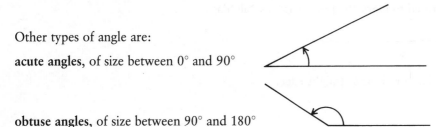

obtuse angles, of size between 90° and 180°

Parallel lines

Lines which do not intersect, no matter how far they are extended, are called **parallel lines**.

There are many examples of parallel lines around us.

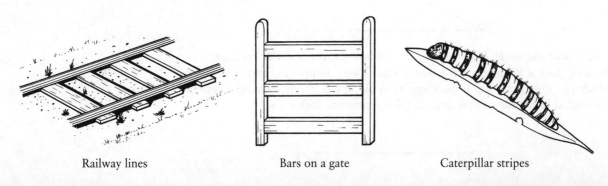

Railway lines   Bars on a gate   Caterpillar stripes

16.2 *Polygons*

Plane figures which are bounded by straight lines are called polygons.

Triangles

A **triangle** is a three-sided polygon.

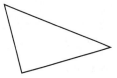

Isosceles triangles

An isosceles triangle has two sides equal in length and the angles opposite these sides equal in size.

In the diagram below, the equal sides are marked with dashes and the equal angles with arcs.

$$AB = AC$$

$$\text{Angle } B = \text{Angle } C$$

which we can also write as

$$\text{Angle } ABC = \text{Angle } ACB$$

$$\text{or} < ABC = < ACB$$

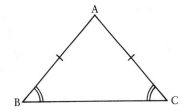

Equilateral triangles

An equilateral triangle has all three sides equal in length and all three angles in size.

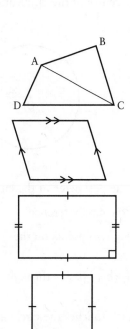

Quadrilaterals

As the name suggests, **quadrilaterals** are four-sided polygons.

A line joining two vertices of a polygon is called a **diagonal**. AC is a diagonal of quadrilateral ABCD.

Some special quadrilaterals are described below:

A **parallelogram** is a quadrilateral which has both pairs of opposite sides parallel.

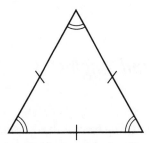

A **rectangle** is a parallelogram which has all its angles of 90°.

A **square** is a rectangle which has four sides of equal length (or a rhombus with angles of 90°).

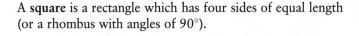

Pentagons

A **pentagon** is a polygon with five sides.

Pentagon

A **hexagon** is a polygon with six sides.

Regular hexagon

A **trapezium** is a quadrilateral which has one pair
of opposite sides parallel.

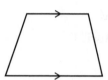

A **regular polygon** has all its sides equal in length and
all its angles equal in size.

16.3 *Circles and angles*

Definitions

A circle is a set of points which are a fixed distance from a given point.
The given point is the **centre** of the circle and the fixed distance
is the **radius**.

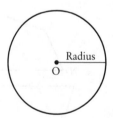

Radius

O

The **circumference** is the perimeter of the circle.

An **arc** is a section of the circumference.

A **chord** is a line joining two points on the
circumference.

A **diameter** is a chord which passes through
the centre.

A **tangent** is a line which touches the circle at
one point only.

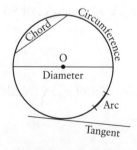

EXERCISE 16.1

In the child's sorting tray below, identify each lettered shape.

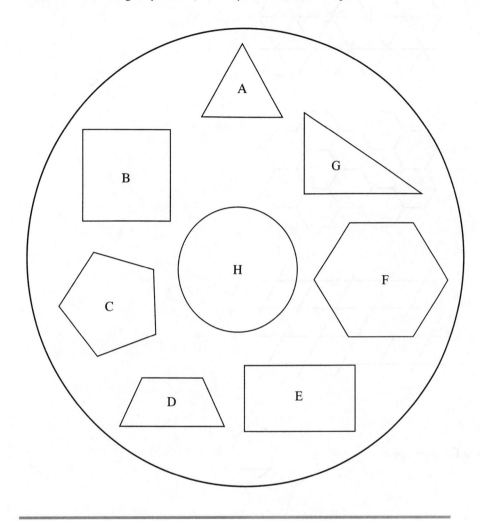

16.4 *Tessellations*

A tessellation is a pattern which when repeated will completely cover a plane without leaving any gaps. The pattern can either be one shape, or a combination of shapes.

Simple shapes which tessellate are:

Squares

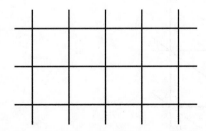

Equilateral triangles

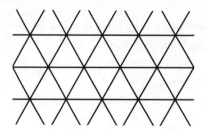

Regular hexagons

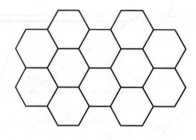

Parallelograms

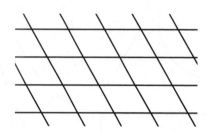

Most shapes, for example regular pentagons, cannot tessellate.

In 1891, a Russian crystallographer named Fedorov showed that there are only 17 different ways in which a basic pattern can be repeated. These repeating patterns are found frequently on dress materials, wallpaper, etc.

Any triangle can be placed with an identical triangle to form a parallelogram. Since parallelograms tessellate, any triangle can be the basis of a tessellation.

Here is an example:

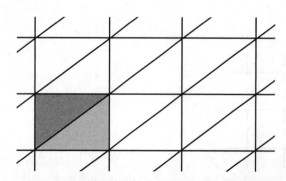

A shape which tessellates need not be regular. Here is an example:

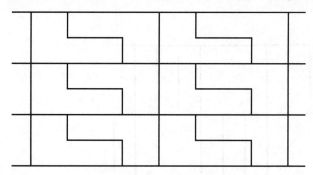

A tessellation can be formed by using two (or more) basic shapes. For example, regular octagons, (polygons with eight sides) and squares form a tessellation. One such pattern is:

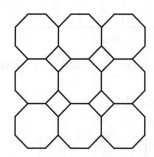

┌─ **EXAMPLE** ─────────────────────────────────
Combine equilateral triangles and squares to form a tessellation.

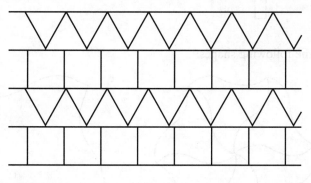

──

EXERCISE 16.2

1 Draw a tessellation based on each of the following shapes:

    a   **b**   **c**

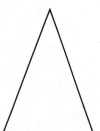
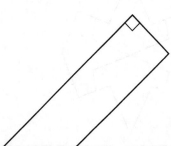
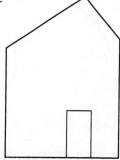

2 Square tiles of side 15 cm and rectangular tiles 5 cm by 15 cm are used to tile a bathroom wall, part of which is shown.

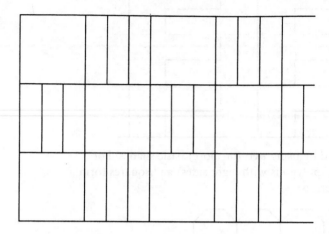

The wall measures 3.3 m by 2.5 m. How many of each type are needed to tile the wall?

3 Which additional shape is needed for this shape to tessellate?

4 Draw a tessellation based on each of the following shapes:

a

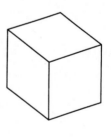

c

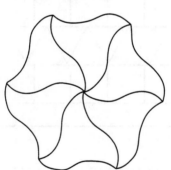

e

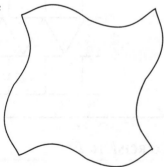

b

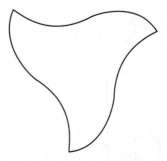

d

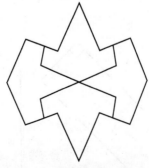

16.5 *2D representation of 3D objects*

It is common to see in newspapers pictures of three-dimensional objects, e.g. boxes, houses, people. These pictures are printed on paper and hence are in two dimensions.

The diagram on the right represents a cuboid. The edges you can see are shown as solid lines and the edges of the cuboid which you cannot see are shown as dotted lines. These diagrams are usually drawn with one of the horizontal directions in the *x* direction (as if it were a graph) with the vertical direction of the body being in the *y* direction. The second horizontal direction is shown at an angle.

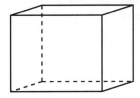

This diagram represents a **cube**.

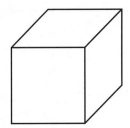

A **cube** is a solid with six square faces (or sides), hence the length, breadth and height of a cube are all equal.

A sphere is drawn as a circle:

Circles are drawn as ovals, and a cylinder is drawn to have two oval ends.

 or r

Similar representations can be shown using isometric paper.

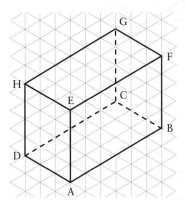

This paper uses a tessellation of equilateral triangles. The lines on the paper go in three directions, each of which represents a dimension. The lines up and down represent the vertical dimension. The other two directions on the isometric paper represent the two horizontal dimensions. Thus on the cuboid shown AB and AD represent the two horizontal dimensions (length and width) and AE is the vertical dimensions (height). The cuboid has a base 6 units by 3 units with a height of 4 units.

EXAMPLE

Draw a triangular prism of length 8 units. The isosceles triangular face has a base of 4 units and a perpendicular height of 4 units.
Note: The base AB is 4 units in length, the length AD is 8 units and the height PQ of the triangular face is 4 units.

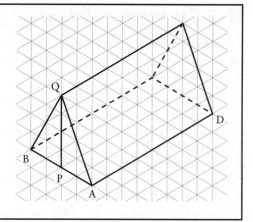

EXERCISE 16.3

Draw two-dimensional representations of:

1 a triangular prism of length 6 units.
   The triangular face is equilateral of side 5 units.

2 a cube of 5 units.

3 a pyramid on a square base of side 4 units.
   The height is 6 units.

4 a house.

5 a triangular prism is drawn on the isometric dotted paper below.

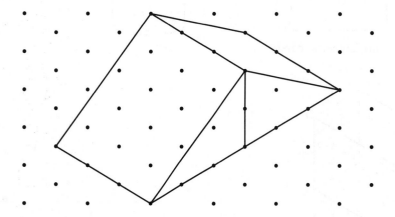

Using a scale factor of 2 draw an enlargement of the triangular prism.   (SEG W94)

17 *Mensuration*

17.1 *Perimeters of polygons*

As we saw in the last unit, a **plane figure** is a two-dimensional shape which is bounded by lines called **sides.**

Here are some examples:

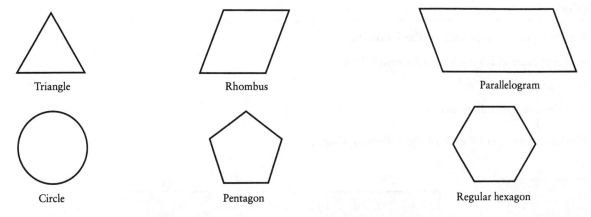

Triangle   Rhombus   Parallelogram

Circle   Pentagon   Regular hexagon

The **perimeter** of a plane figure is the total length of the sides.

EXAMPLE 1

A photograph frame has a metallic surround. The outer and inner perimeters of the surround are edged with gold.

Find the total length of the outer and inner perimeter and hence the length of the gold edging.

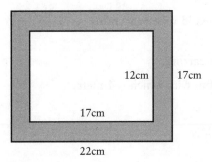

12cm   17cm

17cm

22cm

Length of gold edging = Outer perimeter + Inner perimeter

$$= 2 \times (22 + 17) + 2 \times (17 + 12) \text{ cm}$$
$$= (78 + 58) \text{ cm}$$
$$= 136 \text{ cm}$$

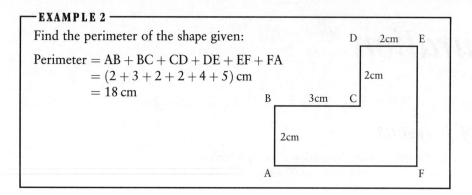

EXAMPLE 2

Find the perimeter of the shape given:

Perimeter = AB + BC + CD + DE + EF + FA
$$= (2 + 3 + 2 + 2 + 4 + 5) \, \text{cm}$$
$$= 18 \, \text{cm}$$

EXERCISE 17.1

1 Find the perimeter of each of the following:

   a a rectangle of length 8 cm and width 3 cm

   b a square of side 7 m

   c a rhombus of side 6 inches.

2 Find the perimeter of each of the following shapes:

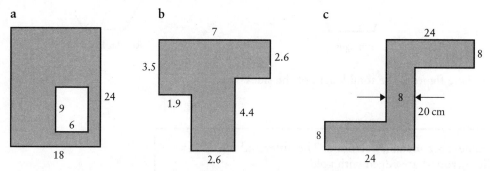

3 A canvas for an oil painting is stretched on a canvas frame 75 cm by 35 cm.

   What is the perimeter of the frame?

4 A craft stall sells earrings which are made from gold wire bent into a rectangle. Each rectangle is 12 mm by 6 mm.

   a How much gold wire is needed for a pair of earrings?

   b How many pairs of earrings can be made from wire which is 1 metre in length?

5 What is the perimeter of a sheet of paper which is:

   a size A4   **b** size A3?

6 A photographic firm supplies cardboard frames for college photographs. The outer measurements of the frame are 25.5 cm wide and 20 cm high and the border is 2.5 cm wide.

   a What are the inside measurements of the frame?

   b What is the total (outer plus inner) perimeter?

7   A child's playpen has sides of length 230 cm by 160 cm.

What is the perimeter of the playpen?

8   The WC in a toilet for the disabled takes up an area of floor space 50 cm wide by 90 cm long. Allowances of 100 cm, in total, on the width and 110 cm on the length are made for wheelchair access.

   a What are the dimensions of the toilet?

   b What is the perimeter of the toilet?

9   A leisure centre marks out its indoor tennis courts with white plastic strip, as shown in the diagram.

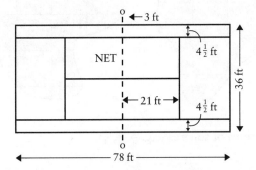

What length of white plastic strip is needed for each tennis court?

10 Shown on the right is the plan of a hotel bedroom. When redecorating, an attractive frieze is pasted, at ceiling height, all round the walls. What length of frieze is needed for this room?

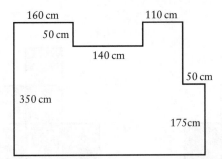

11 A manufacturer of fitted kitchens makes cupboard doors which are 60 cm by 35 cm. The doors are edged with a thin strip of wood. What length of wood is needed for a pair of doors?

12 a A firm makes 1000 piece jigsaw puzzles which are 19 inches by 27 inches.
      What is the perimeter of a completed jigsaw?

   b The firm decides to produce a portable board for its jigsaw puzzles which will be 8 inches wider than the completed puzzle on each side.
      (i) What are the dimensions of the board?
      (ii) What is the perimeter of the board?

17.2 *Area*

Area is a measure of the surface covered by a given shape.

EXAMPLE 1

Consider the shapes below and place them in ascending order according
to their area.

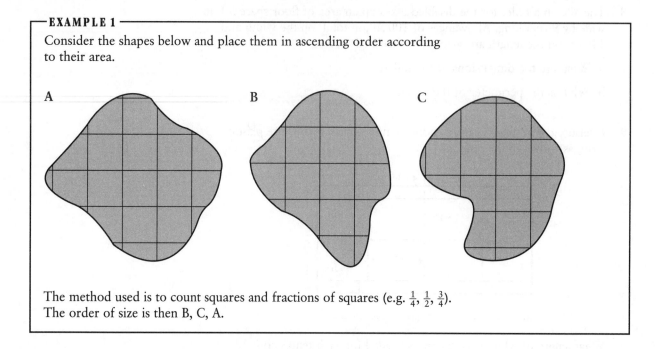

The method used is to count squares and fractions of squares (e.g. $\frac{1}{4}$, $\frac{1}{2}$, $\frac{3}{4}$).
The order of size is then B, C, A.

Figures which have straight sides (polygons) are much easier to compare.

EXAMPLE 2

Consider the following polygons:

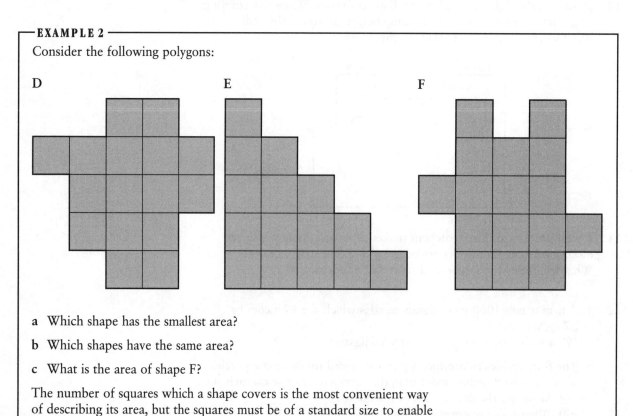

a Which shape has the smallest area?

b Which shapes have the same area?

c What is the area of shape F?

The number of squares which a shape covers is the most convenient way
of describing its area, but the squares must be of a standard size to enable
comparisons to be made.

The square used in the diagrams above is a 1 centimetre square.

The area of a 1 cm square = 1 square centimetre or 1 cm^2.

The area 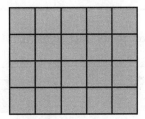 = 1 cm^2.

The answers are: **a** E **b** D and F **c** 16 square centimetres.

The most common measures of an area are based on:

square of side 1 cm: area = 1 square centimetre = 1 cm^2

square of side 1 m: area = 1 square metre = 1 m^2

square of side 1 mm: area = 1 square millimetre = 1 mm^2

The imperial units for area are, 1 square inch = 1 in^2

1 square foot = 1 ft^2

1 square yard = 1 yd^2

Area of rectangle

EXAMPLE 1

What is the area of the rectangle shown?
(Each square represents 1 cm^2.)

The rectangle covers 20 squares, each of area 1 cm^2.

∴ Area of rectangle = 20 cm^2

EXAMPLE 2

What is the area of this rectangle?

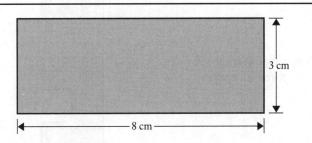

It is not necessary to draw in the 1 cm squares.
It can be seen that
the number of squares fitting along the length = 8
the number of squares fitting along the breadth = 3
the number of squares required for the area = 8 × 3
= 24

∴ Area of the rectangle is 24 cm^2

For a rectangle: **Area = Length × Breadth**
$A = L \times B$

For a square: **Area = Length × Breadth**
$A = L^2$

Some shapes, which are more complicated, can be split up into rectangles in order to find the area.

EXAMPLE 3

Find the area of this shape.

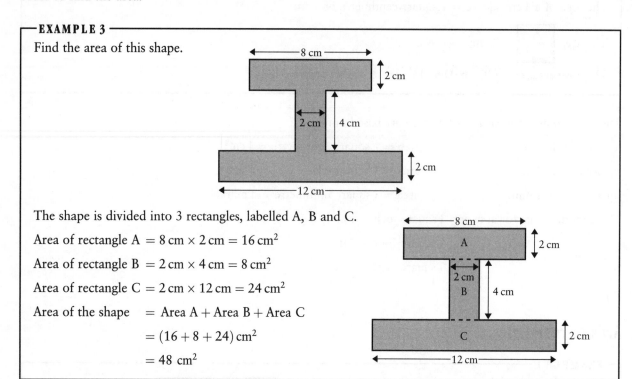

The shape is divided into 3 rectangles, labelled A, B and C.

Area of rectangle A $= 8\,\text{cm} \times 2\,\text{cm} = 16\,\text{cm}^2$

Area of rectangle B $= 2\,\text{cm} \times 4\,\text{cm} = 8\,\text{cm}^2$

Area of rectangle C $= 2\,\text{cm} \times 12\,\text{cm} = 24\,\text{cm}^2$

Area of the shape $\;=\;$ Area A + Area B + Area C

$\qquad\qquad\quad = (16 + 8 + 24)\,\text{cm}^2$

$\qquad\qquad\quad = 48\,\text{cm}^2$

In some cases it is quicker to subtract areas than to add.

EXAMPLE 4

Find the area of this shape.

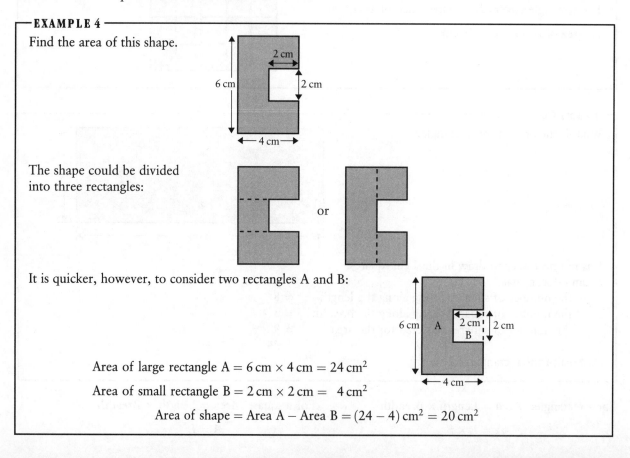

The shape could be divided into three rectangles:

or

It is quicker, however, to consider two rectangles A and B:

Area of large rectangle A $= 6\,\text{cm} \times 4\,\text{cm} = 24\,\text{cm}^2$

Area of small rectangle B $= 2\,\text{cm} \times 2\,\text{cm} = \;\;4\,\text{cm}^2$

Area of shape = Area A − Area B $= (24 - 4)\,\text{cm}^2 = 20\,\text{cm}^2$

EXERCISE 17.2

1   Write down the areas of the following rectangles. (Each square represents 1 cm².)

a 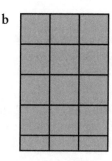   b   c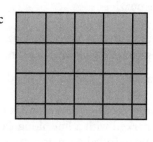

2   Calculate the area of a rectangle with dimensions:

   a 12 cm × 5 cm   **c** 10 cm × 7.5 cm   **e** 22.8 cm × 11.6 cm

   b 15 cm × 20 cm   **d** 17.5 cm × 2.5 cm   **f** 15.5 cm × 15.5 cm.

3 A rectangular piece of land covers an area of 156 m².

   a If its length is 13 m, what is its width?

   b What is its perimeter?

4   A square has its perimeter which is 22 cm long.
    What is the area of the square?

5   A rectangular design is made from 24 panes of coloured glass, each measuring 11.5 cm by 6.5 cm.

   a If the rectangle is at least two panes wide, how many different rectangles can be made?
   State the dimensions of each rectangle.

   b Find: (i) the perimeter   (ii) the area of each of your rectangles.

6   A piece of card, 20 cm square, is used to make a surround for a picture.

   a What size square is cut out if the frame is 4 cm wide?

   b What is the area of the card surround?

7   What is the area of: **a** an A4 sheet of paper   **b** an A5 sheet of paper?

8   What area of card is used in making the photograph frame in question 6 of Exercise 17.1?

9   What area is enclosed by the playpen in question 7 of Exercise 17.1?

10   A doctor's surgery is to have a new sink fitted. A rectangular hole, 40 cm by 30 cm is cut out of a bench top measuring 160 cm by 60 cm.

    What area of bench top remains?

11   The hotel bedroom shown in question 10, Exercise 17.1, is to have a new fitted carpet.

    What area is to be carpeted?

12 Tarquin enjoys doing jigsaw puzzles. He buys the 1000 piece jigsaw and board mentioned in question 12, Exercise 17.1.

When he has completed the puzzle, what is the area of uncovered board surrounding the puzzle?

13 A window manufactured by a double-glazing firm requires 24 panes of glass, each measuring 26.5 cm by 21.5 cm.

What is the total area of glass in the window?

14 A factory produces rectangular steel plates which are 128 cm by 92 cm. The plates are marked with a line along each side, 2 cm in from the edge. Rivet holes are then drilled 4 cm apart along this line.

a What is the perimeter of the plate?

b What is the length of the line marked out for the rivets?

c How many rivets are needed for each plate?

d What is the area of the plate in square metres?

Area of triangle

Draw a rectangle ABCD and mark a point E anywhere along AB.

Join ED and EC.

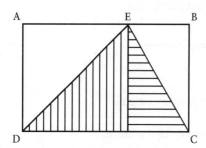

If triangles ADE and BCE are cut out, they can be placed on top of triangle DEC so that they exactly cover triangle DEC.

> Area of triangle DEC = Half the area of rectangle ABCD
> Area of rectangle ABCD = Length DC × Width BC

DC is the base of triangle DEC and BC equals its height.

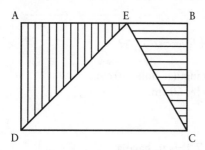

Therefore: **Area of triangle DEC = $\frac{1}{2}$ Base × Height**

$$A = \tfrac{1}{2}bh$$

EXAMPLE 1

Show that the area of the triangle below is $\frac{1}{2}$ Base × Height.

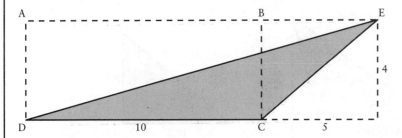

Area of the rectangle ABCD $= 10 \times 4 = 40$

Area of the triangle DEC $\quad = \frac{1}{2}(15 \times 4) - \frac{1}{2}(5 \times 4) = 30 - 10$

$\qquad = 20$

$\qquad = $ Half rectangle ABCD

$\qquad = \frac{1}{2}$ Base × Height

EXAMPLE 2

Find the area of the following:

a

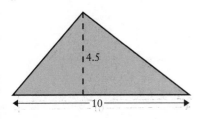

b

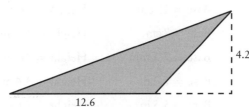

a Area $= \frac{1}{2}bh$

$\quad = \frac{1}{2} \times 10 \times 4.5$

$\quad = 22.5$

b Area $= \frac{1}{2}bh$

$\quad = \frac{1}{2} \times 12.6 \times 4.2$

$\quad = 26.46$

EXAMPLE 3

A triangle has an area of 35 cm^2 and a height of 4 cm.
What is the length of its base?

$\qquad A = \frac{1}{2}bh \qquad\qquad or \qquad\qquad A = \frac{1}{2}bh$

$\qquad 35 = \frac{1}{2} \times b \times 4 \qquad\qquad\qquad b = \frac{2A}{h}$

$\qquad\qquad = 2b \qquad\qquad\qquad\qquad\qquad = \frac{2 \times 35}{4} = 17.5$

$\qquad b = \frac{35}{2} = 17.5$

$\qquad$ Base $= 17.5$ cm $\qquad\qquad\qquad$ Base $= 17.5$ cm

EXERCISE 17.3

1 Find the areas of the following triangles:

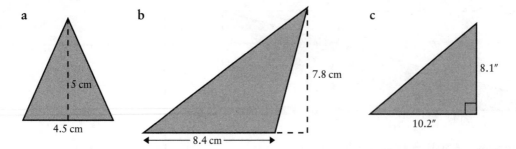

a   5 cm   4.5 cm

b   7.8 cm   8.4 cm

c   8.1″   10.2″

2 Find the area of a triangle with:

a Base = 16 cm, Height = 11 cm   c Base = 10.5 in, Height = 1 ft

b Base = 28 mm, Height = 17.5 mm d Base = 4.6 m, Height = 8.4 m

3 a A triangle has an area of 40 m² and a height of 8 m.
     What is the length of its base?

   b A triangle has a base of length 12 cm and an area of 96 cm².
     What is its height?

4 Calculate the missing dimension in the following triangles:

a Area = 144 cm²   Base = 18 cm   Height = ? cm

b Area = 53 cm²   Base = ? cm   Height = 13 cm

c Area = 45 mm²   Base = 7.5 mm   Height = ? mm

d Area = ? m²   Base = 7.2 m   Height = 3.4 m

e Area = ? in²   Base = 5.5 in   Height = 8.6 in

Area of a parallelogram

A parallelogram is a quadrilateral
(four-sided figure) which has both
pairs of opposite sides parallel.

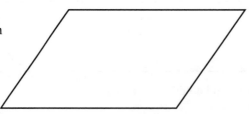

Any parallelogram can be divided into
two identical triangles by drawing
in a diagonal.

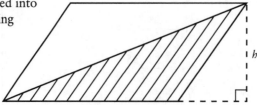

b

Area of the parallelogram = 2 × Area of one triangle

$$A = b \times h$$

EXAMPLE 1

Find the area of a parallelogram with base 12.5 cm and height 8.2 cm.

$$A = b \times h$$

$$= 12.5 \times 8.2 \, \text{cm}^2$$

$$\text{Area} = 102.5 \, \text{cm}^2$$

EXAMPLE 2

A parallelogram has a base of 14 cm and an area of 168 cm^2.
What is the height of the parallelogram?

$$A = b \times h \qquad or \qquad A = b\,h$$

$$168 = 14 \times h \qquad\qquad h = \frac{A}{b}$$

$$h = \frac{168}{14} = 12 \qquad\qquad h = \frac{168}{14} = 12$$

$$\text{Height} = 12 \, \text{cm} \qquad\qquad \text{Height} = 12 \text{cm}$$

EXERCISE 17.4

1 Find the areas of the following parallelograms:

   a Base = 10 cm   Height = 12 cm

   b Base = 12.6 cm   Height = 6 cm

   c Base = 34.7 in   Height = 13 in

   d Base = 1.3 m   Height = 26 cm

   e Base = 19.2 mm   Height = 10.3 cm.

2 Find the missing dimension for the following parallelograms:

   a Area = 24 cm^2 Base = ?   Height = 10 cm

   b Area = 1.3 m^2 Base = 3.9 m   Height = ?

   c Area = ?   Base = 8.4 cm   Height = 16 mm

   d Area = 0.68 m^2 Base = 17 cm   Height = ?

   e Area = 2.4 yd^2 Base = ?   Height = 3 ft.

3 Find the height of a parallelogram which has:

   a area 32 cm^3, base 4 cm   **c** area 42 in^2, base 8 in.
   b area 36 cm^2, base 9 cm

4 Find the base of a parallelogram which has:

   a area 70 cm^2, height 10 cm   **b** area 20 cm^2, height 11.1 cm.

Area of a trapezium

The area of a trapezium is:

$\dfrac{1}{2} \times$ **Sum of parallel sides $\times$ Perpendicular height**

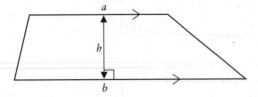

$$\text{Area} = \frac{1}{2}(a+b)h$$

EXAMPLE

Trapezium PQRS has PQ parallel to SR. PQ = 8 cm, SR = 13 cm, and the perpendicular distance from S to PQ is 9 cm.

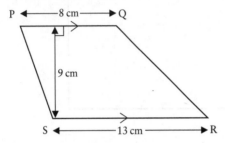

Find area PQRS.

$\text{Area} = \dfrac{1}{2}(13 + 8) \times 9$

$\qquad = \dfrac{1}{2} \times 21 \times 9$ (evaluate inside of bracket first)

$\qquad = 94.5 \text{ cm}^2$

EXERCISE 17.5

1   Find the areas of the following trapeziums.

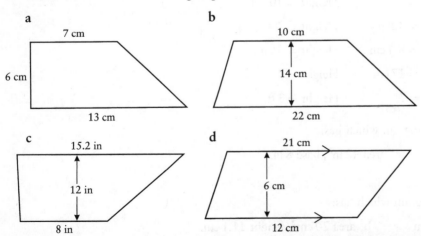

EXERCISE 17.6

1 An architect designs a marble pediment to go above the door of a mansion house. The pediment is triangular in shape with a base length of 2.8 m. The height is a quarter of the length of the base.

What is the area of the pediment?

2 The design opposite is part of a mosaic floor, similar to one in the Grand Master's Palace in Rhodes.

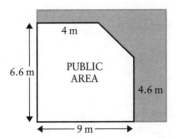

Calculate the area, excluding the surround, covered by each of the four different colours of tiles (shown by the different shading).

3 A building society's new branch has a floor plan as shown in the diagram below.

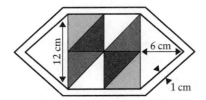

The floor of the public area is to be carpeted.

What area of carpet is required?

4 A stationery business sells envelopes. The net of one of their envelopes is shown in the diagram. The shape is cut out of paper and is then folded along the dotted lines.

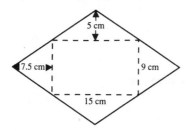

What area of paper is used for each envelope?

5 The tables at a day nursery have tops which are trapeziums, as shown in the diagram.

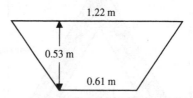

Two tables fit together to form a hexagon.
a What is the area of a single table top?
b What is the area of a hexagonal table top?

6 The same nursery, as in question 5, has a child's sand pit in the garden. The sand pit is 3 m long and 2.5 m wide and is surrounded by a path 0.5 m wide.

What is the area of the path?

7 A hotel lounge has a small stage built at one end for the dance band.

a The shape of the stage is a trapezium, as shown in the diagram. What is the area of the stage?

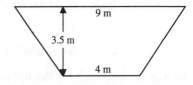

b In front of the stage is a dance floor which is 4 m square. Coffee tables and arm chairs are placed on the remaining floor area. If the hotel lounge is 14 m by 10 m, what area is left on which the hotel can place tables and chairs?

8 The diagram below shows a design for flower beds to be planted out along the promenade of a seaside resort.

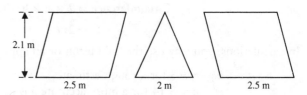

What is the total planting area?

9   Warning triangles are manufactured for a garage to the specifications shown.

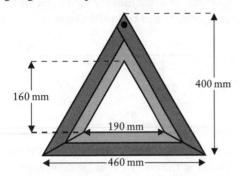

Calculate the surface area of the plastic in the triangle.

10   A carpenter makes a drop-leaf table in walnut. The centre of the table is a 1 m square and the two leaves are trapeziums, as shown in the diagram.

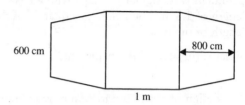

What is the total area of the table top?

17.3 *The circumference and area of a circle*

Circumference of a circle

The **perimeter** of a circle is called the **circumference**.

Take a long piece of thread or thin string and cut off a piece equal to the length of the diameter of the circle on the right.

Cut off a second length equal to the length of the circumference. (You will need to take care when measuring the circumference.)

Compare the two lengths of thread and you should find that the longer piece is just over three times the length of the shorter piece.

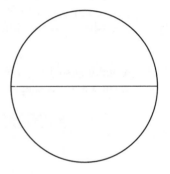

That is:

$$\text{Circumference} \approx 3 \times \text{Diameter}$$

This formula was good enough for the mathematicians of ancient times, but we now have an accurate value for this multiple of the diameter.

The multiple is given the symbol π, the Greek letter for 'p', pronounced 'pi'.

If you have a π button on your calculator, press it and you will see that π =3.141592654.

In fact, the number goes on for ever, but 9 decimal places are adequate for most purposes!

For all circles:

$$\textbf{Circumference} = \pi \times \textbf{Diameter}$$
$$C = \pi d$$

or

$$\textbf{Circumference} = 2 \times \pi \times \textbf{Radius}$$
$$C = 2\pi r$$

In calculations, you may use the 'pi' button or an appropriate approximation,

e.g. $\pi = 3$ for a rough estimate,
$\pi = 3.14$ for a more accurate answer.

You will usually be told in an examination which value of π to use.

EXAMPLE 1

Find the circumference of a circle with radius 6 cm. (Take $\pi = 3.14$.)

$$\text{Circumference} = 2 \times \pi \times r$$
$$= 2 \times 3.14 \times 6 \,\text{cm}$$
$$= 37.68 \,\text{cm}$$

EXAMPLE 2

A circle has a circumference of length 30 m. Find:

a a rough estimate of the diameter
b an estimate of the diameter, correct to 2 d.p.

a For a rough estimate take

$$C \approx 3 \times d$$
$$\therefore d \approx \frac{C}{3} = \frac{30}{3} = 10$$

The diameter is 10 m:

b $$C = \pi \times d$$
$$\therefore d = \frac{C}{\pi} = \frac{30}{3.14} \text{ or } \frac{30}{\pi}$$

and use the π button on your calculator.

The diameter $= 9.55$ m (to 2 d.p.).

EXERCISE 17.7

1 Use the π button on your calculator (or take $\pi = 3.14$) to calculate the missing lengths below. Give your answers correct to 1 d.p.

   a Diameter $= 10$ cm   Radius $= ?$ Circumference $= ?$

   b Diameter $= ?$ Radius $= ?$ Circumference $= 27''$

   c Diameter $= ?$ Radius $= 3.5$ mm   Circumference $= ?$

   d Diameter $= ?$ Radius $= ?$ Circumference $= 51$ cm

   e Diameter $= ?$ Radius $= ?$ Circumference $= 6.12$ m

2 The diameter of a £1 coin is 23 cm.
   What is the length of its circumference, correct to 2 d.p.?

3 The radius of a 1p coin is 5.5 mm.
   What is the length of its circumference in centimetres, correct to 2 d.p.?

4 The Doric columns of the Parthenon in Athens have a height of 35 ft, which is 51 times the diameter of the base.
   What is the circumference of the base of the column?

5   A circular clock face is designed so that the minute hand travels 48 cm in 1 hour and the hour hand travels 27 cm in 12 hours.
What length should the designer make:

   a the minute hand

   b the hour hand?

6   An art shop sells posters which are rolled and packed into cardboard cylinders. The diameter of each cylinder is 7.2 cm.
What is the circumference of the cylinder?

7   A confectioner's decides to tie bows of ribbon around its speciality chocolates for Mother's Day. The chocolates are packed in round boxes which are sold in two sizes.

   a If an allowance of 40 cm is made for tying the bow, what length of ribbon is needed for the 16 cm diameter box? (Give your answer to the nearest cm.)

   b A 70 cm long ribbon (including 38 cm for the bow) is needed for the smaller box of chocolates. What is the diameter of the smaller box, to the nearest centimetre?

8   Amy cycles to keep fit. The wheel of her bicycle has a diameter of 672 mm.

   a What is the circumference of the wheel in centimetres?

   b How many metres has she travelled when the wheels have turned 50 times?

9   An exercise class uses hula hoops made from 290 cm of plastic tubing bent into a circle.

   What is the diameter of a hoop, to the nearest centimetre?

10 Ecuador and Sumatra are on opposite sides of the world.
The radius of the Earth is 6370 km.

   How far is it from Ecuador to Sumatra, travelling along the Equator?

11 A theme park has an aerial railway track around the perimeter of the park. Tourists can travel in carriages to various stations on the track. Sonia and Iain board a carriage at one station and get off at a station which is halfway round the perimeter. They have travelled a distance of 2.5 km.

   How far would they have to walk between the stations, if they could walk straight across the theme park?

12 A rope works produces rope for ship-yards. One of their ropes is 8 cm thick. String is wrapped exactly 9 times around the end of the rope to prevent fraying.

   a What is the circumference of the rope?

   b What length of the string is required for the two ends of a rope?

13 The outer frame of a wrought iron gate requires 548.8 cm of wrought iron. The gate is 82 cm wide.

   What is its overall height?

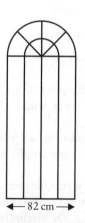

← 82 cm →

Area of a circle

A circle with radius 1 has an area $= \pi$

A circle with radius r has an area $= \pi \times r^2$.

For all circles:

$$A = \pi r^2$$

EXAMPLE 1

A circle is drawn which has a diameter of 6 cm. What is the area of the circle?

$$\text{Diameter} = 6 \text{ cm}$$
$$\text{Radius} = 3 \text{ cm}$$
$$\text{Area} = \pi \times r^2$$
$$= \pi \times 3 \times 3 \text{ cm}^2$$
$$= 28.3 \text{ cm}^2 \text{(to 3 s.f.)}$$

EXAMPLE 2

A circle has an area of 10 m². What is the radius of the circle?

$$\text{Area} = \pi r^2$$
$$\pi \times r^2 = 10$$
$$r^2 = \frac{10}{\pi}$$
$$r = \sqrt{\frac{10}{\pi}} = 1.78 \text{ m (to 3 s.f.)}$$

EXERCISE 17.8

1 Use the π button on your calculator, or take $\pi = 3.14$, to calculate the area of:

a a circle of radius 7.1 cm

b a circle of radius 29.5 in

c a circle of diameter 13.6 mm

d a semicircle of radius 4.9 cm

e a semicircle of diameter 9.28 m

2 By taking an approximate value for π of 3, estimate the length of the radius of a circle with area:

a 27 cm²   b 150 in²   c 108 cm²

d 48 m²   e 300 ft²

3 Calculate the length of the radius, correct to 3 s.f., for each of the circles in question 2 above.

4 A potter's wheel has a diameter of 30 cm or 12 inches.
What is the area of the top surface of the wheel:

a in square centimetres

b in square inches?

5 The pattern shown in the diagram was given to students in Babylonian times to calculate areas. Find the areas of each of the sections labelled **a**, **b** and **c**.

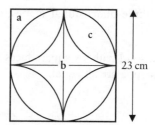

6 Mrs Conway runs a craft stall in the market. One of her lines is lavender bags, which she makes from circles of linen of radius 8 cm.

a What is the area of each circle?

b How many circles can Mrs Conway mark out across the width of a piece of linen if it is 122 cm wide?

7 A Young Enterprise Group at an FE college sets up a business making and selling circular drinks coasters which picture local scenes. Each coaster is made from a square of wood of area 56.25 cm².

   a What is the largest possible diameter of a coaster?

   b What is the largest possible area of a coaster?

8 A flower bed in a rest-home has a radius of 6 m.

   a What is its area?

   b If a rose needs an area of 3 m², approximately how many roses could be planted in the flower bed?

9 A circular table in a geriatric ward is to be recovered with green baize to make a card table. The diameter of the table is 1.5 m and the baize covering costs £6.20 per m².

   What is the cost of the baize covering, to the nearest pound?

10 What is the area of the theme park in question 11, Exercise 17.7, which is enclosed by the railway track?

11 A discotheque has a circular dance floor which covers 50 m².
What is the diameter of the dance floor, correct to 1 d.p.?

12 A glass factory makes circular mirrors.
What surface area has to be 'silvered' if a mirror has a diameter of 48 cm?

13 Mr Swain's firm makes fibre glass fish ponds. Each fish requires a surface area of 1000 cm². If a circular pond is intended to contain 10 fish, what is the smallest radius (correct to the nearest centimetre) that must be used for this pond?

17.4 *Volume*

Volume is a measure of the amount of space which is taken up by a solid shape.

Solids are three-dimensional shapes, i.e. they have length, breadth and height.

A **cube** is a solid with six square faces (or sides), hence the length, breadth and height of a cube are all equal.

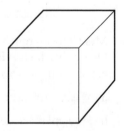

A cube which is 1 cm long, 1 cm wide and 1 cm high has a volume of 1 cubic centimetre (= 1 cm³).

Similarly, the volume of a cube of side 1 metre is 1 cubic metre (= 1 m³).

In imperial units the measures of volume are cubic feet, cubic inches, etc.

A **cuboid** is a solid with six rectangular faces.

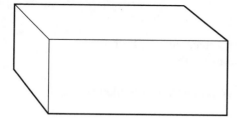

To find the volume of a cuboid we need to find out how many unit cubes it contains.

EXAMPLE

A cuboid which is 6 cm × 4 cm × 3 cm can be divided as shown:

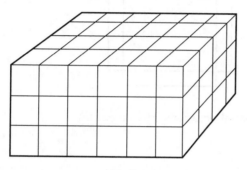

6 one centimetre cubes can be along the length
4 rows (each of 6 cubes) can be fitted into the base $= 6 \times 4$ cubes
3 layers (of 6 × 4 cubes) are needed for the height $= 6 \times 4 \times 3$ cubes
$= 72$ cubes

The volume is therefore 72 cubic centimetres.

Volume of a cuboid = Length × Breadth × Height

$$V = L \times B \times H$$

For a cube, $Length = Breadth = Height$, and

$$V = L^3$$

Exercise 17.9

1 Calculate the volume of the following cuboids:

  a Length = 6 cm   Breadth = 5 cm   Height = 3 cm

  b Length = 3.4 m   Breadth = 2.6 m   Height = 5.8 m

  c Length = 0.7 m   Breadth = 0.6 m   Height = 0.8 m

  d Length = 30 cm   Breadth = 22 cm   Height = 22 mm

  e Length = 2 m   Breadth = 60 cm   Height = 1 m

2 The base of a cuboid has an area of 12 cm². The volume of the cuboid is 40 cm³.

  What is the height of the cuboid?

3 Calculate the volume of a cube of side:

a 8 cm **b** 11 cm **c** 4.1 cm

4 Enrico designs and makes statuary and garden ornaments. A plinth for a statue of Hermes is to be cuboid in shape and measure 56 cm × 60 cm × 66 cm.
What volume of artificial stone mixture will be required for the plinth?

5 A stage set requires a collapsible wall to be made out of polystyrene blocks. Each block measures 42 cm × 28 cm × 10.5 cm and there are 80 blocks in the wall.
What volume of polystyrene is needed to make the wall?

6 What volume of paper is contained in a full box made from the net shown?

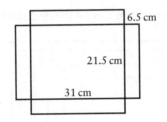

7 **a** Janine makes and decorates cakes for special occasions. Her largest tin is 40 cm square with a height of 9 cm.

What volume of fruit cake would fill the tin?

b The next two sizes of cake tin are 32 cm square by 7 cm high and 24 cm square by 6 cm high.

What volume of cake is there in a wedding cake using all three cake tins?

8 A child at a day nursery has 27 wooden blocks, each a cube of edge 1 inch. She builds one large cube using all the blocks.

a What is the volume of the large cube?

b What is the length of an edge of the large cube?

9 Boxes of toilet rolls are ordered in bulk by the Sundowners Rest Home. Each box measures 46 cm by 23 cm by 24 cm.

How much storage space would be taken up by one dozen boxes?

10 A hotel in the tropics regularly sprays its rooms to kill mosquitoes. Half a fluid ounce of anti-mosquito liquid, when diluted, sprays a volume of 15 m³.

How many fluid ounces of liquid are required to spray a room 7 m × 5.5 m × 3 m?

11 A dining room in an hotel in Spain is air-conditioned. The dining room is 32 m by 18 m by 3.8 m high. The air needs to be changed every 20 minutes.

What volume of air per minute does the air conditioning unit supply?

12   Delicate dental equipment is packed into boxes full of polystyrene beads for protection. The boxes are 40 cm by 15 cm by 12 cm, and the dental equipment occupies a volume of 3500 cm³.

What volume of polystyrene is needed for each box?

13   A microwave is manufactured with an oven capacity of 0.8 cubic feet. The oven is 16 inches wide and 8 inches high.

What is the depth of the oven?

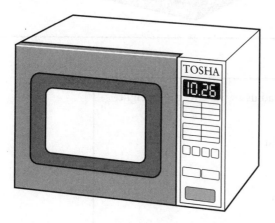

Volume of a prism

A **prism** is a solid which has a constant cross-section (i.e. the cross-section of the top is exactly the same as the cross-section of the base).

Some common prisms are:

(i) a **cylinder** (with a cross-section which is a circle)

(ii) a **triangular prism**

(iii) a **rectangular prism** or cuboid

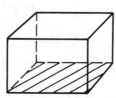

For a prism:

   Volume = Area of cross − section × Height

For a cylinder:

   Volume = Area of circle × Height

   $V = \pi r^2 h$

---**EXAMPLE 1**---

A Toblerone packet is a triangular prism.
The triangular cross-section has an area of 2.25 cm² and the length of the packet is 16.8 cm.
What is the volume of the Toblerone packet?

Volume = Area of cross-section × Length

$$= 2.25 \text{ cm}^2 \times 16.8 \text{ cm}$$

$$= 37.8 \text{ cm}^3$$

---**EXAMPLE 2**---

Find the volume of a cylinder with a base radius of 3.5 cm and a height of 8 cm.

Volume of cylinder = Area of base × Height

$$= \pi r^2 h$$

$$= \pi \times 3.5 \times 3.5 \times 8 \text{ cm}^3$$

$$= 307.9 \text{ cm}^3$$

---**EXAMPLE 3**---

Find the volume of a block of wood of length 12 cm which has a constant cross-section as shown in the diagram.

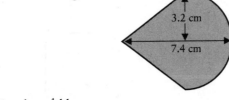

3.2 cm

7.4 cm

$$\text{Area of triangle} = \tfrac{1}{2}bh$$

$$= \tfrac{1}{2} \times 6.4 \times 4.2 \text{ cm}^2$$

$$= 13.44 \text{ cm}^2$$

$$\text{Area of semicircle} = \tfrac{1}{2}\pi r^2$$

$$= \tfrac{1}{2} \times \pi \times (3.2)^2 \text{ cm}^2$$

$$= 16.08 \text{ cm}^2$$

$$\text{Area of cross-section} = 13.44 + 16.08 \text{ cm}^2$$

$$= 29.52 \text{ cm}^2$$

$$\text{Volume} = \text{Area of cross-section} \times \text{Height}$$

$$= 29.52 \times 12 \text{ cm}^3$$

$$= 354 \text{ cm}^3$$

EXERCISE 17.10

1 Calculate the volume of a cylinder with:

    a Radius = 4 cm   Height = 12 cm

    b Radius = 9 cm   Height = 12 cm

    c Diameter = 14 in   Height = 11 in

    d Diameter = 8.4 cm   Length = 7 cm.

2 Find the volume of the following solids which have a length as given and a uniform cross-section as shown in the diagram.

    a Length = 15 cm

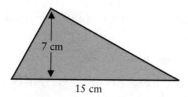

    b Length = 5 cm   **c** Length = 10.5 cm

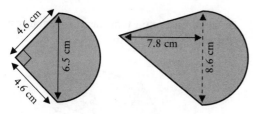

3 A greenhouse is 10 m long and has a cross-section which is a square of side 5 m on top of which is a triangle, as shown in the diagram.

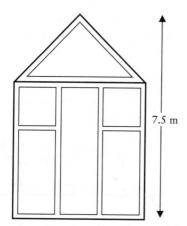

The overall height of the greenhouse is 7.5 m. Calculate the volume of air inside the greenhouse.

4 A tunnel is excavated from a hillside. The length of the tunnel is 300 m and its cross-section is as shown:

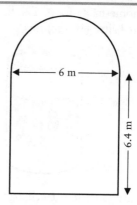

Calculate the volume of earth which is removed to make the tunnel.

5 A glassblower makes triangular prisms of crystal for chandeliers.
Each prism has a cross-section as shown in the diagram and a length of 9 cm.

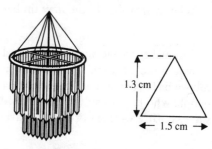

    a Calculate the volume of glass in one crystal.

    b Calculate the total volume of glass required for a chandelier with 54 crystals.

6 Clay pots for the garden have an internal diameter of 30 cm and an internal height of 28 cm.

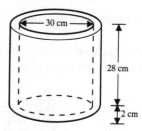

    a What volume of soil will a pot hold? The thickness of the clay is 2 cm.

    b What is the external diameter of a pot?

    c What is the external height of a pot?

    d Find the external volume and hence the volume of clay used in making the pot.

7   Mrs Andrews has a small business making and
selling home-made food. The home-made soup
is sold in $\frac{1}{2}$ litre (500 cc) tins.

Mrs Andrews decides to change the shape of
the tin while keeping the capacity the same.

a   She decides on a height of 12 cm.
What diameter should she order for the new
tins?

b   She decides to have another tin which is
broader than its height and orders a diameter
of 12 cm.
What height should the new tin be?

8   A firm makes wedge-shaped foam cushions, as
shown in the diagram. These are designed to
relieve back pain and are particularly useful for
people who have to sit for long periods of time,
such as office workers or people travelling.

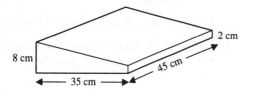

What volume of foam is used in each cushion?

9   A house needs to be adapted for wheelchair
access.
Concrete ramps are to be build outside the
front and back door, as shown.

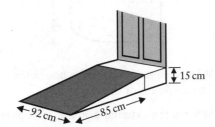

a   What is the volume of one ramp?
b   What volume of concrete is required for the
ramps?

10   A pharmacist stocks oxygen
cylinders for customers who
have breathing problems.
The shape of the container
is a cylinder on top of which
is a hemisphere. The overall
height of a container is 120 cm
and the diameter is 20 cm.
The volume of a hemisphere
is given by $V = \frac{2}{3}\pi r^3$, where
r is the radius of the
hemisphere.

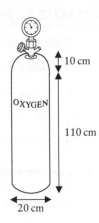

a   Calculate the volume of the hemisphere.

b   Calculate the volume of the cylindrical
section.

c   What is the total volume of the container?

d   What is the capacity of the oxygen cylinder?
($1000\text{ cm}^3 = 1$ litre.)

11   A small mountain tent has the dimensions
shown in the diagram.

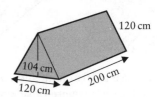

a   Calculate the volume of the space inside the
tent.

b   Calculate the area of canvas used in making
the tent, including the base.

12   A charter air company gives canvas flight bags
to its business-class customers.

The bags are cylindrical in shape, as shown in
the diagram. They have a length of 60 cm and a
diameter of 30 cm.

a   Calculate the capacity of a bag to the nearest
100 cm^3.

b   What is the bag's capacity to the nearest
0.01 m^3?

13 A firm manufactures two sizes of cocoa tin. The height of the larger tin is 10 cm and its diameter is 4.46 cm.

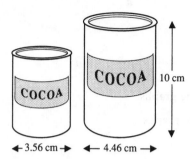

a What is the volume of the tin?
The smaller tin has a diameter of 3.56 cm and a volume of 79.6 cm³.

b What is the height of the smaller tin to the nearest cm?

14 A section of metal pipe has an outer diameter of 5 cm and the metal is 3 mm thick. The section of pipe is 18 cm long.

a What is the internal diameter of the pipe, in cm?

b What is the area of metal in the cross-section of the pipe?

c What volume of metal was used in making this section of pipe?

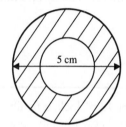

18 *Time and Travel Graphs*

18.1 *Distance–time graphs*

Graphs which connect distance and time are called distance–time graphs.

Graphs which connect velocity and time are called velocity–time graphs.

---EXAMPLE---

One Sunday at 12 o'clock, a family set out for a picnic at a well-known beauty spot, 25 miles from their home.

They travelled at a steady speed and arrived at their destination at 12.45 pm.

After $3\frac{1}{4}$ hours at the picnic spot they set off for home.

Unfortunately the traffic was very heavy and they only managed to average 20 mph.

The family's day can be represented by a 'travel graph' which measures distance from home along the vertical axis and time along the horizontal axis.

The vertical axis is scaled from 0 to 25 miles and the horizontal axis from 12 noon to 6.00 pm.

At 12 noon they were at 0 miles (home) and at 12.45 pm they were at 25 miles (the picnic spot). These two points are plotted and the line joining them represents the family's outward journey.

For $3\frac{1}{4}$ hours they are not travelling and this is represented by a horizontal line from 12.45 pm to 4.00 pm, 25 miles from home.

If their average speed on the return journey was 20 mph then after 1 hour they were 5 miles from home.

The point (5.00, 5) is plotted and a line is drawn through it to meet the horizontal axis.

The graph is shown in the column opposite.

They arrived home in time for their favourite programme.

Find:

a the time at which they arrived home

b at what times they were 10 miles from home

c their average speed on the outward journey.

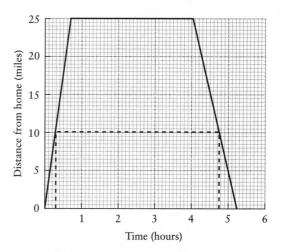

From the graph we can see that:

a they arrived home at 5.15 pm.

b on the outward journey they were 10 miles from home after 0.3 hours, i.e. at 12.18 pm; on the homeward journey they were 10 miles from home after 4.75 hours, i.e. at 4.45 pm.

c Their average speed on the outward journey is given by

$$\text{Average speed} = \frac{\text{Total distance}}{\text{Total time}} = \frac{25 \text{ miles}}{45 \text{ mins}}$$

$$= \frac{25 \text{ miles}}{0.75 \text{ hours}}$$

$$= 33.3 \text{ mph}$$

EXERCISE 18.1

1   Nessa is invited to stay with her French agent in Nice. Below is Nessa's itinerary for travelling from Calais to Nice along the A6 and a map showing the distances involved.

Arrive Calais   1400   Continental time
Arrive Paris   1700   Dinner stop
Depart Paris   1800
Arrive Valance   0400   Refreshment stop
Depart Valance   0430
Arrive Nice   0800

Draw a travel graph of Nessa's journey and use it to calculate the average speeds, to the nearest km/h, for the three sections of the journey:

a   Calais to Paris,   b   Paris to Valance,

c   Valance to Nice.

2   The graph below represents Mr Phillip's journey to work one morning. The first 10 miles of his journey is through a built-up area and then he joins the motorway. Unfortunately, there has been an accident and he is held up for some time. He leaves the motorway at the next exit and completes his journey on the ordinary roads.

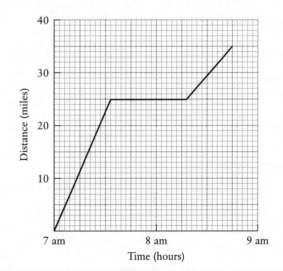

a   How long did the journey through the built-up area take him?

b   What was his average speed on the motorway section of the journey, until he had to stop?

c   For how long was he held up?

d   At what time did he arrive at work?

e   How far did he travel from home to work?

f   What was his average speed for the whole journey?

3   Barry and Ali have been told to cycle to keep fit.

a   They live 5 miles apart and decide to meet at a barn 2 miles from
Barry's house. His friend, Ali, leaves home at 9.00 am and cycles at a
steady speed of 12 mph. Barry does not leave until 10 minutes later.
He arrives at the barn 10 minutes after Ali.

Draw a graph to represent their journeys.
  (i) When did each man arrive at the barn?
  (ii) At what speed did Barry cycle?

b   On another occasion they decide that they will keep cycling towards
each other until they meet.
Ali leaves home at 9.30 am and Barry leaves at 9.35 am, both cycling
at 12 mph.

Draw a graph to find:
  (i) at what time they meet,
  (ii) how far each man will have travelled.

4   Draw a graph to represent the following journey:

Susan left home at 10.00 am and drove to her friend Valerie's house,
15 minutes away, for coffee. Her average speed was 32 mph. The two
friends chatted for 45 minutes and then Susan drove her friend to the
local leisure centre, 2 miles away, arriving at 11.12 am. They spent
1 hour 24 minutes swimming. Then Susan drove home, dropping Valerie
off on the way. Her average speed for the return journey was 25 mph.

a   How far did she drive to her friend's house?

b   At what time did they leave Valerie's house?

c   At what time did Susan arrive home?

5   Roy delivers spare parts to garages in his area.

a   Roy made three deliveries.
  (i) How long did his longest
      delivery take?
  (ii) How long did his shortest
      delivery take?

b   Give a possible explanation for his
third stop.

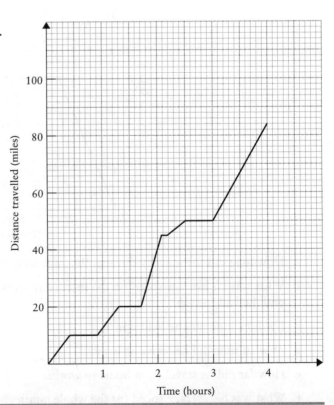

18.2 *Growth and decay*

Another type of function which is connected with time is a growth (or decay) function. Examples of growing functions are bacteria and rabbit populations, the value of an antique car or work of art, compound interests.

A decaying, or shrinking, function becomes smaller as time passes. Examples are: the value of a car that is not antique, the radioactivity of some substances, the value of factory machinery, and the population of an endangered species.

Functions that are getting smaller are said to **depreciate**; functions that are getting larger **appreciate**.

EXAMPLE

The number of bacteria in a piece of cheese doubles every hour.

Assuming there are 100 bacteria present at the beginning, draw a graph to show the number present over the next 6 hours and find:

a the number of bacteria after $2\frac{1}{4}$ hours

b the rate of growth after $4\frac{1}{4}$ hours.

The table of values for time t and number of bacteria n is:

t	0	1	2	3	4	5
n	100	200	400	800	1600	3200

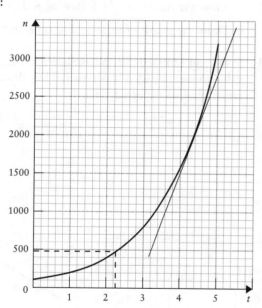

a Read along the dotted line from $t = 2.25$.
After $2\frac{1}{4}$ hours the number of bacteria is 475.

b The rate of growth is the gradient of the tangent at $t = 4\frac{1}{4}$.

$$\text{Rate of growth} = \frac{2800 - 1000}{5 - 3.6} = \frac{1800}{1.4} = 1286 \text{ bacteria per hour}$$

It is not possible to draw curves, or tangents to a curve, with a high degree of accuracy and, therefore, values taken from graphs are only correct to a limited number of significant figures.
By calculation, the rate of growth is 1319 bacteria per hour.
The graphical answer is therefore correct, if given to 2 s.f.,
i.e. 1300 bacteria per hour.

EXERCISE 18.2

1 The spread of moss in a lawn is represented on the graph below.

   a What area of lawn was covered by moss at the beginning?

   b After how long had the area of moss doubled?

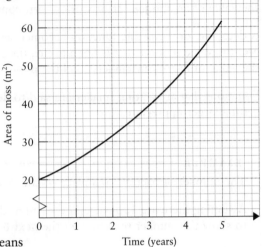

2 A radioactive substance has a *half-life* of one day. This means that at the end of each day the mass of the substance remaining radioactive is half the mass at the beginning of that day.

   a If the mass at the beginning of day 1 was 200 g, draw up a table to show the mass over the following 6 days.

   b Draw the graph of mass against time and find after how long the mass is 70 g.

3 Sasha and Elizabeth buy an antique painting for £1000. They expect its value to increase by 5% per year. They draw a graph to show their estimate of its expected value.

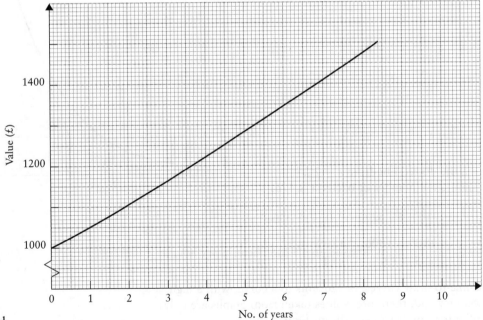

Find:

   a the value which Sasha and Elizabeth expect their painting to be worth after 6 years

   b the rate of increase in the painting's value after 5 years.

4 A sum of £1000 was invested in a building society. The amount of money in the account at the end of each of the following 6 years is shown on the graph.

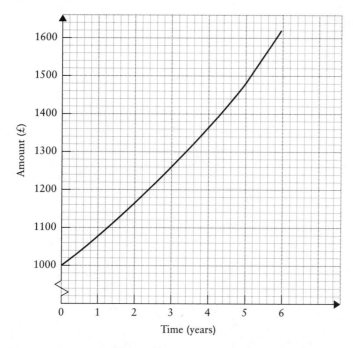

Time (years)

a If no money is withdrawn, how much is in the account after:
(i) $2\frac{1}{2}$ years   (ii) 5 years?

b Is the rate of growth increasing or decreasing? Give a reason for your answer.

5 A tube containing an isotope of radon is implanted in a patient and emits alpha rays. The radon has a half-life of 4 days and is implanted for 8 days. The graph shows the mass of radon during the 8-day period.

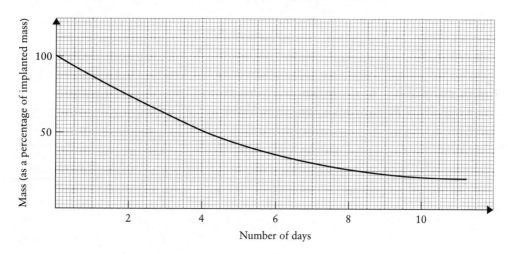

Number of days

Find:
a (i) the mass of radon remaining after 8 days
   (ii) the mass of radon remaining after 3 days

b the rate of decay after 6 days.

6   A company depreciates the value of a CNC lathe every year. Using the reducing balance method, the company gives the value of the lathe at the end of each year.

Time (years)	0	1	2	3	4	5
Value (£)	5000	4000	3200	2560	2048	1638

a   Draw the graph of value V against time t.

b   What is the value of the lathe (to the nearest £10) after $2\frac{1}{2}$ years?

c   What is the rate of depreciation after: (i) 1 year, (ii) 5 years?

7   Zoë is a scientist checking the ages of artefacts by carbon-dating. This is based upon the presence of carbon-14, which has a half-life of 5730 years. The presence of carbon-14 is 0.02% in any living item and it starts decaying on death.
The graph below shows the presence of carbon against time.

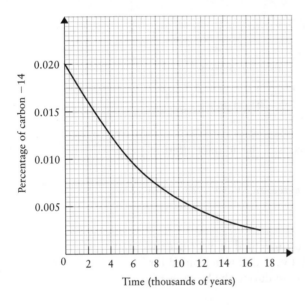

Find:

a   the age of a Sumerian sailboat with 0.012% carbon-14

b   the rate of decay of carbon after 10 000 years.

c   The Chalcolithic period was from 4000–3150 BC. What percentage of carbon-14 would you expect to find in any artefact from this period?

19 *Pythagoras and Trigonometry*

19.1 *Pythagoras' theorem*

The name of Pythagoras must be the most widely recognised of all the famous Greek mathematicians.

The theorem attributed to his name appears in all school geometry and trigonometry textbooks.

He was born in 582BC on the island of Samos. He later lived in Crotona where he founded a secret society known as the Pythagoreans. The main purpose of this 'brotherhood' was political, but they were also interested in mathematics and astronomy. They believed that everything could be explained in terms of numbers and number patterns.

The theorem for which they are best known, concerning the sides of a right-angled triangle, had been known in a limited form for many hundreds of years.

Egyptian surveyors, or rope-stretchers, knew that a triangle with sides of lengths 3, 4 and 5 units always contained a right angle.
They used a rope with 12 equally spaced knots.

The ends could then be joined together and the rope stretched to form a right-angled triangle which could be used for marking out fields after the Nile floods or for building.

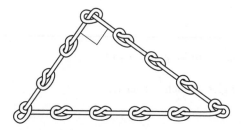

Even before the Egyptians, the Babylonians knew of hundreds more of these triangles.

For example, triangles with sides of 5, 12 and 13 units or 8, 15 and 17 units are always right-angled triangles.

It was Pythagoras, or one of the Pythagoreans, however, who discovered the relationship which connects the sides of these triangles.

Pythagoras' theorem states that in any right-angled triangle:

The square of the hypotenuse is equal to the sum of the squares of the other two sides.

(The **hypotenuse** is the side of a triangle which is opposite to a right angle.)

The theorem can easily be illustrated for the Egyptians' 3, 4, 5 triangle:

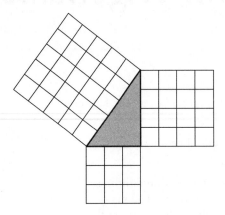

It was about two hundred years later that the theorem was proved, by Euclid when he was writing his textbook of geometry theorems.

For a triangle ABC with sides of length *a*, *b* and *c*, as shown:

$$c^2 = a^2 + b^2$$

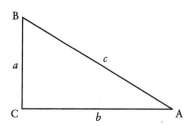

EXAMPLE 1

John is building a garage with a rectangular base, 6.5 m long and 3.4 m wide.
John knows that to ensure he marks out right angles at each corner he must also mark out one of the diagonals.[‡]
Calculate the length of this diagonal.

By Pythagoras' theorem:

$$x^2 = 6.5^2 + 3.4^2$$
$$= 42.25 + 11.56$$
$$= 53.81$$
$$\therefore \quad x = 7.34$$

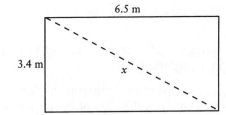

; The diagonal has a length of 7.34 m.

[‡]If the three sides of a triangle satisfy Pythagoras' theorem $(a^2 + b^2 = c^2)$ the angle opposite the largest side is a right angle. Thus when John measures the diagonal in his garage base he knows that he will create a right angle when the diagonal is of the correct length.

EXAMPLE 2

In PQR, R = 90⁸, PQ = 17 in, QR = 10 in. Find PR.

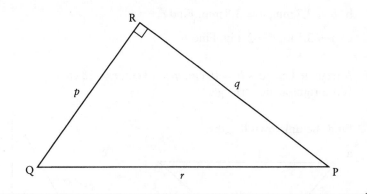

By Pythagoras' theorem:
$$r^2 = p^2 + q^2$$
$$\therefore \quad 17^2 = 10^2 + q^2$$
$$\therefore \quad q^2 = 17^2 - 10^2$$
$$= 189$$
$$\therefore \quad q = \sqrt{189}$$
$$= 13.7$$
$$; \quad \text{PR is 13.7 in.}$$

EXAMPLE 3

In the diagram below, ∠ CAB = ∠ CBD = 90⁸. AC = 8 cm, AB = 6 cm, and CD = 12 cm.

Find BC and BD.

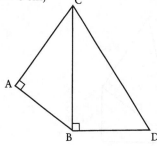

Insert all the known lengths and angles on the diagram.

Two lengths are known in triangle ABC. Therefore use triangle ABC first.

In △ ABC
$$x^2 = 6^2 + 8^2$$
$$= 100$$
$$\therefore \quad x = 10$$

x is 10 cm.

In △ BCD
$$x^2 + y^2 = 12^2$$
$$\therefore \quad 10^2 + y^2 = 12^2$$
$$100 + y^2 = 144$$
$$\therefore \quad y^2 = 144 - 100$$
$$= 44$$
$$\therefore \quad y = \sqrt{44}$$
$$\therefore \quad y = 6.633$$

y is 6.63 cm.

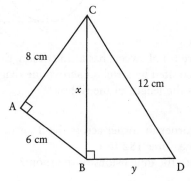

EXERCISE 19.1

1   **a**   Construct a triangle with sides 6 cm, 8 cm, 10 cm and check that it is right-angled by measuring the largest angle.
An accuracy of between 89⁸ and 91⁸ should be obtained.

     b   Measure the two remaining acute angles in the triangle.

2 The following questions refer to the diagram opposite:

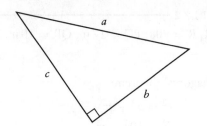

   a $b = 5$ cm, $c = 12$ cm. Find a.

   b $b = 2.7$ mm, $a = 3.8$ mm. Find c.

   c $a = 3.5$ in, $c = 2.1$ in. Find b.

3 A triangle has sides $p = 10$ cm, $q = 17$ cm, $r = 13$ cm.
Is it a right-angled triangle?

4 Find the unknown lengths:

   a

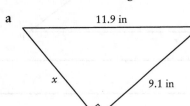

   c

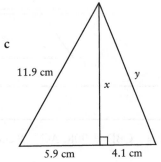

   b

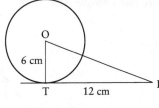

   d

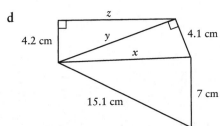

5 Find the length of OP.

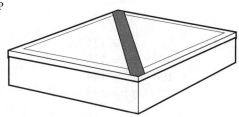

6 A square tin of sweets has a side of length 17 cm.
It is decorated by a ribbon across one diagonal.
What is the length of the ribbon?

7 From corner to corner across the floor of a square
room measures 182 feet.
What are the dimensions of the room?

8 A concrete fence post, TY, is supported by two wire
struts, XY and YZ, of equal length.
Calculate the length of a strut.

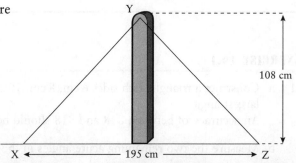

9   A house has a dormer window, as shown in the diagram. Calculate the length of the roof, over the dormer window, from the ridge to the gutter edge.

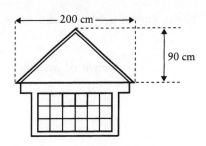

10 A side-view of the dormer window in question 9 is shown here. Calculate how far the window projects from the roof of the house.

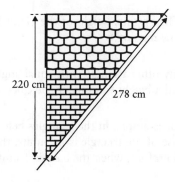

19.2 *Trigonometrical ratios*

The tangent ratio

The word **trigonometry** means triangle measurement.
The surveyors of ancient times were able to find the height of a tall object by comparing its shadow with the shadow of an object (e.g. a stick) of known height.

Because the angle of the Sun's rays was the same for both objects, two similar triangles were formed, in which the lengths of the shadows and the heights were in the same ratio.

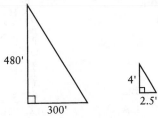

$$\frac{\text{Height of pyramid}}{\text{Length of pyramid's shadow}} = \frac{\text{Height of stick}}{\text{Length of stick's shadow}} = \frac{4.0}{2.5}$$

The unknown height could then be calculated.

$$\text{Height of pyramid} = \frac{4.0}{2.5} \times \text{Length of its shadow}$$

$$= 1.6 \times 300\,\text{ft}$$

$$= 480\,\text{ft}$$

(The original height of the Great Pyramid was 481.4 ft, although 31 feet are now missing.)

Any other triangle with equal angles will also have its sides in the same ratio and a height can quickly be calculated if the ratio is known.

For example, in the triangles below, the angle at the base is 588. When the base of the triangle is 2.5 units, the height of the triangle is 4.0 units. Therefore, when the base is 1 unit the height is 1.6 units.

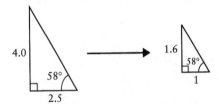

The height of any similar triangle can be found by multiplying the length of its base by 1.6.

Height of tree = 5.5 m × 1.6

$\qquad = 8.8\,\text{m}$

The ratio 1.6 is called the **tangent of 588.**

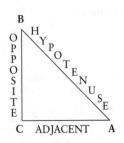

In about 150 BC, a Greek mathematician working in Alexandria, called Hipparchus, realized that a great deal of time could be saved if a table of values for different angles was constructed.

In a triangle ABC, if A is the angle involved in a calculation, the sides are named as shown in the diagram on the right:

The tangent ratio is therefore:

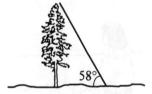

$$\text{Tangent of angle A} = \frac{\text{Side opposite to angle A}}{\text{Side adjacent to angle A}} = \frac{\text{BC}}{\text{CA}}$$

or
$$\text{Tan A} = \frac{\textbf{Opposite}}{\textbf{Adjacent}}$$

EXAMPLE 1

In the triangle shown, find angle A.

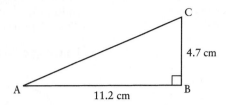

$$\tan A = \frac{\text{Opposite}}{\text{Adjacent}} = \frac{CB}{AB} = \frac{4.7}{11.2}$$

$$= 0.4196428$$

$\angle A = \boxed{\text{INV}} \ \boxed{\text{tan}} \ 0.4196428 \ \left(\text{or} \ \boxed{\text{tan}^{-1}} \ \text{or} \ \boxed{\text{arctan}} \ \text{key}\right)$

$\angle A = 22.88$

EXAMPLE 2

In the triangle below, find PQ.

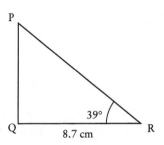

$$\tan R = \frac{\text{Opposite}}{\text{Adjacent}}$$

$$\tan 39° = \frac{PQ}{8.7}$$

$\therefore \quad PQ = \tan 39° \times 8.7$

$$= 7.05 \text{ cm}$$

EXAMPLE 3

In the triangle shown, find XY.

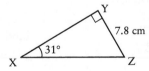

$$\text{Tan } X = \frac{\text{Opposite}}{\text{Adjacent}}$$

$$\text{Tan } 31° = \frac{7.8}{XY}$$

$\text{Tan } 31° \times XY = 7.8 \text{ (multiplying by XY)}$

$$XY = \frac{7.8}{\tan 31°}$$

$$= 13.0 \text{ cm}$$

EXERCISE 19.2

1 Find AB.

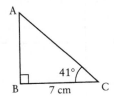

2 Find angle R.

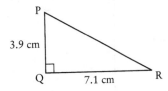

3 Find XY.

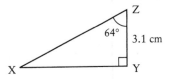

4 Find x and y.

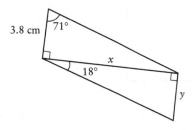

5 ABC is an isosceles triangle with AB = AC.

  a Find the altitude of triangle ABC.

  b Calculate the area of triangle ABC.

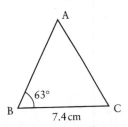

6 In the diagram, PT is a tangent to the circle, centre O, which has a radius of 6.5 cm. PT = 20 cm.

Find angle RST.

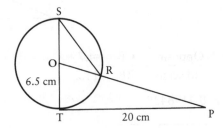

7 A chord of length 4 cm subtends an angle of 408 at O, the centre of the circle.
Find:

  a the distance of the chord from the centre

  b the radius of the circle.

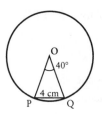

8 CA and CB are tangents to the circle.
Find ∠ ACB.

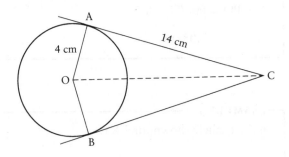

9 Find the length of the chord RQ.

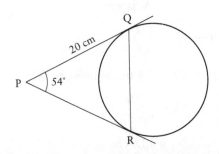

Sine and cosine ratios

The tangent ratio does not involve the hypotenuse, but the sides of a triangle can be paired in two more ways to give ratios which do involve the hypotenuse.

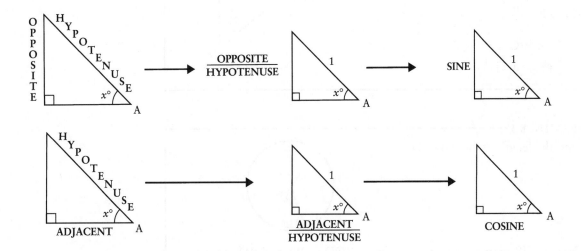

i.e.

$$\text{Sine of angle A} = \frac{\text{Side opposite angle A}}{\text{Hypotenuse}}$$

or

$$\textbf{Sin A} = \frac{\textbf{Opposite}}{\textbf{Hypotenuse}}$$

and

$$\text{Cosine of angle A} = \frac{\text{Side adjacent to angle A}}{\text{Hypotenuse}}$$

or

$$\textbf{Cos A} = \frac{\textbf{Adjacent}}{\textbf{Hypotenuse}}$$

EXAMPLE 1

In the triangle shown, find angle A.

$$\text{Sin A} = \frac{\text{Opposite}}{\text{Hypotenuse}} = \frac{\text{BC}}{\text{AC}} = \frac{4}{10}$$

$$= 0.4$$

Angle A = | INV | | sin | 0.4

$$= 23.68$$

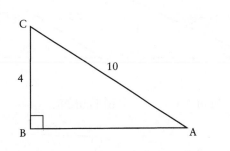

EXAMPLE 2

In the triangle shown, find BC.

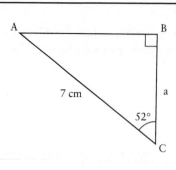

$$\text{Cos C} = \frac{\text{Adjacent}}{\text{Hypotenuse}}$$

$$\text{Cos } 52° = \frac{a}{7}$$

$$a = \text{Cos } 52° \times 7$$

$$BC = 4.31 \text{ cm}$$

EXAMPLE 3

Find the length of the radius OQ.

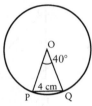

Draw in OR perpendicular to PQ, then ∠ ROQ = 208 and RQ = 2 cm.

$$\text{Sin Y} = \frac{\text{Opposite}}{\text{Hypotenuse}}$$

$$\text{Sin } 20° = \frac{2}{OQ}$$

$$\text{Sin } 20° \times OQ = 2$$

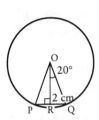

$$OQ = \frac{2}{\text{Sin } 20°} = 5.85 \text{ cm}$$

EXERCISE 19.3

1 a Find PQ. **b Find XY.**   **3 a Find angle C.** **b Find angle R.**

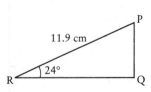 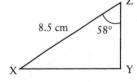   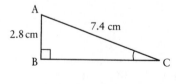 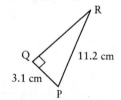

2 a Find AB. **b Find PR.**   **4 a Find angle A.** **b Find angle P.**

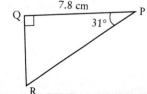 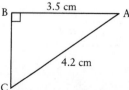

5 Find x and y.

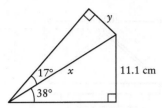

6 Find p and q.

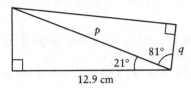

7 Find AC and angle CAD.

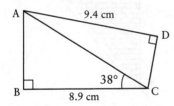

8 Draw in the altitude AD.
Hence find angle BAC.

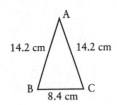

9 PQ and PR are tangents to the circle.
Calculate the length of the chord QR.

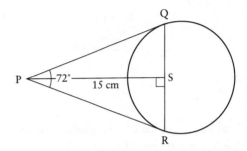

Choosing the ratio to solve a problem

When an angle is to be found in a right-angled triangle, first decide which two sides have been given. Then use the trigonometric ratio which includes these two sides.

When a side is to be found in a right-angled triangle and one angle (other than the right angle) is given, consider which side is given (opposite, adjacent or hypotenuse), and which is the side required. Then use the trigonometric ratio which includes these two sides.

EXERCISE 19.4: MISCELLANEOUS QUESTIONS

1 Find angle X.

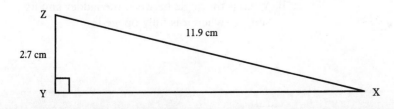

2 Find PQ.

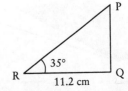

3 Sides AB and AC are equal.
Draw in the altitude AD.
Find AB.

4 Sides AB and DC are parallel.
Find *p* and *q*.

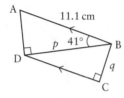

5 A ladder, 3.6 m long, rests against a window sill which is 3.3 m above the ground.
How far from the wall is the foot of the ladder?

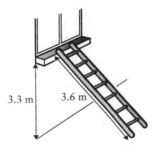

6 A ramp is to be constructed to allow a wheelchair access to a building.

The height of the step into the building is 15 cm.
The slope of the ramp is to have an angle of 108.

a What is the length of the top of the ramp?

b How far from the doorstep will the ramp protrude?

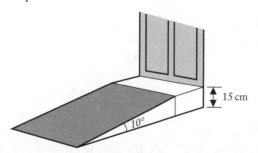

7 A dormer window is shown in the diagram below.

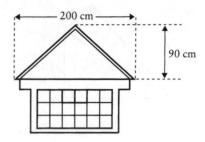

Calculate the pitch of the dormer roof (i.e. the angle the roof makes with the vertical).

8 The diagram shows the side view of the dormer window.
Calculate the pitch of the roof of the house.

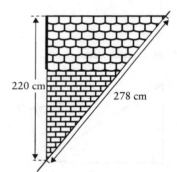

9 A step ladder is 125 cm long. When fully opened the distance between the foot of the ladder and its support is 82 cm.

a How high above the ground is the top of the ladder?

b What is the angle between the ladder and its support when it is fully opened?

19.3 *Bearings*

An instrument for measuring the direction, on the
ground, of one location from another, is called a
compass.

The compass direction is called a **bearing**.

A compass rose, often shown on maps, gives the
bearings in terms of the four cardinal points, north,
south, east and west.

A mariner's compass, or a surveyor's prismatiç
compass, gives a bearing as an angle measured from
north in a clockwise direction.

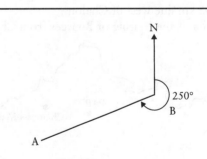

This is the most usual method of giving a bearing, which is always
written as a three-digit number. For example:

SW is 225 8
E   is 090 8
N   is 000 8

To find the bearing of a point B from a point A,

1 Join A and B.

2 Draw in the **north** line at A.

3 Find the angle between north and AB, measured
   clockwise.

4 Record the angle, in degrees, as a three-digit figure.

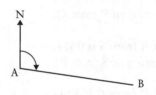

EXAMPLE

In the diagram, the bearing of A from B is 250 8.

Find the bearing of B from A.

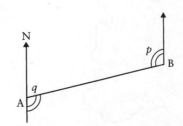

Draw the north line at A.

The bearing of A from B is 250 8.

$$\therefore \quad \text{Angle } p = 360° - 250°$$
$$= 110°$$

$$\therefore \quad \text{Angle } q = 180° - 110°$$
$$= 70°$$

;   The bearing of B from A is 070 8.

EXERCISE 19.5

1 Write the following directions as three-digit bearings:

a East

b SE

c NW

d N 308 W

e S 158 W

2 In each of the following, find the bearing of B from A.

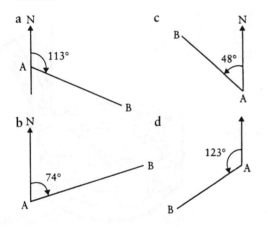

3 The bearing of Q from P is 1928. What is the bearing of P from Q?

4 The bearing of R from S is 0618. What is the bearing of S from R?

5 The bearing of D from C is 3248. What is the bearing of C from D?

6 Paris is 200 km due north of Bourges and 145 km due west of Chalons. What is the bearing of Bourges from Chalons?

7 New Orleans is 360 miles due south of Memphis and Jacksonville is 500 miles due east of New Orleans.

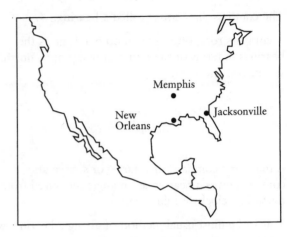

a On what bearing will a plane fly when travelling from Memphis to Jacksonville?

b On what bearing will a plane fly when travelling from Jacksonville to Memphis?

8 A ship leaves harbour, H, on a bearing of 3108. After sailing 3 miles, the ship is due north of a coastal town, T, which is due west of the harbour.
How far from the harbour is the town?

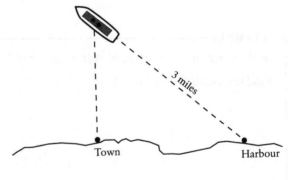

19.4 *Angles of elevation and depression*

If you look at an object, the angle formed between the horizontal and your
line of sight is called

the angle of elevation, if it is above the horizontal,
the angle of depression if it is below the horizontal.

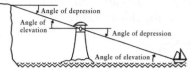

EXAMPLE 1

Bill stands 200 m from a church and measures the angles of elevation of
the top and the bottom of the steeple. These are 198 and 158 as shown
below.

Calculate the height of the steeple.

$$\frac{PR}{200} = \tan 19°$$

$$\therefore \quad PR = 200 \tan 19°$$

$$= 68.86$$

$$\frac{QR}{200} = \tan 15°$$

$$\therefore \quad QR = 200 \tan 15°$$

$$= 53.59$$

$$PQ = PR - QR = (68.86 - 53.59) = 15.27 = 15.3 \text{ (to 3 s.f.)}$$

; The height of the steeple is 15.3 metres.

EXAMPLE 2

A coastguard watching a yacht race sees a yacht at an angle of depression
of 48. He knows that he is 300 ft above sea level.
How far from him is the yacht?

Draw a figure.

From the figure
$$\frac{300}{x} = \tan 4°$$

$$300 = x \tan 4°$$

$$x = \frac{300}{\tan 4°}$$

$$= 4290 \text{ ft}$$

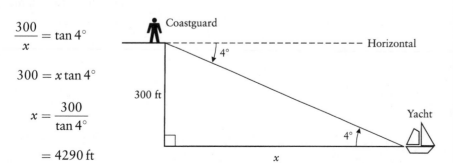

; The distance is 4290 feet.

EXERCISE 19.6

1   From a boat, the angle of elevation of the top of a cliff is 748.
The height of the cliff is known to be 800ft.
How far is the cliff from the boat?

2   The height of a tree is 58 m. Jacky, who is 2 m tall, is 200 m away from the tree on horizontal ground.
What is the angle of elevation of the top of the tree from Jacky's eyes?

3   John sees a plane at an angle of elevation of 3.88.
The plane is 2.1 miles horizontally from John.
What is its height?
Give your answer in feet.
(5280 ft = 1 mile.)

(*Note*. In this type of question, where the distances are large, the height of a person is negligible and can be ignored.)

4   A plane flies horizontally over Sue at a height of 2 miles. When she first sees it, the plane is at an angle of elevation of 748 and it takes 9.2 seconds to pass over her and once again to be at an elevation of 748.

What is its speed? $\left(\text{Speed} = \dfrac{\text{Distance}}{\text{Time}}.\right)$

5   Ken is 30 m from a flagpole. The angle of elevation of its top is 12.48, and the angle of depression of the bottom is 2.18.

How high is the flagpole?

6   In a penalty shoot-out, the player is 36 ft away from the goal mouth, and the goal has height 8 ft. What is the maximum angle of elevation at which the ball can be kicked to go into the goal if it travels in a straight line?

7   A space shuttle is rising at 2000 ft per second. Avril is 2 miles away from the launch pad. What is the angle of elevation of the space shuttle after:

a 2 minutes   b 5 minutes?

8   A balloon is positioned 420 metres above a showground.

Angus is 3 miles away from the showground. What is the angle of elevation of the balloon?
(1 mile = 1.6 kilometres.)

20 *Assignments*

20.1 *Introduction*

It is desirable for all students to obtain their own data by means of individual research. This could involve the student conducting a survey, doing an experiment, or using the Internet. There is little doubt that the enthusiasm with which any student completes an assignment reflects whether they can relate to the specific task which they are undertaking. For example, there is little point in a student producing an assignment on the increase in sales of popcorn unless they are interested either in popcorn or the spread of American culture.

The examples of assignments given are chosen to demonstrate topics related to the student's study which could show the required evidence. Most GNVQ students should be able to show the vast majority of the skills required in 'what you must do' in two substantial assignments, leaving them with only a minority of 'evidence' to supply from their other work. Advanced and Advanced Subsidiary students should be able to show most of these skills in areas associated with the subjects they are studying on their own particular interests.

To enable students to carry out the assignments detailed in this section, we have often supplied some useful data. However, it cannot be emphasised too forcefully that students should find their own data wherever possible. One of the criteria of Application of Number is 'to obtain the relevant information' from **two** different sources and therefore, to demonstrate this skill, the students must obtain their own data in at least one assignment from some other source.

As the number and levels of areas of study are so extensive, only **one** assignment is suggested for each GNVQ area and level. In a number of topics, the assignment is specific to that study – for example, rate of flow from an inverted cone in A/AS Physics or GNVQ Advanced Science. In many cases, however, it is possible to use the assignments described in this book in other areas – for example, the use of the internet in Foundation Information Technology can be used readily in most areas of study at level I.

An example of the way in which an assignment can be developed to show the majority of the evidence needed for level 2 is shown below.

Example for Intermediate Media: Time spent watching television

Survey 20 students, aged 16–20, and 20 adults, aged over 50 years, to discover how much television each person interviewed had watched during the last three days.

Compare the two groups of people and discover any differences or similarities between them.

You should design your assignment so that it shows most of the evidence needed for Level 2 Key Skills, i.e. **N2 1**, **N2 2** and **N2 3**.

For **N2 1**, your assignment should include evidence to show:
  (i) how you chose which information was required
 (ii) how you obtained this information, and
(iii) how you chose the actual people to survey.

For **N2 2** you should write up the calculations used to find the mean, median, mode and range of each set of data. This could include using a formula for the mean and a check on the accuracy of your mean, median and mode.

For **N2 3** you should show your results: (i) as a bar chart for each group, and (ii) as a frequency table for each group.

You should highlight the main points of your findings and explain how the results of your calculations enable you to meet the purpose of the activity, which was 'to compare the two groups of people and discover any differences or similarities between them'.

In the section below on Intermediate level Media, you will find data which could be used by students who were unable to carry out a suitable survey.

An example of the way in which an assignment can be developed to show the majority of the evidence needed for level 3 is shown below.

Example for Advanced Science: Rate of flow from an inverted cone

The standard formula for the rate of flow out of an inverted cone of semivertical angle α is:

$$\frac{8}{15} C_D \, \tan \alpha \sqrt{2gh^5}$$

where C_D is the coefficient of discharge.

Because of the vena contractor phenomenon, the flow can be easily measured.

Use an experiment to confirm that the rate of flow is proportional to $h^{\frac{5}{2}}$ and find C_D.

The requirements for Key Skills level 3 could be satisfied in the method identified below.

N3 1 In your assignment you should show clearly:

(i) how you plan to obtain the information required to confirm the rate of flow,
(ii) how you did obtain the information, and
(iii) why you chose this particular method of obtaining the information.

This could be shown by a write up of the experiment.

N3 2 Your work should include relevant calculations probably plotting the volume leaving the cone at intervals, possibly every second, against $h^{\frac{5}{2}}$. You will need to rearrange the formula to find C_D, and this rearrangement must be shown clearly in your working.

This should be achieved by showing the working which you used, but *not* by simply showing calculator results.

N3 3 In this section you will need to present your findings clearly, identifying why you chose to present your findings in this way. You could use a diagram to explain the experiment and a graph to show the results. Naturally, you must also explain how the results of your calculations relate to the purpose of your task.

In the section on Advanced Science you will find data which could be used by students who were unable to carry out a suitable experiment.

20.2 *Foundation Art and Design: Operating an exhibition*

A group of artists exhibit their work for five weeks in a local hall. To see whether the exhibition is a success, the organisers record the number of visitors who visit the exhibition each week. Their findings are shown in the table below

Week	1	2	3	4	5
Number of visitors	234	581	1213	948	725

a Illustrate this data by means of an appropriate statistical diagram.

b Identify the fluctuations in attendance over the five weeks.

c Find the total number of visitors during the five-week period.

The exhibition was open for six days each week.

d Calculate the mean number of visitors per day.

The artists charge an entrance fee of £1 per person, and the cost of operating the exhibition was £105 per day.

Using the formula   Profit = Revenue − Cost:

e calculate the average profit made per day.

f discuss whether the artists should have exhibited their work for a sixth week.

20.3 *Intermediate Art and Design: Replacing a Photocopier*

A small design studio is considering updating its photocopier.

The studio contacts four different suppliers whose charges are given in the table below:

Supplier	Rental per year	Price per sheet (Monochrome)	Price per sheet (Colour)
Copious Copies	£800	3.8p	42p
Careful Copier	£1200	4.3p	29p
Perfect Photocopies	£750	3.9p	45p
Quality Photocopier	nil	4.2p	41p

The design studio anticipates that it will make 12000 black and white copies and 590 colour copies in a year.

a Find the anticipated cost of each supplier's photocopier.

b Show the costings for each photocopier by means of a sectional bar chart.

c Apart from the cost, what other criteria should the designers consider when deciding which photocopier to choose?

The studio is considering a change of policy so that it produces a greater proportion of photocopies.

d Discuss how this would affect the choice of supplier.

20.4 *Advanced Art and Design: Golden Ratio*

When asked to select one of the following shapes for a picture frame, most people would select shape R.

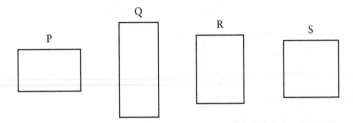

In shape R, the ratio of the length of the shorter side to the length of the longer side is the same as the ratio of the longer side to the sum of both sides.

i.e.
$$\frac{a}{b} = \frac{b}{a + b}$$

This ratio is known as the **golden ratio**.

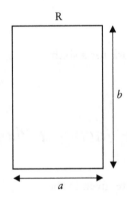

The golden ratio has been commonly used in architecture throughout history – for example, in the Parthenon in Athens, where the ratio of the gap between the columns to the height of the columns is a golden ratio. It is found in innumerable other examples – for example, in the construction of a violin, where the ratio of the length of the neck to the length of the body, and the length of the body to the overall length of the violin are both golden ratios.

(i) If k is the golden ratio, $\dfrac{a}{b} = \dfrac{b}{a + b} = k$

Show that $k^2 a + ka - a = 0$

and hence $k^2 + k - 1 = 0$

(ii) Using the formula for the solution of a quadratic equation
$ax^2 + bx + c = 0$

$$x = \frac{-b \pm \sqrt{b^2 - 4ac}}{2a},$$

show that $k = \frac{1}{2}(\sqrt{5} - 1)$

The golden ratio can also be found in a five-pointed star, the **Star of David**, as shown below. The mathematical name for this shape is a **pentagram**.

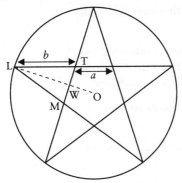

The polygon within the circle is a regular pentagon. Find:
- (iii) the angle TOM
- (iv) the length of MW, and
- (v) angles LMW and MLT
- (vi) Hence find $\sin 18°$ in terms of a and b.
- (vii) Using the value of k found in part (ii) above, show that $\sin 18° = \frac{1}{4}(\sqrt{5} - 1)$
- (viii) Find LW and hence find the area of the five triangles in the pentagram.

20.5 *Foundation Business: Customer Survey*

A business wishes to discover whether people who come into its office leave with a positive view of the company. Visitors are asked to complete the following questionnaire, the results of which are as shown:

	Agree Strongly	Agree	Neither Agree nor Disagree	Disagree
I did not have to wait for attention	25	13	2	0
I was made to feel welcome by the receptionist	18	14	8	0
The receptionist answered my enquiry promptly	25	8	6	1
The receptionist was competent	12	23	1	4

Please complete the remainder of the questionnaire if you were seen by a member of our staff in addition to a receptionist.

I was happy with the information I was given	7	6	2	0
The materials I was given were of a high standard	11	3	1	0
My needs from the business were fully satisfied	8	5	1	1
I hope to use this business again	9	2	2	2

a Show each of the responses for the receptionist by means of a statistical diagram.

b Find the percentage of clients who:
- (i) agree strongly that they were made to feel welcome by the receptionist
- (ii) hope to use the business again.

c Identify any weakness which the company should address.

20.6 *Intermediate Business: Employment Costs*

The cost of employing a member of staff is not solely the wage which the worker receives.

In addition the employer needs to pay National Insurance costs, employers' pension contributions, overalls or uniform costs, together with additional costs involved with additional payroll, staff accommodation needs, etc.

For a person earning £21 000 per year these additional costs for one particular company would amount to:

a National Insurance costs which are levied at the rate of 12.2% on all earnings in excess of £84 per week

b pension contributions which would be 6.8% of the worker's wage

c uniform costs which amount to £85 per year

d the additional costs which would be £15 per week.

Taking one year as 52 weeks, calculate the total annual cost of employing this worker and show the breakdown of the cost as:

  (i) a bar chart, and
  (ii) a pie chart.

20.7 *Advanced Business: Three-dimensional Model*

Jenny is making a three-dimensional model of a new development to a scale of 1:100. Next to the new development is an industrial development which includes a high chimney.

In order to show her model in proportion to established buildings, Jenny decides to include the chimney.

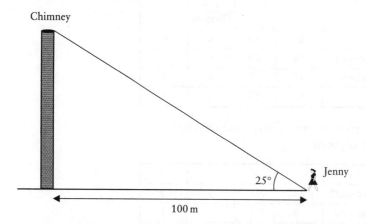

To find its height, Jenny walks 100 m away from the chimney and notes that the angle of elevation of the top of the chimney is 25°, as shown in the diagram. The ground is horizontal.

a Find the height of the actual chimney.

b Jenny measures the circumference of the chimney to be 11 m.
   Calculate the radius of the chimney.

c Hence find the volume of the actual chimney.

Jenny's model is on a scale of 1:100.

d Find the dimensions of the chimney on her plan

e Hence find the volume of the chimney on her plan.

20.8 *Foundation Construction: Using MDF*

Ken buys a sheet of MDF in its regular size which is 2440 cm by 1220 cm.

He cuts pieces 800 cm by 300 cm to make the front of cupboards.

Ken decides to allow 2 mm between two adjacent pieces to ensure a smooth finish after the cut has been made.

a How many cupboard fronts can Ken cut from the sheet?

b Draw a diagram to indicate how the MDF may be cut to enable Ken to obtain the largest number of pieces from the sheet.

c What percentage of the sheet is wasted?

The whole sheet of MDF weighs 45 kg.

d What is the weight of each cupboard front?

20.9 *Intermediate Construction: Hard Wood*

A block of hardwood has a density of 44 pounds per cubic foot.

1 pound = 453.6 grams   1 inch = 2.54 cm   12 inches = 1 foot

a What is the density of this hard wood in kilograms per cubic metre?

A post made out of this hardwood is 10 cm by 14 cm by 2.4 m.

b Using your answer to part **a**, find the weight of the post.

c Consider your answer and discuss whether it is realistic.

20.10 *Advanced Construction: Models*

Joanna is constructing a carving of an elephant from wood.

The density of a number of different substances is given in the table below.

Substance	Density in grams/cm^3
Aluminium	2.0
Brass	8.9
Iron	7.8
Wood	0.8

The carving will be 0.4 metres in height, and Joanna expects it to have a total volume of 0.123 cubic metres.

a Find the expected weight of the carving.

Joanna thinks she will make a second, larger carving of an elephant.
The volume of the new carving, V, is given by the formula

$$V = k^3 \times M$$

where M is the volume of the initial carving and k is the scale factor of the enlargement.

Joanna knows that the crane which she will use to lift this second, larger carving into its position can lift a maximum weight of 1.1 tonnes.

b Find the maximum scale factor that Joanna could use which would allow this crane to lift her carving into position.

20.11 *Foundation Engineering: Cost of wiring a garage*

Tom wants to install electricity into his detached garage to enable him to fit a light and operate a deep freezer.

He measures the relevant distances and decides which electrical goods he will need to buy.

Tom prices the following items:

1 double electricity socket	£2.65
1 metal fixing box for the socket	£1.89
1 light switch	£4.43

12 m internal specification wiring at 60p per metre

4 m heavy duty outside specification wiring at £2.10 per metre.

It is recommended that students find for themselves the actual cost of these items at a local supplier.

a Calculate the total cost of these electrical items exclusive of VAT.
VAT at $17\frac{1}{2}\%$ is levied on the total cost.

Tom intends to carry out the work himself.

b Calculate the final cost to Tom of wiring the garage.

c Set out the bill which Tom would be given if he bought all these electrical items at the local supplier.

20.12 *Intermediate Engineering: Scale diagram*

John is making a scale diagram of a house. He is using a scale of 1:50.

For this assignment, use the relationship between actual and image dimensions:

$$\text{Image length} = \text{Scale factor} \times \text{Actual length.}$$

One door of the actual house is 2 metres by 0.9 metres.

a Find the dimensions of a door on John's scale diagram.

The area of a window in John's diagram is 0.0045 square metres. The width of the window is 0.09 metres.

b Find the height of the window on John's scale model.

c What are the dimensions of the actual window of John's house?

d What is the area of the actual window of John's house?

e Draw a graph which will convert actual lengths to scale lengths.

20.13 *Foundation Health and Social Care: Comparing life expectancy with prosperity*

Helen is investigating whether there is a relationship between life expectancy and prosperity in different areas of England.

Helen obtains the data given below.

KEY - Unemployment: % rate 1999. Exam results: five or more GCSEs A*-C grade, 1998/99 (*=1996/1997).
Mortality: standardised mortality ratio (UK = 100), 1997.
Crime: notifiable offences recorded by police, 1997.
Household income: disposable household income per head, 1997.

WEST MIDLANDS	
Unemployment	7.0%
Exam results	43.5%
Mortality	101
Crime	9,055
Average house price	£71,168
Household income	£8,640

LONDON	
Unemployment	7.8%
Exam results	43.6%
Mortality	96
Crime	10,527
Average house price	£127,814
Household income	£11084

EAST MIDLANDS	
Unemployment	5.2%
Exam results	43.3%
Mortality	98
Crime	9,187
Average house price	£64,289
Household income	£8,926

YORKSHIRE AND THE HUMBER	
Unemployment	7.1%
Exam results	40.5%
Mortality	101
Crime	10,857
Average house price	£59,414
Household income	£8,676

NORTH EAST	
Unemployment	10.1%
Exam results	39.4%
Mortality	110
Crime	9,713
Average house price	£57,049
Household income	£8,080

SOUTH WEST	
Unemployment	5.0%
Exam results	50.2%
Mortality	90
Crime	7,490
Average house price	£81,540
Household income	£9,543

EASTERN	
Unemployment	4.3%
Exam results	49.9%
Mortality	92
Crime	6,643
Average house price	£86,968
Household income	£10,371

SOUTH EAST	
Unemployment	3.7%
Exam results	51.2%
Mortality	93
Crime	7,276
Average house price	£107,035
Household income	£10,559

NORTH WEST	
Unemployment	6.9%
Exam results	44.1%
Mortality	107
Crime	9,422
Average house price	£61,525
Household income	£8,703

(Map of the United Kingdom with region labels: SCOTLAND, NORTHERN IRELAND, NORTH EAST, NORTH WEST, YORKSHIRE & THE HUMBER, EAST MIDLANDS, EASTERN, WEST MIDLANDS, SOUTH WEST, LONDON, SOUTH EAST)

a Arrange the regions in order for:
(i) mortality
(ii) income
(iii) unemployment.

Is there any apparent connection between these orders?

Each of the four regions, South West, West Midlands, Yorkshire and the Humber and Eastern, has a population of 5 000 000.

b Find the mean for these four regions of:
   (i) household income
   (ii) unemployment, and
   (iii) mortality

c Which region is:
   (i) more than the mean, and
   (ii) less than the mean in all these measures?

d London has a population of 7 million people.
   Do the statistics for London place it above or below the means found in part **b**?

e Do these statistics tend to confirm that there is a link between life expectancy and prosperity in different areas of England?

20.14 *Intermediate Health and Social Care: Factors affecting a person's health and well-being*

This is an assignment considering the nation's health. It is not only desirable for an individual's well being to be healthy, but the healthier the nation, the less the Government will need to spend on health care.

The assignment could consider the relationship between physical exercise and health. One measure of physical exercise is the time spent on physical exercise, and one measure of a person's health is their body mass index. A person's body mass index or BMI is the person's weight in kilograms divided by the square of their height in metres.

To find a relationship between these two measures, consider a sample of twenty people of similar age, for example twenty teenagers or twenty people in their forties.

Using a survey, find the time spent by each person on physical exercise and their body mass index.

Show clearly how you have used the BMI to find the body mass for each person.

Find the mean and median of each of these measures.

To present the findings, include at least:
   (i) one diagram – for example, a scatter diagram of BMI against time spent exercising
   (ii) one bar chart – for example, showing BMI in a grouped form for each of the two groups of people.

You should include a table to show how the range of BMI from 10 to 45 indicates whether a person is underweight, normal, overweight, obese or very obese.

A person is normally said to be neither underweight nor overweight if the BMI is between 18 and 25.

Claire is 5 feet 8 inches tall.

a Convert Claire's height into metres

b Hence determine in kg the range in which Claire's weight should be.

c Convert the weight you have found in part **b** into stones and pounds.

You may use: 2.54 cm = 1 inch   1 pound = 453.6 grams
               12 inches = 1 foot   14 pounds = 1 stone

20.15 *Advanced Health and Social Care: Constructing a slide*

You are going to construct a slide in a children's home. Health and safety requirements in your area determine that the maximum slope of the slide is 50° to the horizontal. You want the slide to be 10 feet in (sloping) length, and to be as steep as possible.

a Find the height of the top of the slide above the ground.

The slide is to be 2 feet wide, and there will be a platform $2\frac{1}{2}$ feet in length at the top of the slide. The platform and the sloping part of the slide will be constructed from material which costs £1.20 per square foot.

b Find the cost of this material.

The platform is to be supported by four cylindrical poles each of which will be buried one foot into the ground. The poles cost 60p per foot.

c Find the cost of the poles.

You are going to paint the four poles, which are each 6 inches in diameter.

d Find the area in square feet which you will paint, assuming that the area to be painted is that part of each pole above the ground together with the circular top of the pole.

20.16 *Foundation Hospitality and Catering: Yorkshire pudding recipe*

The recipe to make 12 individual Yorkshire puddings for a dinner by the British Beef Marketers' Association is:

4 oz plain flour   a pinch of salt   two eggs   half a pint of milk

Create a recipe which would make 30 individual Yorkshire puddings.

20.17 *Intermediate Hospitality and Catering: Airport shuttle bus*

An hotel is six miles from an airport. The manager is considering whether to introduce an airport shuttle bus. The manager anticipates that he would need three buses which will be operated by three full-time drivers, and six additional part-time drivers.

The cost of operating the shuttle will be composed of:

   (i) driver's pay and benefits
  (ii) maintenance of the buses
 (iii) lease of the buses
 (iv) fuel for the buses, and
  (v) airport taxes

The full-time drivers will be paid £18 000 per annum. The part-time drivers will each work ten hours per week, and be paid an hourly rate of £6.20 per hour. Additional National Insurance, pension, and holiday costs will add an additional 16% to these payments.

The pie-chart below shows the breakdown of the annual costs into the five categories above.

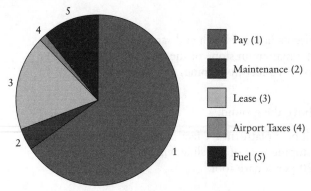

a Estimate the cost of each of the remaining four items (ii) to (v).

b Show this information by means of a bar chart.

c Find the total cost of operating the airport shuttle.

The manager anticipates that his hotel will gain an extra 20 guests every night if he operates the shuttle.

d How much will the shuttle cost per additional guest per night?

20.18 *Advanced Hospitality and Catering:* *Air conditioning and plan of a restaurant*

You are building a restaurant. It will be constructed as a regular hexagon of side 10 metres with a ceiling height of 4 metres. You will install air-conditioning. To remove any traces of second-hand smoke, you will require that, on average, all the air is changed every 5 minutes.

a Find the volume of air in the restaurant.

The cost of various air-conditioners is shown below, together with the amounts of air they displace every minute.

b Which is the cheapest air-conditioner you can choose? You will need a number of units which must be of the same type.

	Cost (£)	Capacity (m³/min)
Air-conditioner A	700	200
Air-conditioner B	400	120
Air-conditioner C	120	50
Air-conditioner D	250	70
Air-conditioner E	100	20

20.19 *Foundation Information Technology:* *Use of computers*

A college has two suites of rooms containing computers which are linked to the Internet. Their use is monitored throughout the working week of a ten-week term, so that the college's management can discover which courses the students who use the Internet are following, and whether a third room needs to be created.

The use of the computers was as follows:

	Number of hours computers used per term	Number of students on the course
Students following a GCSE course	50	30
Students following a GNVQ Foundation course	1110	110
Students following a GNVQ Intermediate course	2835	230
Students following a GNVQ Advanced course	6070	475
Students following a GCE programme	2120	920
Students following other vocational courses	2750	700

a For each of these groups, find the mean number of hours per student enrolled spent using the Internet.

There are 20 computers in each room.

b Find the number of hours each computer is used per week.

20.20 *Intermediate Information Technology: Buying a house*

You want to buy a house and ask estate agents to send you information on houses for sale.

Draw up a spreadsheet so that you can identify for each house:

(i) the area in which it is situated
(ii) the number of bedrooms it has
(iii) the number of bathrooms it has
(iv) whether the house is detached, semi-detached, terraced, bungalow, or an apartment.
(v) its price
(vi) its area in square feet.

The information on the first ten houses sent to you is as follows:

House A is in Newcastle. It has 3 bedrooms, 1 bathroom, is detached with an area of 1200 sq ft and costs £82 000.

House B is in Gateshead. It is semi-detached, with 1 bathroom, 2 bedrooms, and costs £47 000 for its area of 620 sq ft.

House C is in Whitley Bay. It is semi-detached, with an area of 810 sq ft, and has 3 bedrooms, 1 bathroom. It costs £53 000.

House D is in Ponteland. It is a 1500 sq ft detached house for sale at £182 000, with 2 bathrooms and 4 bedrooms.

House E is in Newcastle. This has 2 bedrooms, 1 bathroom, is terraced, with an area of 480 sq ft, and is on sale at £32 000.

House F is in Tynemouth. A 3-bedroomed detached house with 1 bathroom for £51 000, it has an area of 1100 sq ft.

House G is in Washington. This 1050 sq ft 1 bathroom, 3-bedroomed semi-detached house is on offer at £41 000.

House H is in Birtley. This bungalow is £46 000, with an area of 910 sq ft, including 2 bedrooms and 1 bathroom.

House I is in Gosforth. This detached house has 2 bathrooms, for £87 000. There are 3 bedrooms in its 1450 sq ft area.

House J is in Longbenton. This is a 2-bedroomed apartment, with a bathroom, offered at £38 000. The area is 580 sq ft.

Use your spreadsheet to find:

a the mean price of the ten houses

b the mean price of the detached houses

c the mean area in square feet of the semi-detached houses.

20.21 *Advanced Information Technology: Hard disk capacity*

a A computer has a hard disk with a storage capacity of 8 gigabytes.

1 gigabyte or Gb is 1024 megabytes or Mb

1 megabyte is 1024 kilobytes or kb

1 kilobyte is 1024 bytes

1 byte is 8 bits.

(i) How many bits can be stored on the hard disk?

(ii) Convert your answer to part (i) into standard form correct to 4 significant figures.

When you operate your hard disk which has 8 Gb of storage space, you find that:

- 300 mb of the hard disk is used to operate Windows
- a further 450 mb is used to operate Office
- 400 mb is needed when Windows is running for 'swap' files
- 1.05 Gb is used for a video.

b What percentage of the hard disk is available for you to use?

20.22 *Foundation Land and Environment: Irrigating crops*

Dan is a farmer in East Anglia. In one field, Dan grows lettuce which need a constant water supply during the summer months. His father has told him that an allotment measuring 6 m by 3 m needs 0.05 m^3 of irrigation water on a normal sunny day.

Dan's field is 70 m by 50 m.

a How much irrigated water is needed by the lettuce plants in the whole field on a normal day?

The actual amount of water required varies according to the weather, as shown in the table below:

Types of weather	Actual weather	Irrigation water required
A	Sunny and Hot all day	20% more than normal
B	Normal	Normal
C	5° cooler than normal	10% less than normal
D	Rains most of the day	None

b Find the amount of irrigation water required when the weather is hot and sunny all day.

c Calculate the amount of irrigation water required when it is 5° cooler than usual.

For two weeks Dan keeps a record of the types of weather in his area.

These types are: B, C, D, D, B, A, A, B, A, D, D, B, A, B.

d Calculate the total amount of irrigation water required for these two weeks.

e Find the mean amount of irrigation water needed per day.

f Show the number of days requiring each type of watering as a bar chart.

20.23 *Intermediate Land and Environment:*
Land use in European countries

You are investigating differences in land use in the United Kingdom and four other European countries. You want to determine whether these differences can be explained by the difference in latitude and climate of these countries.

You obtain the following data on types of land use of land which is not built upon.

Land use	UK	Portugal	France	Italy	Spain
Arable land	29%	32%	32%	32%	31%
Permanent crops	0%	6%	2%	10%	10%
Meadows and Pasture	48%	6%	23%	17%	21%
Forest and woodland	9%	40%	27%	22%	31%
Other	14%	16%	16%	19%	7%
Irrigated land in sq km	1570	6340	11 600	41 000	33 600
Total area of country in sq km	2.42×10^5	9.16×10^4	5.47×10^5	2.94×10^5	4.99×10^5

a Show this information for each of the UK and Portugal by means of a pie chart.

b Find the average percentages for each category for the three countries: France, Italy and Spain.

c (i) Find the area irrigated in each country as a percentage of the total area of that country.
  (ii) Does this data show that the percentage varies with latitude?

d Give two other differences between the land use of these countries and explain how the climate of the countries causes these differences.

20.24 *Advanced Leisure and Recreation:*
Heating a swimming pool

You are calculating the cost of installing and operating a swimming pool.

The pool will be rectangular, measuring 15 metres by 5 metres. The pool will slope from 1.3 metres in depth at the shallow end to 2.2 metres at the deep end. In addition, you will build an area of constant depth 1.3 metres in the shape of a semi-circle at the shallow end.

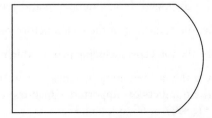

The inside of the pool will be tiled.

a Find the total area to be tiled; include the base and the sides. Assume that the depth of the pool, for example 2.2 metres, is the distance from the floor of the pool to the top of the sides.

The cost of heating the pool throughout the year depends on the volume of water in the pool. A typical cost is £90 per m^3.

b What is the expected cost of heating this pool?

20.25 *Foundation Leisure and Tourism: Credit card payments*

To investigate whether the average payments made by credit card are greater or less than those made by cheque or cash, you have found the income which a sports centre had received over the past week. These were as given below.

Amounts paid by credit card

£21	£19.24	£22.34	£32.80	£72.10
£24.20	£11.05	£9.60	£26.80	£40.80

Amounts paid by cheque or cash

£7.12	£27.20	£6.20	£21.10	£2.70
£13.59	£21.10	£4.40	£6.30	£34.98
£23.19	£6.59	£20.70	£8.40	£6.29

1   Represent this data by means of a bar chart, grouping the data where appropriate.

2   Find the average amount paid by: (i) credit card   (ii) cheque or cash.

3   Show:
     a a completed credit card payment slip for £22.35 which you would have accepted
     b a cheque for £19.40 which you would have accepted.

20.26 *Intermediate Leisure and Tourism: Costing transport for a football match*

Ann and Jeff operate coaches taking football supporters to matches. They are calculating how much to charge for transport to an away match when Southampton play Aston Villa. The cost of the coach, including fuel, is 45p per mile for the journey which is 152 miles each way. The cost of parking is expected to be £10.

The driver of the coach will be paid £6 per hour from 10 am until 9.30 pm. Meals for the driver will cost an additional £10.

Incidental costs are an extra £90, which includes insurance in case the match is postponed. In addition, Ann and Jeff add on a 15% profit margin. Find:

a the total cost of the coach before profit is added, and

b the total cost including profit, which Ann and Jeff intend to charge supporters.

On the last ten away matches which Ann and Jeff organised for Southampton, the numbers of supporters which travelled with them were: 44, 35, 40, 52, 31, 49, 46, 40, 39, and 47.

Ann and Jeff price the trip to Aston Villa assuming that the number of people travelling with them will be the mean of these last 10 trips (rounded up to the next integer).

c Find the amount which Ann and Jeff will charge each supporter for the trip to Aston Villa.

After having set the price in part **c**, they found that only 39 supporters travelled with them to Aston Villa.

d What percentage profit did they actually make?

e Use a pie chart to show the breakdown of the costs Ann and Jeff charge the supporters.

20.27 *Foundation Manufacturing: Bottled water*

Terry and Jane are planning to sell the water which comes from a spring on their land. The bottling plant which they install can bottle 1 litre of water every 10 seconds.

a How many litres of water can they bottle in one hour?

Their spring produces 30 000 litres of water a week.

Terry and Jane can sell the first 5 000 litres at 40p per bottle.

The next 20 000 litres can be sold at 30p per bottle.

The cost of bottling the spring water is 15p per bottle.

b How much profit can Terry and Jane make if they bottle 25 000 litres per week?

c How many hours per week must they operate the bottling plant if they are going to bottle 25 000 litres of water per week?

20.28 *Intermediate Manufacturing: Energy sources*

You are investigating various types of electricity generation. The types of methods used in the generation of electricity in the United Kingdom is shown in the bar chart below, showing the percentages generated by each in 1980, 1990 and 1995.

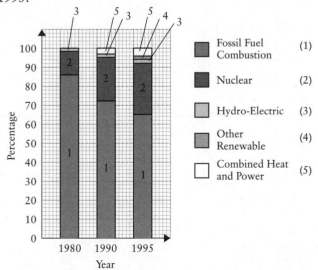

The table below shows these percentages of electricity generated in the United Kingdom for the year 1995.

Non-renewable sources:	fossil fuels	67.6%
	nuclear generation	25.0%
	combined heat and power (CHP)	5.1%
Renewable sources:	hydroelectric	1.6%
	other (wind, landfill gas, burning refuse, etc.)	0.7%

In addition to electricity generated in this country, the UK also imports electricity from France.

In 1995, this imported electricity was 6% of the total electricity used in the UK and the capacity of the Channel Link was 15% of the daily usage in the UK.

On one particular day, 10% of the electricity used in the UK is imported from France.

a Assuming that this imported energy was all nuclear electricity, find:
   (i)   the percentage of electricity used in the UK which has been made by nuclear generation
   (ii) the percentage of electricity used in the UK produced from non-renewable energy sources
   (iii) the proportion of electricity used in the UK which comes from renewable energy sources.

b Use a pie chart to show the proportions of electricity generated in the UK from renewable and from non-renewable sources.

c Draw a line graph to show how the percentage of the electricity generated in the UK from renewable energy sources has been growing over the last 15 years. You should find the percentage for the latest year to ensure your graph is as up to date as possible.

d Find the similar distribution of renewable/non-renewable energy sources of another country.

20.29 *Advanced Manufacturing: Efficiency of a cool box*

A cool-box is placed in a room at noon. The room has a constant temperature of 11°C. When placed in the room, the contents of the cool-box are at −5°C. The graph below shows the temperature of the contents over a period of 24 hours.

Find

a the temperature at 6 pm

b the temperature at midnight

c the time at which the temperature of the contents reaches 0°C

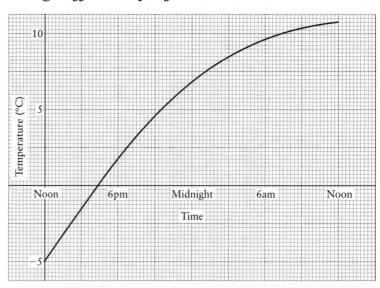

If the efficiency of the cool box is increased, the cool-box will take more time for its contents to warm. In such a cool box, the rate of change of temperature is half that of the original cool box.

d Draw a graph to show the temperature against time for this new cool box.

e Hence find the time taken for the contents of this new cool box to reach 0°C.

When placed in another room, the temperature of the cool box, T°C is given by

$$T = T_0 - Qe^{-kt},$$

where k is a measure of the efficiency of the cool box, T_0 is the temperature of the room, t is the time in hours after the cool box is placed in the room, and Q is the original difference in temperature between the room and the contents of the cool box.

f Find the temperature of the room when a cool box with $k = 0.45$ takes 5 hours for the contents to rise in temperature from -5°C to 0°C.

20.30 *Intermediate Media: Time spent watching television*

Please refer to page 223 for details of the assignment 'Time spent watching television'.

Data which you could use from a survey carried out on a Tuesday:

No. of hours spent watching TV	Students aged 16–20 years	Adults aged over 50 years
Saturday	1,1,1,3,0,2,4,2,1,1, 3,0,6,3,0,1,3,3,3,0.	4,3,1,0,5,2,9,3,2,5, 5,1,4,7,2,3,7,6,4,3.
Sunday	2,0,3,1,4,1,2,3,1,0, 4,0,0,1,1,2,3,2,0,1.	1,5,3,6,2,2,0,1,4,3, 5,1,3,2,7,2,5,6,3,2.
Monday	0,1,1,2,0,0,0,1,1,2, 1,1,1,3,5,2,1,1,2,1.	2,1,3,0,0,2,5,4,6,1, 0,3,3,0,2,1,2,2,1,4.

20.31 *Advanced Media: Newspaper sales*

Newspapers regularly try to attract new readers with offers, promotions or special articles.

The fifteen newspaper best-sellers in 1999 are listed below.

Newspaper bestsellers 1999

Increase (000s)	%	Newspaper	Subject
411	15	Mirror	10p
348	8	Sun	Grand National
291	8	Sun	Millionaire
244	6	NoW	Changing Rooms
244	7	Sun	Christmas TV
242	19	S Times	Rich list
220	12	S Mirror	Toper horoscope
209	11	S Mirror	Toper horoscope
203	5	NoW	Free calendar
198	5	Sun	Sophie topless
194	8	Mail	Just the Ticket
194	7	Mirror	Lucky Bags
190	9	Mirror	M Magazine
185	8	Mail	Lucky Wallets
184	4	NoW	Bug's Life comic

The top bestseller in 1999 was one edition of the *Mirror* when its cover price was reduced to 10 pence, and 411 000 extra copies were sold. This was an additional 15% of its normal sales.

a Using the formula:

$$\text{Normal sale} = \frac{100}{\text{percentage increase}} \times \text{number of extra copies sold}$$

find the normal sale of the Mirror.

b The percentages are given to the nearest integer. Using the figures for the second and third bestsellers, find the range of possible values for the normal sale of the Sun.

c *The Times* normally sells 730 000 copies. The highest increase in the sales of *The Times* is 17% which occurred when it reported the budget. Why is this increase not on the list of bestsellers?

d Find:

    (i) the mean percentage, and

    (ii) the mean number of increases shown.

e Find the bestsellers list either:

    (i) for another year, or

    (ii) for another country

and compare the topics which led to the increase in sales.

20.32 *Foundation Performing Arts: Advertising evening events*

A theatre advertises two events. The first is a play performed by a travelling group of performers, and the second is a concert performed by a local orchestra. The cost of advertising the two events is given below.

Advertising Expenditure (£)

	Play	Concert
Posters	80	95
Local radio	20	145
Newspapers	210	124
Direct mail shot	50	212

a Represent the amount spent on each type of expenditure by means of a pie chart for:

    (i) the play, and

    (ii) the concert.

b Contrast the ways in which the advertising expenditure was divided. The audience was 800 for the play and 700 for the concert.

c What was the average cost of publicity for each person for:

    (i) the play, and

    (ii) the concert?

20.33 *Intermediate Performing Arts: The orchestra*

The string section of an orchestra has 60 musicians:

- 30 who play violins,
- 14 who play violas
- 12 who play cellos
- 4 who play double basses.

a Draw a pie chart to show the composition of the string section of the orchestra.

The remainder of the orchestra is composed of:

- 2 flutes
- 2 oboes
- 2 clarinets
- 2 bassoons
- 2 trumpets
- 3 trombones
- 4 horns
- 3 percussionists.

b Show the composition of the complete orchestra by means of a bar chart.

c By grouping the whole orchestra into its four musical sections, show this composition by means of a pie chart.

d Investigate whether a major orchestra composed of 100 or more players has the same proportion when broken down into its musical sections.

20.34 *Advanced Performing Arts: Open-air stage*

A stage 10 feet above the ground has been constructed in a park for an open air music concert. During the concert, the performers could be as far back as 15 feet behind the front of the stage.

a How far from the stage must the audience stand if they want to be able to see at least the heads of the performers at all times?

You can assume that the lowest part of the head of the performer is 4 ft 8 in from the floor of the stage and that the eyes of the audience are at least 5 ft 5 in above the ground.

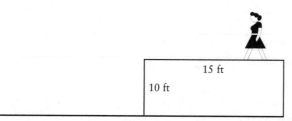

Tracey is 5 ft 8 in tall and is 30 feet from the stage.

Wayne is standing behind Tracey and his eyes are 5 ft 5 in above the ground.

b How far behind Tracey must Wayne stand if he is going to be able to see all the stage?

20.35 *Foundation Retail and Distribution: Marketing potatoes*

A farmer receives £2.20 for each 25 kg sack of potatoes. The wholesaler adds an extra 60p per bag as the cost of taking the potatoes to the market.

At the market an additional 20% is added before selling it to a retailer.

The retailer splits the bag into 5 kg packs, which costs the retailer 20p per 25 kg sack. After this charge, the retailer adds on 60% of the total cost for profit and overheads.

a Find the selling price, per kilogram, to the customer.

b Show the cost which the customer pays as:
  (i) a pie-chart
  (ii) a bar-chart

  identifying the breakdown in cost to the customer.

20.36 *Intermediate Retail and Distribution: Household expenditure*

The dual bar chart compares weekly household spending in the years 1968 and 1999.

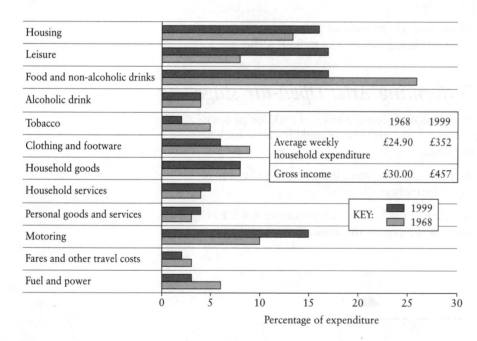

	1968	1999
Average weekly household expenditure	£24.90	£352
Gross income	£30.00	£457

KEY: ■ 1999 ■ 1968

Percentage of expenditure

In 1968, the gross income of a household was £30.

a What was the percentage of this gross income which was spent?

b How much was spent per week on motoring in
  (i) 1999
  (ii) 1968?
  (iii) Hence find the increase on money spent on motoring as a percentage of the amount spent in 1968.

Inflation had been 881% during this 31 years.

c Find the increase **in real terms** in spending on motoring, as a percentage of the amount spent in 1968.

d State the area of expenditure which in real terms has shown:
   (i) the greatest
   (ii) the least increase in spending, and give these increases as a percentage of the amount spent in 1968.

To gain further credit for this assignment, students could carry out their own research and present appropriately actual price differences – for example, differences in the price of petrol and of cars in 1968 and 1999.

20.37 *Advanced Retail and Distribution: Advertising*

The manager of a store has been given new promotional objectives, and needs to increase sales in a particular area.
She decides to have posters printed which will be distributed with the local free paper.
She considers two firms which could produce the posters.
Adbreeze would cost £c for n posters, where $c = 5 + 8nd^2$.

In this formula, d is the perimeter of the poster in metres.

She could go to France and use *Affiches Maintenant* who charge $20 + 5nd^2$ for n posters. This price is given in euros (€).
You can use the exchange rate of €1.61 to £1.

a Find the cost in pounds of producing 1000 posters measuring 40 cm by 20 cm from each company.

b The manager does not wish to spend more than 40 pence per poster when obtaining the 1000 posters. What is the maximum size of square posters which she could obtain?

20.38 *Foundation Science: Temperature in a bucket*

A bucket of ice at temperature -7°C is placed in a room which is at a constant temperature of 15°C.

A thermometer is embedded in the ice and the temperature of the bucket is recorded every 5 minutes.

Time (minutes)	0	5	10	15	20	25	30	35	40	45
Temperature (°C)	−7	−4	−1	−0.1	0.0	0.0	1.1	3.5	5.9	8.3

a Draw a line graph of temperature against time.

b Comment on the graph, including a comment on the time taken to get from −1°C to 1°C.

c Find the time interval when the temperature rose the most.

20.39 *Intermediate Science: Ohm's law*

You are carrying out an experiment to confirm Ohm's law. This states that for a constant voltage the current in a circuit is inversely proportional to the electrical resistance of that circuit.

You record the current on a number of occasions when the resistance is changed.

Resistance (ohms)	5	10	15	20	25	30
Current (amps)	16	8.1	4.8	4.0	3.2	2.6

a Plot these values on a graph of resistance against current.

b You suspect that one reading could have been incorrect. Which reading was this?

c Does this experiment support the hypothesis that the current is inversely proportional to the resistance?

20.40 *Advanced Science: Rate of flow from an inverted cone*

Please refer to page 228 for details of the assignment on the rate of flow from an inverted cone. Here is some data which could be used for a cone with vertical angle 60°:

Height of water in cone (in cm)	Rate of flow (in cm³)
0	0
1	0.19
2	1.02
3	2.81
4.5	7.74
6	16.0
10	57.0

20.41 *Advanced Travel and Tourism: Holiday travel*

In this assignment, students should select their own destination and find the current costs for the journey.

David and Sarah and their two children are going to St Tropez for their two-week family holiday. Their local travel agent informs them that:

(i) the price of return travel from London to St Tropez by rail is £130 per person

(ii) the price by air from London to Nice is £90 per person each way from where they could catch a train to St Tropez or hire a car

(iii) the price of return travel by coach from London to Nice is £60 per person from where they could catch a train to St Tropez or hire a car.

David and Sarah also calculate the cost of using their own car.

The cost of the ferry crossing for their car and four people is £195 including breakdown insurance.

The journey from Calais to St Tropez is 1145 kilometres each way and their car averages 42 miles per gallon.

a How many gallons of petrol would the car use in the round trip?
You may use 8 km = 5 miles.
In France, petrol costs 6.57 francs per litre.

b What is this cost in pounds per gallon?
You may use the conversion 4.55 litres = 1 gallon.
The exchange rate is 10.5 French francs to £1.

David and Sarah would not travel at a weekend.

They would expect to average 70 mph as there are motorways from Calais to St Tropez, nearly all of which have a speed limit of 130 kmph.

c How many hours do David and Sarah calculate that the journey by car to St Tropez would take?

d Compare the costs to travel by air with the costs given by the travel agent.

The travel agent reminded David and Sarah that the flight takes only 2 hours, much less than by any other means.

e Give one advantage of each of the four modes of transport.

f Which method of transport would you use? Justify your decision.

g Would **your** choice be affected
(i) if you decided to travel on Saturday 1 August
(ii) if you were travelling on your own
(iii) if you were travelling with four other people?

Solutions to Exercises

Note. Solutions are given for exercises with a 'closed' numerical answer. They are not provided for 'open-ended' questions and for some questions leading purely to an illustration (e.g. a pie-chart or a graph).
Numerical answers are generally given correct to 3 significant figures.

Exercise 1.1

1 a 5 tens   b 7 hundreds   c 3 thousands
   d 4 units   e 6 tenths   f 2 hundredths
2 a 10, 17, 21, 45, 54, 86
   b 14, 23, 32, 104, 203, 230
   c 6, 60, 61, 600, 601, 610
   d 11, 99, 101, 110, 999, 1001
   e 297, 300, 399, 400, 420
3 7510   4 2369
5 a 430   d 132   g 516
   b 16 700   e 590   h 7030
   c 20 000   f 935.8   i 130
6 a   32   d 40.3   g 0.0027
   b   3   e 0.65   h 0.051
   c   40   f 0.065   i 0.0002
7 a 100   b 400   c 4100   d 6200

Exercise 1.2

1 41.9   2 180.3   3 133.97   4 16.7   5 16.71
6 51.75   7 169.4   8 702.36   9 1770   10 7.8
11 72.31   12 47.86

Exercise 1.3

1 26   2 36   3 5   4 1   5 1   6 7
7 0   8 66   9 133   10 2   11 £4.96
12 4   13 £78.01   14 a 988   b £4755
15 a 2 h 7 min (127 min)   b £19.05
16 7 packs, £1.35   17 a 47.5 miles   b £12.92
18 £1183.80   19 £160.50
20 a 7.39 kg   b 135   21 a 9   b 14.6 cm

Exercise 1.4

1 2   b −4   c −10   d 4   e 6   f 40   g 0   h −49
2 a −1   b 17   c −13   d 20   e −3   f 0   g 50   h 36

Exercise 1.5

1 a −18   b −3   c 28   d $1\frac{3}{4}$ e −15
   f −27   g 8   h 36   i −1   j −10

Exercise 1.6

1 1, 4, 9, 16, 25, 36, 49, 64, 81, 100
2 1, 8, 27, 64, 125, 216
3 a 5   b 11   c 25   d 15   e 14
4 a (i) 3   (ii) −4   (iii) 9
   b 2   c (i) 3   (ii) 5
5 1 + 3 + 5 + 7 + 9
6 8   7 27   8 a 2   b 3   c 6   d $\frac{1}{2}$ e −4
9 3   10 100

Exercise 1.7

1 a 1 × 15   b 1 × 27   c 1 × 36   d 1 × 64
     3 × 5   3 × 9   2 × 18   2 × 32
                                 3 × 12   4 × 16
                                 4 × 9   8 × 8
                                 6 × 6
   e 1 × 100
     2 × 50
     4 × 25
     5 × 20
     10 × 10
2 a (i) 1, 2, 3, 4, 6, 8, 12, 16, 24, 48
     (ii) 1, 2, 3, 4, 6, 8, 9, 12, 18, 24, 36, 72
   b 1, 2, 3, 4, 6, 8, 12, 24
3 64, 144, 116, 2620
4 a 5, 10, 20, 25   b 5, 10, 25   c 5, 10
   d 5, 25   e 5, 10, 20
5 a 240, 87, 96, 255   b 240, 96   c 240, 255

Exercise 2.1

1 9.74   2 0.36   3 147.5   4 29
5 0.53   6 4.20   7 1250   8 0.004
9 270   10 460.0

Exercise 2.2

1 a 3500   b 240   c 1200   d 300   e 250
   f 10   g 40   h 5
2 a 9   b 0.06   c 24
3 Incorrect calculations are c, d, e, f, h, i.

Exercise 2.3

1 52p   2 6 tins   3 5   4 a 27p   b 3p
5 2m   6 25p   7 £10.91   8 £13.86
9 £1458.90   10 26

Exercise 2.4

1 11.8   2 73 700   3 2.70   4 0.173   5 88.9
6 29.0   7 21.4   8 26.0   9 0.786   10 882.65
11 0.829   12 11   13 3.3

Exercise 2.5

1 a 7.9×10^5 b 4.6×10^{-3} c 3.13×10^4
   d 9.41×10^{-5} e 1×10^5 f 2.82×10^{-4}
   g 1.57×10^4 h 4.7×10^7 i 3.4×10^{-2}
   j 2.7×10^{-6} k 5×10^{-1} l 1.4×10^{-7}
2 a 7530   b 240   c 0.0019   d 0.837   e 0.0451
   f 40 420   g 192 000   h 0.000974   i 0.000 0068
3 a 6×10^4 b 5.18×10^0 c 4×10^1 d 1.35×10^4
   e 2.174×10^3 f 4×10^{-2} g 4.32×10^{-5}
   h 2.84×10^4 i -5×10^{-4} j 6×10^1
4 390   5 8 minutes 20 seconds

Exercise 2.6

1 a 2.3×10^{-5} kg   b 8.70 m
2 3.5×10^4, 266.6 m   3 W\$756.25
4 4.096×10^7 5 2.303×10^{13} 6 1.34×10^7
7 a 1.32×10^5 b 362   8 106 days   9 \$4595
10 228 years

Exercise 3.1

1 a 8 b 8 c 18 d 9 e 7 f 9
2 a $\frac{2}{3}$ b $\frac{3}{4}$ c $\frac{2}{9}$ d $\frac{1}{3}$ e $\frac{3}{4}$ f $\frac{2}{3}$ g $\frac{6}{13}$ h $\frac{2}{3}$
3 $\frac{2}{3}$ 4 a $\frac{9}{16}$ b $\frac{3}{16}$ 5 $\frac{3}{16}$ 6 $\frac{1}{4}$ 7 $\frac{4}{7}$
8 a $\frac{20}{9}$ b $\frac{31}{6}$ c $\frac{59}{12}$ d $\frac{111}{10}$ e $\frac{35}{4}$ f $\frac{38}{3}$ g $\frac{143}{20}$ h $\frac{143}{7}$
9 a $1\frac{2}{7}$ b $7\frac{1}{5}$ c $3\frac{1}{3}$ d $7\frac{5}{8}$ e $13\frac{10}{11}$ f $10\frac{7}{12}$
  g $8\frac{4}{5}$ h $23\frac{1}{2}$

Exercise 3.2

1 $1\frac{3}{20}$ 2 $\frac{1}{24}$ 3 $\frac{2}{3}$ 4 $\frac{3}{4}$ 5 $\frac{1}{2}$ 6 $5\frac{1}{20}$ 7 2 8 $\frac{7}{8}$
9 $\frac{3}{20}$ 10a 6 b (i) $\frac{1}{4}$in (ii) $\frac{11}{16}$in 11 $\frac{1}{12}$
12 $\frac{2}{15}$ 13 a $\frac{1}{12}$ b 3
14 a $\frac{3}{25}$ b 400 mg aspirin, 40 mg ascorbic acid,
60 mg caffeine
15 $3\frac{5}{12}$ 16 7in 17 $\frac{3}{16}$ in 18 $1\frac{7}{8}$ in

Exercise 3.3

1 $\frac{7}{10}$ 2 $1\frac{1}{3}$ 3 12 4 $1\frac{1}{9}$ 5 $7\frac{3}{20}$ 6 $1\frac{5}{7}$
7 a $\frac{3}{5}$ b 1in 8 a $1\frac{1}{4}$ cm b 3cm 9 £7.60
10 a $\frac{1}{4}$ b 6 11 $\frac{3}{4}$ stone 12 a 13g b $\frac{3}{4}$g 13 13
14 a £288 b 15 15 $1\frac{1}{8}$ in 16 a $7\frac{1}{2}$ in b $2\frac{1}{2}$ in

Exercise 3.4

1 a $\frac{8}{12}=\frac{2}{3}$, 0.$\dot{6}$, b $\frac{1}{4}$, 0.25 c $\frac{5}{8}$, 0.625
2 a 0.1 b 0.5 c 0.75 d 1.45
  e 4.84 f 2.8$\dot{3}$ g 7.$\dot{4}$ h 3.$\dot{1}4\dot{2}857$
3 a $\frac{1}{2}$ b $\frac{1}{4}$ c $\frac{2}{3}$ d $1\frac{1}{3}$ e $1\frac{3}{10}$
  f $2\frac{4}{5}$ g $3\frac{3}{5}$ h $2\frac{3}{20}$ i $\frac{1}{8}$ j $\frac{3}{8}$
5 a Insert d.p. into numerator 1 place from right.
  b Multiply numerator by 2 and change to tenths.
  c Insert d.p. into numerator 2 places from right.
  d Change to tenths then divide by 2.
  e Multiply numerator by 4 and change to hundredths.
6 34 7 a (i) $1\frac{2}{3}$ (ii) 1.67 b 80p
8 a 20 sheets b (i) $20\frac{5}{6}$ (ii) 20.83
9 (i) $4\frac{2}{3}$ hours (ii) 4.67 hours
10 (i) $3\frac{1}{5}$ hours (ii) 3.20 hours 11 (i) $1\frac{3}{4}$ (ii) 1.75

Exercise 4.1

1 5 : 6 2 4 : 5 : 10 3 20 : 9
4 a 3 : 2 b 10 : 1 c 12 : 1 d 1 : 4 e 4 : 3
  f 3 : 2 g 3 : 8 h 3 : 2 i 2 : 3
5 a 8 b 2 c 1.2 d 0.6 e 3.2 f 2.6
6 410 and 1025 7 $13\frac{1}{2}$ kg 8 3 : 20
9 a 125 b 200 10 3 : 16 11 28 fl oz
12 1 : 8 13 a 720 b 480 14 40 : 1 15 66

Exercise 4.2

1 £260, £390 2 £1500, £4500, £6000
3 £48, £32, £24 4 £1750, £1250, £1000
5 1360 g, 240 g 6 20
7 a £6318, £4212 b £15 760 c £9924
8 £26 154, £34 872, £17 436, £26 154
9 27, 45 10 40
11 a (i) 5 : 3 (ii) £7.50, £4.50 b 7.33, £4.67
12 £24 13 1813 14 a 192 b 720

Exercise 4.3

1 £3.18 2 £2.66 3 £1.26 4 £1.84 5 £4.40
6 £242 7 £430.50 8 44 9 200 10 4 hours
11 £1845 12 84 13 $\frac{11}{16}$ in

Exercise 4.4

1 a 1 cm b 4.8 cm c 1.1 m (110 cm) d 2.88 cm
2 a 20 cm b 1.24 m (124 cm) c 1.68 m (168 cm)
  d 75 ft e 90 in (7.5 ft)
3 a 45 in b 60 in × 24 in
4 a 1 : 40 b 48 in
5 a 1.05 m × 0.40 m b 0.65 m
6 100 m × 450 m 7 12.8 m²
8 a 1 : 72 b 11 ft × 8 ft 9 3.65 m, 1.25 m
10 a 1 : 200 b 3.24 m²

Exercise 4.5

1 a (i) 7 cm (ii) 14 cm × 12 cm (iii) 8 mm
  b (i) 93 cm (ii) $13\frac{1}{2}$ cm (iii) 69 cm × 60 cm
2 a 9 ft × 2 in b 39.7 cm
3 a 20.4 m b 68 ft
4 a 6 cm × 3 cm b 1.24 m
5 a 8.8 cm b 5 m
6 a 1 : 150 b $2\frac{2}{3}$ cm
7 a 1 ft : 30 m b 6.3 ft
8 a 1 : 130 b 3.0 cm c 39 m

Exercise 5.1

2 a metres b millimetres c kilograms
  d kilometres e millimetres
3 5000 mm 4860 cm $\frac{1}{2}$ km 750 m
4 $\frac{3}{8}$ kg
5 a 1.232 km b 32 mm c 0.626 kg d 73.1 cl
  e 16.2 ml f 12 700 m g 0.0591 litres
6 230 g 7 20 days 8 1.55 kg 9 2.65 cm
10 665 litres (665.8 litres including disinfectant)

Exercise 5.2

2 a 3.25 ft b 2 lb 8 oz c 5.5 yards d 27 in
  e 55 oz f 2.5 gal g 28 pt h 14 fl oz
3 $\frac{3}{4}$ pint 4 a 46.5 ft b 15.5 yards
5 $6\frac{1}{8}$ (6.125) oz 6 5 yd × $2\frac{1}{2}$ yd 7 40
8 5 9 20 yd 2 ft 4 in 10 $1\frac{1}{2}$ ft × $1\frac{1}{6}$ ft

Exercise 5.3

1 9 km
2 a 15 oz b 15.5 oz c 14.6 oz
3 a 454 g b 5.3 oz c 2.3 kg d 336 g e 0.5 oz
4 a 0.219 gal b 4.4 gal 5 3.52 miles per litre
6 a 152 (150) mm b 14.6 (14.8) in
  c 17.5 (16) ft 7 80 kph
8 a 42 lb b 2 lb 9 6 in 10 25.4 kg
11 1.60 m–1.83 m b 22.9 m
12 a 77.8 g b 0.579 troy ounces
13 57 mm, 89 mm, 22 mm, 32 mm
14 28

Exercise 5.4

1 6.4 cm, 2.5 in Approx, 2.3 m to 5 m 2 66 865
3 335 g 4 98.5°F 5 15 min 10.6 s
6 a 30 mph b 50 kph 7 5 psi

Exercise 5.5

1 81p 2 £374.50
3 a 90 miles b 7 gallons c approximately 8 miles/litre
4 £167.75 5 6 hours 43 minutes 6 9.7 kg
7 a 8p b £42.24 8 1.17 g/cm³

Exercise 5.6

1 a 54 mph b 8.6 m/s (31.0 km/h) c 88 km/h
2 a 204 km b 2760 miles
3 a 3 hours b 7 hours 39 minutes 4 $7\frac{1}{2}$ miles
5 a 3 hours 52 minutes b 6 km/h

Exercise 6.1

1 a 20% b $12\frac{1}{2}$% c 70% d 65% e $66\frac{2}{3}$% f 36%
  g 175% h 250%
2 a $\frac{3}{5}$ b $\frac{1}{4}$ c $\frac{1}{10}$ d $\frac{17}{20}$ e $\frac{3}{20}$ f $1\frac{3}{20}$ g $\frac{3}{8}$ h $\frac{1}{3}$
3 a   0.75   75%
  b $\frac{1}{2}$ 50%
  c   0.125 $12\frac{1}{2}$%
  d $\frac{1}{3}$ 0.$\dot{3}$
  e $\frac{3}{8}$ $37\frac{1}{2}$%
  f   0.7   70%
  g $\frac{7}{20}$ 0.35
  h $\frac{2}{3}$ $66\frac{2}{3}$%
  i   0.6   60%
  j $\frac{5}{8}$ 0.625

Exercise 6.2

1 a £1.38 b £318.62 c £22.12 d £13.91 e £5.17
  f £8.73 g £97.20 h £44.20

Exercise 6.3

1 a £10.12 b £4.07 c £5.50 d £10.79 e £10.04
2 a £108.18 b £1.05 c £792.00 d £233.75
  e £156.00 f £21.69

Exercise 6.4

1 a £24.00 b £8.40 c £14.08 d 36p e £10.39
2 a £49.77 b 59p c £51.20 d £23.76 e £59.43
  f £1.09

Exercise 6.5

1 a 80.0% b 3.45% c 175% d 50%
  e 54.5% f 130%
2 a +23.1% b +20.0% c +375% d −20.0%
  e −45.5% f +464%

Exercise 6.6

1 a 18% 2 a 260 b 78 3 12%
4 a 20 000 b 7500 c 36.2%
5 a 406 b 146 6 £2.64 7 £3.43
8 £1335.70 9 616 10 £2240

Exercise 7.1

1 £172.20 2 £479.67 3 £6.43 4 £11582.40
5 £134.28 6 £23 700 7 £7320 8 £186.82
9 £5244 10 £194.36 11 £5.526 12 £36.95
13 a £259.70 b £155.75 c £441 14 £4.2667

Exercise 7.2

1 £344.10 2 a £4.50 b 4 3 £187.68 4 £257.30
5 £8.43 6 £253.80 7 £279.90 8 £218.40
9 £268.80 10 £166.50 11 £266.40
12 Andrews £204.18
   Collins £268.92
   Hammond £263.94
   Jali £318.72
   Longman £308.76
13 £5.45

Exercise 7.3

1 £1560 2 £24.72 3 £1883.20 4 £493.20
5 £1138 6 £1456
7 a Firm B by £500 b Firm A by £250
8 £283.55 9 £94 10 £60 11 £99.40
12 £304 13 £380.70

Exercise 7.4

1 £59.04 2 £56.40 3 £3.99 4 £228.70
5 £182 6 £362 7 £243.50 8 £31 9 £440
10 1570 Fr 11 £62.08 12 £98.20

Exercise 7.5

1 a (i) £4385 (ii) £115 (iii) £11.50
  b (i) £4385 (ii) £565 (iii) £56.50
  c (i) £4385 (ii) Nil (iii) Nil
2 £132 3 £9.31 4 a £85.80 b £106.50
5 £10.76 6 £136.50 7 £9.96
8 a (i) £4385 (ii) £815 (iii) £81.50
  b (i) £4385 (ii) £1387 (iii) £138.70
9 £9.70 10 £9.35 11 £133.50 12 £147.50
13 £146

Exercise 7.6

1 a £1503.90 b £934.98 c £2429.20
2 a £2935.20 b £2935.20
3 a £61.45 b £35.59 c £96.60 4 £5186.70
5 £370.08 (or .07) 6 £5593.04 7 £391.71
8 £206.91 9 £331.21 10 £4759.20
11 £389.88 (or .87) 12 £239.41 13 £5704.14

Exercise 7.7

1 a £3.67 b £25.74 c £53.93 d £8.37 e £4.44
2 a £31.20 b £4232.80
3 a £184 b £10.80 c £143.95

Exercise 8.1

1 a 137.76 kunas b 128.24 lats c $152.47
2 a £76.34 b £4549.18 c £3.82
3 £8.47 4 a £80.31, 40.2
5 a 3913.20 b 291.28
6 a 177, 940 b 70270 c £201.33 d £1.86
7 a 771.50 b £93.99 c £6.01

Exercise 8.2

1 a £1 b £1 c £8.01 2 a £3 b £6
3 a 1251.32 kuna, 245.52 swiss francs, 749.70 litas
  b (i) £560 (ii) £5.60 c £223.90

Exercise 8.3

1 6.15 am; 0615
2 Ten past eleven in the evening, 2310
3 Half past nine in the morning, 9.30 am
4 Twenty to two in the morning; 0140
5 Ten to two in the afternoon, 1.50 pm
6 Twenty past ten in the evening; 10.20 pm
7 9.50 pm; 2150
8 Quarter to eleven in the morning; 1045
9 12.25 am; 0025
10 Four minutes to five in the afternoon; 4.56 pm

Exercise 8.4

1 14 minutes 2 0655 3 9.30 am 4 0942
5 a 1623 b 28 minutes 6 1 hour 45 minutes
7 a 1945 b 2030

Exercise 8.5

1 a 20 minutes b 4 c 39 minutes
   d 1451, 1543 (or 1551)
2 a 5 b 0030 Belgian time c 25 minutes d 0930
   e 1 hour f 1335

Exercise 8.6

1 £101.51 2 a 1155 b 1650
3 a Ease of access to airport; Departure time or arrival
     time in Naples; Experience of the airline.
   b American: 2335; Virgin: 0040
4 £86.54 5 1313 6 £217.03 7 £307.22
8 5.09 pm 9 52.5% 10 a 1045 b 2100 British time

Exercise 9.1

1	Discrete	2	Continuous	3	Continuous
4	Continuous	5	**Qualitative**	4	Continuous
7	Continuous	8	**Qualitative**	9	Discrete
10	Qualitative	11	**Discrete**	12	Qualitative

Exercise 10.1

1 a total population of the town
   b people asked at a particular time in a particular
     shopping street
   c Specify the intended catchment area of the new
     shopping centre. Use the electoral role for this area
     to select a random sample.
2 a all the students in the College
   b She only asks people in the common room, and she
     only asks girls.
   c Find students' enrolment numbers, and select 50
     random numbers in the range of numbers given.
3 a all cars in the UK
   b The police only check cars between 5 pm and 6 pm.
   c Sample at different times of day on different days of
     the week on different roads.
4 a the soil in his garden
   b only one sample. Soil beyond the range of his throw
     cannot be sampled.
   c Draw a plan of the garden and divide into numbered
     squares. Use random sampling to choose several
     squares and take samples from these areas.
5 a all teenagers
   b Carol only asked people entering a tobacconist's.
     The sample is biased towards smokers. Carol should
     only ask teenagers.

c Obtain a list of pupils in the school; select a random
  sample from the list.
6 a any homes in the telephone area
   b The salesgirl only asks those with a telephone. The
     sample includes only those who are at home when
     the salesgirl rings.
   c The salesgirl needs to know the number of homes in
     the area. She needs to use the rating register (used in
     water rates) to identify homes; use their reference
     numbers to obtain a random sample.
7 a all cars owned by people in an area
   b Peter only asked people at home during one
     afternoon. The responses came from a small part of
     the town.
   c Use the DVLC in Swansea to produce a list of cars
     registered as being owned by people in the required
     area. Use random numbers to obtain a sample of the
     required size.
8 a all people who travel to work in John's area
   b People at the station would be biased towards those
     using a train to go to work.
   c Use the electoral role and ask a random sample from
     this how they travel to work. If they do not work,
     delete them from the sample. Continue with a
     random selection until you have a suitable number
     who do work.

Exercise 10.3

1 a Analyse rainfall for the given period over several years.
   b Devise a questionnaire, survey, or experiment.

Exercise 11.1

(Frequencies only are given)
1 8, 7, 5, 5, 4, 3, 1, 2, 1, 1, 1, 0, 1, 0, 1
2 1, 3, 5, 10, 19, 6, 6
3 18, 17, 13, 7, 4, 2, 1, 0, 1
4 4, 8, 9, 8, 9, 6, 2, 2, 2
5 a 1, 4, 4, 4, 8, 5, 4, 3, 5, 1, 1
   b 1, 8, 15, 8, 6, 2
6 1, 14, 23, 19, 6
7 5, 6, 2, 8, 10, 12, 3, 4
8 9, 11, 8, 11, 5, 8, 12, 11, 5
9 1, 7, 15, 16, 9, 2
10 31, 13, 15, 1
11 1, 0, 5, 16, 13, 4, 1

Exercise 12.1

1 a East Lynne b 50 c 410
4 a 175 b 8.3% c 4 : 1
7 a Soft white baps b 6 c 61.9(62)%
9 a 20 b Evensong c 110
11 a Plymouth–Roscoff b $3\frac{3}{4}$ hours c $2\frac{1}{2}$ hours
13 a 5 b Train c 150

Exercise 12.2

1 a Oak b Oak 80; Elm 10; Chestnut 20;
     Beech 40; Conifer 70; Cedar 25 c 245
6 a A; Adverts on hoarding B are aimed at more
     prosperous suburban inhabitants.
   b 2 c Football club and health education
10 a £30 000 b £27 500 c £2500 d Central
17 a Estate 1 has more occupants in professional jobs;
      Estate 2 has more occupants in 'blue collar' jobs.
    b (i) 10% (ii) 38% c 30%

18 a (i) 15　(ii) 4　**b** 70%　**c** The Maples
20 a Chandler　**b** 20　**c** 18 : 7　**d** 44%

Exercise 12.3

1 a 160　**b** 120　**c** 220　**d** 140
6 a 40°　**b** 25　**c** 50　**d** $\frac{5}{18}$
10 54 762, 5952, 85 714
12 a 298　**b** 46　**c** 306
16 a 325　**b** 290　**c** 210, 87.8%
18 a 72.2%　**b** 458 300 acres

Exercise 12.4

5 a 1 040 000　**b** 1927, 1951, 1974　**c** 1940
6 a Tiredness as the week goes by　**b** 226
7 a £180　**b** £209　**c** Line beginning to curve upwards
　slightly.
　d 1990
8 b 8 am–9 am heating was turned on
　c after 8.20 pm
9 a 52.5 (±0.5) in　**b** 4–6 years
　c It will slow down and eventually stop.
11 a continuous line
　b December (London), October (Nice)
　c June (both)　**d** February
12 b Summer is peak time, but numbers of passengers
　could be declining, whereas winter numbers seem to
　be increasing.
14 a September; new registration letter
　b 15　**c** 171　**d** 28.5

Exercise 12.5

2 b A low absence rate is more likely on Mondays and a
　high one on Fridays.
3 b Book 1: Science fiction.
　Book 2: Child's story.
　Book 1 has a greater number of long words and
　Book 2 has a greater number of short words.
4 There has been a move to 'Traditional Style' from
　'Modern Design'.
6 There are more women than men over the age
　of 45.
7 b The experimental results are very close to the
　expected results.
8 There were less faults on the new model.

Exercise 13.1

1 £130　**2** 68.27 mph　**3** 38.58
4 The ages are given to the last completed year. A person
　aged 17 is between 17 years 0 days and 17 years 364
　days old. Therefore, the true mean is probably above
　$28\frac{3}{4}$, hence John is probably correct.
5 1.848 m　**6** 104.8　**7 a** 1.29 m　**b** Yes
8 a 1125　**b** 75 w.p.m.
9 a £496.14　**b** £5.04　**10** 13.5
11 a 164 lb　**b** 32.8 lb　**c** $13\frac{2}{3}$ (13.7) lb per week
12 a 21.9°C　**b** (i) 18.75°C　(ii) 24°C
13 a 51.78　**b** 57.89 m
　c Considerable improvement (over 6 m)
14 Average is 40.9 mpg. Therefore, taking values to 2 s.f.,
　he is justified.
15 6 min 5 seconds

Exercise 13.2

1 a 4　**b** 4　**2** Blue　**3** 110–114
4 a 12.5　**b** 11　**5** 6.35 kg　**6** 1
7 a James and Linda　**b** 5 ft $2\frac{1}{2}$ in　**c** Mode
8 a 50p　**b** 44p
9 a £10 000　**b** £10 000　**c** £16 800
　d Mode or median
10 a 9.00–11.00　**b** 70–75
11 a 18　**b** 16　**12** St Lucia
13 a £112　**b** £112　**14 a** 4　**b** 2.5
15 4:55 (4 min 55 sec)

Exercise 13.3

1 Mode　**2** Median　**3** Mode　**4** Median　**5** Mean
6 Mean or median　**7** Median　**8** Mean　**9** Mean
10 Any, but the mean is preferable.

Exercise 13.4

1 6　**2** 26.60 min (= 26 min 36 s)　**3** 7.79 words
4 a 1.43　**b** 1　**c** 0　**d** Median
5 a 4.17　**b** 4　**6 a** 7.5　**b** 7.06
7 a 3.5　**b** 3.28　**8 a** 1　**b** 1
9 a 4.08　**b** 4　**c** Median
10 a 2.62　**b** 3　**11 a** 2.94　**b** 3
12 a 0.52　**b** 0　**c** Mean
13 a 19　**b** 19.3
　c Close match between mean and median

Exercise 13.5

1 20 in　**2 a** 12.6 min　**b** 10 min
3 a (i) 31.8　(ii) 36.3
　b (i) 50　(ii) 25　**4** 34　**5** 8.9
6 a 38.2, 41　**b** 56, 22　**c** Beach 2. It has a slightly
　higher average number of shells and is more
　consistent.
7 a £16.10, £2.55, £16.82, £2.60
　Similar ranges, but club 2 has a higher mean.
　b £15.80, £16.95
　c Club 1: distribution is possibly skewed since
　median < mean; Club 2: distribution is negatively
　skewed since median > mean.
8 a 122.3, 82.5　**b** (i) 30　(ii) 30
　c Blood pressure high on day 8, both pressures below
　normal on day 10.
9 a 55.8 cm, 55.5 cm　**b** 51.0 cm, 114 cm
　c The first archer, who is more consistent
10 a 50.3, 48.7　**b** 4.47, 2.94　**c** Machine 3 has a mean
　close to 50 but is variable.
　Machine 5 is producing ball bearings which are
　consistently below size and should be adjusted.

Exercise 13.6

1 a 32　**b** 28　**c** 35　**d** 7　**e** 8
2 a 73 cm　**b** 66 cm　**c** 79 cm　**d** 13 cm
　e (i) 4　(ii) 55
3 a £12 700　**b** £11 200　**c** £13 800　**d** £2600
　e £14 100
4 a 58　**b** 44　**c** 71　**d** 27　**e** (i) 84　(ii) 83
5 b (i) 190 g　(ii) 74　**c** (i) 34 kg　(ii) 21 kg

Exercise 14.1

1 $7x + 5y$　**5** $2p - q$ or $q - 2p$　**3** $\dfrac{2a}{b}$

4 $5x - 8$　**5** $\dfrac{y}{4} + 6$　**6** $4a + 3c$　**7** $4b + 6r + 2w$

8 $4r + 3p + 2t$ **9** $6l + 8p + 2i$ **10** $22n + 3p$
11 $4t + 5r + 3s$ **12** $3a + 5c$ **13** $7f + 5s + 3e$
14 $2h + 3i + 22s$ **15** $28f + 12m + 15w$

Exercise 14.2

1 $5x$ **2** $7n$ **3** $8a$ **4** $2y$
5 $7a + 6b + 4c$ **6** $x + 5y + 9z$ **7** $9p + 2q + r$
8 $5x - 3y + z$ **9** $-a - b + 4c$ **10** $3x + 5y$

Exercise 14.3

1 **a** 11 **b** −1 **c** 13 **d** 6 **e** $\frac{1}{2}$ **f** 2 **g** −30 **h** −4
  i 0 **j** 17 **k** −1 **l** −2
2 **a** 1 **b** −9 **c** −5 **d** −6 **e** 0.3 **f** −14 **g** 6
  h 8 **i** 10 **j** −5 **k** 1 **l** −2
3 **a** 9 **b** −24 **c** 8 **d** $\frac{4}{3}$ **e** −5 **f** $-\frac{3}{4}$ **g** 38
  h 7 **i** 28 **j** 1 **k** 0 **l** 14
4 **a** $\frac{1}{2}$ **b** 1 **c** 2 **d** −4 **e** $2\frac{1}{2}$ **f** $-\frac{1}{4}$ **g** $8\frac{1}{2}$
  h $\frac{3}{5}$ **i** 3 **j** −1 **k** −8 **l** $4\frac{1}{2}$

Exercise 14.4

1 $5x$ **2** $3mn$ **3** $\dfrac{2y}{z}$ **4** abc **5** $6pqr$ **6** $\dfrac{4bc}{d}$

7 $6xy$ **9** $\dfrac{-2p}{q}$ **9** $\dfrac{9xy}{z}$ **10** a^3 **11** a^2b^2 **12** $3a^3$

13 $3a^3b^2$ **14** $-6a^2b^2c$ **15** $6a^2b^4c^2$ **16** $9a^2b$

17 $-18ab^3$ **18** $-2a$ **19** x^3y^3 **20** $\dfrac{-9a^2b}{c}$

Exercise 14.5

1 x^8 **2** x^6 **3** x^3 **4** x^{-1} **5** $x^0 = 1$

6 $\dfrac{1}{x^2}$ **7** 1 **8** $\dfrac{3x^2}{2^2}$

Exercise 14.6

1 $n + 5 = 12$ **2** $n - 7 = 13$ **3** $2n + 4 = 10$
4 $7n = 21$ **5** $5n - 6 = 29$ **6** $\frac{1}{2}n + 10 = 22$
7 $2n - 3 = 3$ **8** $\frac{1}{4}n - 3 = 3$ **9** $2(x + 2x) = 18$
10 $x + (x - 2) + (x + 5) = 27$ **11** $3x + x = 20$
12 $2x + x + 2x + 20 = 135$ **13** $2(x + 2x) = 12.6$
14 $14x + 10(x + 6) + 6(x - 4) = 906$
15 $2(2x) + 3x = 77$ **16** $4 + 2x + (x - 3) = 37$
17 $4x + 2x + x = 1750$
18 $4(3x) + 2(3x) + x + 2(2x) = 10\,350$

Exercise 14.7

1 7 **2** 20 **3** 3 **4** 3 **5** 7 **6** 24 **7** 3 **8** 24
9 3 cm **10** 13 cm **11** 5 **12** 66 **13** 4.2 ft **14** 35
15 22 **16** 9 **17** 250 **18** 1350 **19** 4 **20** 3 **21** 6
22 8 **23** 3 **24** 6 **25** 10 **26** 8 **27** 9 **28** 20

Exercise 14.8

1 4 **2** 3 **3** 2 **4** $\frac{1}{3}$ **5** 9 **6** 2 **7** 0 **8** 10 **9** 4
10 1 **11** 3 **12** −5.2

Exercise 14.9

1 **a** (i) $(x + 25)$ pence (ii) $12x$ pence (iii) $10(x + 25)$
  b (i) $12x + 10(x + 25) = 690$ (ii) $x = 20$p (iii) 45p
2 **a** £$(2x + 2.50)$ **b** £1.25 **3** 55p
4 **a** $3x + 4.40 = 50 - 7.50$ **b** £12.70
5 **a** $x + 0.3$ **b** $4x + 7(x + 0.3) = 19.70$ **c** £1.60

6 **a** $8x + 5(x + 0.26) = 6.63$ **b** 41p **7** £1.20
8 68 kg **9** 15 min
10 **a** £$9x$ **b** £$5(20 - x)$ **c** £$(4x + 100)$
  d $4x + 100 = 148$ **e** 12 matches
11 **a** (i) $2x$ (ii) $2x - 5$
  b $2x - 5 + 2x + x + 15 = 80$; 23
12 **a** $x + (x - 4) + (x + 6) = 35$ **b** 7
13 **a** (i) $2x$ (ii) $2x + 20$
  b $x + 2x + (2x + 20) = 110$; 56

Exercise 14.10

1 **a** $x \longrightarrow$ [Multiply by 7] $\longrightarrow$ [Add 5] $\longrightarrow y$

  b $x \longrightarrow$ [Multiply by 3] $\longrightarrow$ [Subtract 11] $\longrightarrow y$

  c $x \longrightarrow$ [Square] $\longrightarrow$ [Multiply by 3] $\longrightarrow$ [Add 5] $\longrightarrow y$

  d $x \longrightarrow$ [Multiply by 2] $\longrightarrow$ [Add 1] $\longrightarrow$ [Square] $\longrightarrow y$

2 **a** $y = 3x + 3$ **b** $y = \left(\dfrac{x}{5} + 4\right)^2$ **c** $y = \{3(x + 6)\}^2$

Exercise 14.11

1 **a** (i) 30 m/s (ii) 36 m/s
  b (i) 67.5 mph (ii) 81 mph
2 5 **3** **a** 10 **b** 25 **c** −10
4 **a** 7.2 **b** 4.2 **5** **a** £137.50 **b** £82.80
6 £1918.44
7 **a** (i) £16.20 (ii) £115.20 **b** 12.3p
  8 **a** 838 860 800 **b** 9.223×10^{20} **c** 819 200
9 **a** 426 cm^3 **b** 551 cm^3 **10** 5832 in^2
11 **a** 3000 m^3 **b** 2475 m^3 **12** 2.79 ohms
13 £142

Exercise 14.12

1 **a** 26.03 mm **b** $T = \dfrac{2(L - C)}{3} = \dfrac{2(L - \pi D)}{3}$
  e 0.08 mm
2 **a** 72 **b** $y = \frac{1}{2}(N - 4) - x$ **c** 53 cm
  d $N = 4x + 4$, 124 **e** $x = \dfrac{N - 4}{4} = \frac{1}{4}N - 1$
  f 36 cm square

3 **a** £9700 **b** (i) $b = \dfrac{T - 350s - 50c}{1200}$ (ii) 2
  c (i) $c = \dfrac{T - 1200b - 350s}{50}$ (ii) 21

4 **a** 31.5% **b** $P = \dfrac{CR}{100}$ **c** £1690

5 **a** 4550 **b** (i) $H = \dfrac{C}{S}$ (ii) 76 beats per min

6 **a** 340 calories **b** $t = \dfrac{230b - c}{6}$ **c** 1 h 55 min

7 **a** $3\frac{1}{2}$ hours **b** $d = 4t - \dfrac{h}{150} = 4\left(t - \dfrac{h}{600}\right)$
  c 17 km

8 **a** £138 **b** $N = \dfrac{10(D - 50)}{C}$ **c** 6

9 **a** 823 watts **b** (i) $R = \dfrac{V^2}{P}$ (ii) 19.2 ohms
  c (i) $V = \sqrt{PR}$ (ii) 424 volts

Exercise 15.1

1 Rough estimate   **a** $5\frac{1}{2}$%   **b** £10
2 'Exact'   **a** 5   **b** 72 cm
3 'Exact'   **a** $1\frac{1}{2}$ hours   **b** £2500
4 'Exact'   **a** £2.19 (£2.20)   **b** $1\frac{1}{4}$ min
5 'Exact'   **a** 1 h 38 min (± 2 min)
  b No, should be cooked for at least 1 h 12 min
  c To ensure that all bacteria are destroyed and prevent food poisoning.
6 Rough estimate   **a** 30 miles
  b 3.8 hours (= 3 h 48 min)
7 'Exact'   **a** £540   **b** 450
8 Rough estimate   **a** 56   **b** £360 per week
9 Rough estimate   **a** 15 years   **b** 20 years
10 Rough estimate   **a** 3.0 mm   **b** 23 500 miles

Exercise 15.2

1 **a** 10 st 4 lb (±1 lb)   **b** 10 st 8 lb
  c February 1990 and August 1991   **d** Yes
2 **a** 60 cm^2 **b** 4.1 cm^2 **c** 90 cm^2
3 **a** October and February   **b** 14.8 and 15.8 hr
  c December to January and May to June
4 **a** 25 mm   **b** 0.7 minutes   **c** 235 mm
5 **a** 2.6 s   **b** −10 cm   **c** 0.45 s   **d** 1.75 s

Exercise 15.3

1 **a** 68°F   **b** No, too low   **c** 35°C   **d** 90°F
  e Yes (≈14°C)
2 **a** 29 cm × 42 cm   **b** 1.8 cm
3 **a** £22.73 (£22.70)   **b** 1690 yen
4 **a** 8 lb 13 oz   **b** 6 lb 1 oz
5 **a** 66 miles, 153 miles, 219 miles, 350 miles
  b 102 km
6 **a** 95 litres   **b** 285 miles

Exercise 15.4

7 **a** (i) The same coefficient of x (ii) the same gradient
  b The coefficient of x is the gradient of the line
8 **a** All the lines pass through the origin.
  b A graph of the form $y = ax$ passes through the origin.
9 The point on the y-axis through which the line passes.
10 The line slopes downwards, i.e. the gradient of the line is negative.

Exercise 15.5

1 **a** £18   **b** 34 in
2 **a** $y = 10$ cm, $w = 3.8$ cm   **b** $x = 4$ cm, $w = 2.5$ cm
3 **a** (i) 50%   (ii) −40%   **b** £6250
4 **a** £450   **b** £4195
5 **a** 164 cm, 178 cm   **b** 90 cm
6 **a** $8\frac{1}{2}$ min   **b** $4\frac{1}{4}$ min
7 **a** £13   **b** £2125   **c** 6 hours
8 **a** £A22   **b** $7\frac{1}{2}$ miles
9 **a** 19.8 kg (20 kg)   **b** 1.3 litres
10 **a** 440 mm   **b** 60 kg   **c** 300 mm

Exercise 15.6

1 **a** 3   **b** 2   **c** −2   **d** $\frac{1}{2}$ **e** $\frac{2}{3}$ **f** −2   **g** −1
  h −2   **i** $-\frac{1}{3}$
2 **a** 2   **b** −5   **c** 4   **d** −1   **e** 2   **f** $\frac{1}{2}$ **g** −2   **h** −4
  i 2

3 **a** $y = 2x + 1$ **b** $y = 3x - 1$ **c** $y = -x - 1$
  d $y = -\frac{1}{2}x + 2$
4 **a** (v)   **b** (iii)   **c** (vi)   **d** (iv)   **e** (i)   **f** (ii)
5 **a** $S = \dfrac{A}{1400}$ **b** $\dfrac{1}{175}$
6 **a** $y = -0.9x + 24$ **b** 19 500
  c The relationship is not linear outside the given values.
7 $D = \frac{1}{2}Q$
8 **b** $P = -0.6A + 132$ **c** (i) 99   (ii) 121
9 **a** $4y = x + 4$ **b** 4 mm

Exercise 16.1

A Equilateral triangle   **E** Rectangle
B Square   **F** Hexagon
C Pentagon   **G** Right-angled triangle
D Trapezium   **H** Circle

Exercise 16.2

2 176 large and 528 small
3

Exercise 17.1

1 **a** 22 cm   **b** 28 cm   **c** 24 in
2 **a** 114   **b** 28   **c** 136 cm
3 220 cm   4 **a** 72 mm   **b** 13
5 **a** 101.4 cm   **b** 143.4 cm
6 **a** 20.5 cm × 15 cm   **b** 162 cm   7 780 cm
8 **a** 150 cm × 200 cm (1.5 m × 2 m)
  b 700 cm (= 7 m)
9 480 ft   10 1720 cm (17.2 m)   11 3.8 m
12 **a** 92 in   **b** (i) 35 in × 43 in   (ii) 156 in (= 13 ft)

Exercise 17.2

1 **a** 12 cm^2 **b** 13.5 cm^2 **c** 15.75 cm^2
2 **a** 60 cm^2 **b** 300 cm^2 **c** 75 cm^2
  d 43.75 cm^2 **e** 264.48 cm^2 **f** 240.25 cm^2
3 **a** 12 m   **b** 50 m   4 30.25 cm^2
5 **a** 6: 23 × 78, 138 × 13, 34.5 × 52,
    19.5 × 92, 46 × 39, 26 × 39
  b (i) 202 cm, 302 cm, 173 cm, 223 cm, 170 cm,
    130 cm
6 **a** 12 cm × 12 cm   **b** 256 cm^2
7 **a** 624 cm^2 **b** 312 cm^2
8 202.5 cm^2 9 3.68 m^2 10 8400 cm^2
11 14.5 m^2 12 992 in^2 13 1.37 m^2
14 **a** 440 cm   **b** 424 cm   **c** 106   **d** 1.18 m^2

Exercise 17.3

1 **a** 11.25 cm^2 **b** 32.76 m^2 **c** 41.31 in^2
2 **a** 88 cm^2 **b** 245 mm^2 **c** 63 in^2 **d** 19.32 m^2
3 **a** 10 m   16 cm
4 **a** 16 cm   **b** 8 cm   **c** 12 mm   **d** 12.24 m^2
  e 23.65 in^2

Exercise 17.4

1 **a** 120 cm^2 **b** 75.6 cm^2 **c** 451 in^2
  d 3380 cm^2 (0.338 m^2)   **e** 1978 mm^2 (19.78 cm^2)
2 **a** 2.4 cm   **b** 0.33 m   **c** 13.4 cm^2 **d** 4 m   **e** 2.4 yd
3 **a** 8 cm   **b** 4 cm   **c** 5.25 in
4 **a** 7 cm   **b** 1.80 cm

Exercise 17.5

1 a 60 cm^2 b 224 cm^3 c 139 in^2 d 99 cm^2

Exercise 17.6

1 0.98 m^2
2 36 cm^2, 36 cm^2, 108 cm^2
3 54.4 m^2 4 278 cm^2
5 a 0.485 m^2 b 0.970 m^2 6 6.5 m^2
7 a 22.8 m^2 b 101 m^2 8 12.6 m^2
9 768 cm^2 10 2.28 m^2

Exercise 17.7

1 a 5 cm, 31.4 cm b 8.6 in, 4.3 in
  c 7 mm, 22.0 mm d 16.2 cm, 8.1 cm
  e 1.9 m, 1.0 m
2 72.3 mm 3 3.46 cm
4 20.0 ft 5 a 7.64 cm b 4.30 cm
6 23.6 cm 7 a 90 cm b 10 cm
8 a 211 cm b 106 m 9 92 cm
10 20 000 km 11 1.59 km
12 a 25.1 cm b 452 cm 13 210 cm

Exercise 17.8

1 a 158 cm^2 b 2730 in^2 c 145 mm^2 37.7 cm^2
  e 33.8 m^2
2 a 3 cm b 7 in c 6 cm d 4 m e 10 ft
3 a 2.93 cm b 6.91 in c 5.86 cm d 3.91 m
  e 9.77 ft
4 a 707 cm^2 b 113 in^2
5 a 28.4 cm^2 b 114 cm^2 e 75.5 cm^2
6 a 201 cm^2 b 7 7 a 7.5 cm b 44.2 cm^2
8 a 113 m^2 b 37 9 a 1.77 m^2 b £11
10 1.99 m^2 11 8.0 m 12 1810 cm^2
13 56 cm

Exercise 17.9

1 a 90 cm^3 b 51.3 cm^3 c 0.336 m^3
  d 1450 cm^3 e 1.2 m^3
2 a 3.33 cm
3 a 512 cm^3 b 1331 cm^3 c 68.9 cm^3
4 0.222 m^3 (= 222 000 cm^3) 5 0.988 m^3
6 4330 cm^3 7 a 14 400 cm^3 b 25 000 cm^3
8 a 27 cu in b 3 in
9 0.305 m^3 (= 305 000 cm^3) 10 3.85 fl oz
11 109 m^3 12 3700 cm^3 13 10.8 in

Exercise 17.10

1 a 603 cm^3 b 3050 cm^3 c 1690 in^3 d 388 cm^3
2 a 788 cm^3 b 136 cm^3 c 657 cm^3
3 313 m^3 4 15 800 m^3
5 a 8.78 cm^3 b 474 cm^3
6 a 19 800 cm^3 b 34 cm c 30 cm
  d 27 200 cm^3, 7450 cm^3 (7400 cm^3)
7 a 10.3 cm b 8.84 cm
8 7880 cm^3 (7875 cm^3)
9 a 58 700 cm^3 (= 0.0587 m^3)
  b 117 000 cm^3 (= 0.117 m^3)
10 a 2090 cm^3 b 34 600 cm^3 c 34 800 cm^3
  d 34.8 litres 11 a 1.25 m^3 b 8.45 m^3
12 a 42 400 cm^3 b 0.04 m^3
13 a 156 cm^3 b 8 cm
14 a 4.4 cm b 4.43 cm^3 c 79.7 cm^3

Exercise 18.1

1 a 88 kph b 58 kph c 80 kph
2 a 18 minutes b 60 mph c 45 minutes
  d 8.45 am e 35 miles f 20 mph
3 a (i) Ali: 9.15 am; Barry: 9.25 am (ii) 8 mph
  b (i) 9.45 am (ii) Ali, 3 miles; Barry, 2 miles
4 a 8 miles b 11 am c 12 noon
5 a (i) 30 minutes (ii) 21 minutes
  b Traffic hold-up; call of nature, refreshment stop

Exercise 18.2

1 a m^2 b 3 years

2 a

Time	1	2	3	4	5	6	7
Mass	200	100	50	25	12.5	6.25	3.125

  b 1$\frac{1}{2}$ days
3 a £1350 b £60
4 a (i) 1230 (ii) 1500
  b increasing; gradient is increasing
5 a (i) 25% (ii) 60% b 8.5% − 9%
6 b £2900 c (i) £890 per year (ii) £370 per year
7 a 4200 (4300) b −7 × 10^{-7} (or 0.7 parts per million)
  c 0.0125% − 0.014%

Exercise 19.1

1 b 37°, 53°
2 a 13 cm b 2.67 mm c 2.8 in
3 no 4 a 7.67 in b 8.94 cm, 7.35 cm
  c 10.3 cm, 11.1 cm d 13.4 cm, 12.7 cm, 12.0 cm
5 13.4 cm 6 24.0 cm 7 129 ft 8 145.5 cm
9 134.5 cm 10 170 cm

Exercise 19.2

1 6.09 cm 2 28.8° 3 6.36 cm 4 11.0 cm, 3.59 cm
5 a 7.26 cm b 26.9 cm^2 6 36.0°
7 a 5.49 cm b 5.85 cm
8 31.9° 9 18.2 cm

Exercise 19.3

1 a 4.84 cm b 7.21 cm 2 a 7.28 cm b 9.10 cm
3 a 22.2° b 16.1° 4 a 33.6° b 51.1°
5 18.0 cm, 5.27 cm 6 p = 13.8 cm, q = 2.16 cm
7 11.3 in, 33.7° 8 34.4° 9 21.8 cm

Exercise 19.4

1 13.1° 2 7.84 cm 3 7.77 cm 4 8.38 cm, 5.50 cm
5 1.44 m 6 a 86.4 cm b 85.1 cm 7 48.0°
8 37.7° 9 a 118 cm b 38.3°

Exercise 19.5

1 a 090° b 135° c 315° d 330° e 195°
2 a 113° b 074° c 312° d 237° 3 012° 4 241°
5 144° 6 216° 7 a 126° b 306° 8 2.30 miles

Exercise 19.6

1 229 ft 2 15.6° 3 736 ft 4 449 mph 5 7.70 m
6 12.5° 7 a 87.5° b 89.0° 8 5.00° 9 49.8 m

Solutions to Assignments

A free set of solutions is available for teachers and lecturers. Please write to: Mathematics Education Promotion Department, Oxford University Press, Great Clarendon Street, Oxford OX2 6DP.

Index to Main Text